Ireland
TravelBook™

Fifth Edition

AAA

President & CEO: Robert Darbelnet
Executive Vice President, Administration
& Publishing: Rick Rinner
Managing Director, Travel Information:
  Bob Hopkins

Director, Product Development & Sales:
  Bill Wood
Director, Publishing Marketing &
  Communications: Patty Wight
Business Manager: Linda Indolfi
Director, Purchasing & Corporate Services:
  Becky Barrett
Director, Business Development: Gary Sisco
Director, Tourism Information Development:
  Michael Petrone
Director, Travel Information/Publishing
  Operations: Jeff Zimmerman
Director, GIS/Cartography: Jan Coyne
Director, Publishing Systems: Ramin Kalhor
Manager, Business Line Publicity: Heather Hunter

Manager, Content and Product Development:
  Nancy Jones, CTC
Manager, Electronic Media Design: Mike McCrary
Manager, Publishing Design: Sonya Hester
Manager, Pagination, Photo & Pre-press Services:
  Tim Johnson
Photo Research: Denise Campbell &
  Kelly Canova
Managers, Club Sales: Roberta Hodak
  and Tina Franzzo
Manager, Club and Retail Sales: John Coerper
Manager, Marketing Communications:
  Renuka Sastri
Travel Services: Linda Marsh, CTC

Published by AAA Publishing, 1000 AAA Drive,
  Heathrow, Florida 32746

This product includes mapping
based upon data licensed from
Ordnance Survey of Northern
Ireland ® reproduced by permission of the
Chief Executive, acting on behalf of the
Controller of Her Majesty's Stationery Office
© Crown copyright 2008. Permit No. 80013.

Republic of Ireland mapping based on Ordnance
Survey Ireland. Permit No. 8430 © Ordnance
Survey Ireland and Government of Ireland.

Mapping produced by the Cartographic
Department of The Automobile Association.

Traffic signs © Crown copyright. Reproduced
with the permission of the Controller of
Her Majesty's Stationery Office.

The AAA Ireland TravelBook was created and
produced for AAA Publishing by Automobile
Association Developments Limited, Fanum
House, Basing View, Basingstoke, Hampshire,
RG21 4EA, England.

Written by Susan Poole
Managing Editor: Sheila Hawkins
Fifth edition verified by Apostrophe S Limited

Cover photos
Front cover and spine: Belfast, Northern Ireland
© iStock/Christian Zimmerle'
Back cover: Dublin, Ireland
© Martin Moos/Lonely Planet Images

ISBN-13:   978-1-59508-250-3
ISBN-10:   1-59508-250-6

Cataloging-in-Publication Data is on file with the
Library of Congress.

Color separations by Keenes, Andover U.K.
Printed in Dubai by Oriental Press

A03438

A Celtic cross silhouetted against the night sky, Ireland

Foreword

Pleasures are in store for you in the unique and beautiful country of Ireland. As you plan your trip to this magical land, this book will spark your imagination. Introduce yourself to Dublin, with its buzzing streets, stately Georgian buildings and haunting echoes of turbulent Irish history. Explore Belfast, where industry thrives and street entertainers enliven appealing city-center areas. Discover the wild and dramatic coastline of the West, the towering cliffs and the sandy beaches of Achill Island and the eerie limestone landscapes of the Burren.

This is a land that wears its personalities on its sleeve. The poetry of William Butler Yeats reverberates through Sligo. The day of Ireland's patron, St. Patrick, puts the country's citizens and others throughout the world in a festive mood. Shadows of great authors such as James Joyce and Jonathan Swift fall on Dublin's streets, where the literary heritage still flourishes. Stories of Finn MacCool and other folk heroes pervade the Irish psyche.

But Ireland's people, among the most smiling and welcoming you'll find anywhere, are its best attraction. Enjoy relaxing with them as they celebrate – at festivals and sporting events held all over the country.

Let the AAA Ireland TravelBook inspire your adventures. There are maps to help you get your bearings; descriptions and photos of places to see and things to do; and useful suggestions for eating, drinking and shopping – everything you need to get the most out of your trip to Ireland.

Ireland TravelBook™

Contents

Map of Ireland   8

▶ **Introduction to Ireland**   7

Feature: A Way with Words   12
Feature: Saints and Scholars   15
Feature: "And All Their
   Songs are Sad"   17
Feature:
   Ireland in a Festive Mood   19
Timeline   22
Survival Guide   24

▶ **Connacht**   27
Introduction and Map   28

Galway   32
Introduction and Map   32
Essential Information   34

Galway Sights   35
Walk: Stroll Back in Time   37

Regional sights   38
Feature: Journey Through
   Silence – Connemara   44
Drive: Yeats Country   50
Drive: Achill Island and
   County Mayo   55

▶ **Leinster**   59
Introduction and Map   60

Dublin   64
Introduction and Map   64
Essential Information   69

Dublin Sights   70
Feature: Dublin Specials   75
Feature: Enjoy Exploring   78
Walk: South of the Liffey   86
Feature: Dublin's Literary
   Greats   88

Lough Key, Connacht, lies amid acres of woodland

Regional sights   90
Drive: Boyne Valley   94
Drive: Witches and
    Castles   100
Feature: A Long Tradition
    of Spectacular Gardens   106

▶ Munster   111
Introduction and map   112

Cork   114
Introduction and Map   114
Essential Information   116

Cork Sights   117
Walk: Cork's Mercantile
    Past   120
Feature: Cork's Cultural
    Scene   122
Drive: Island City, Magic
    Stone   123

Regional Sights   126
Drive: Ring of Kerry   138
Feature: Medieval Castle
    Banquets and
    Traditional Céilí   144
Feature: Kerry's Festivals   147

▶ Ulster
and Northern Ireland   151
Introduction and Map   152

Belfast   155
Introduction and Map   155
Essential Information   159

Belfast Sights   160
Walk: Between Old
    and New   167
Drive: Strangford Lough   169

Regional Sights   172
Feature: American
    Connection   176
Feature: In St. Patrick's
    Footsteps   182
Drive: Fermanagh Lakeland   186
Feature: The Inishowen
    Peninsula   198
Feature: Finn MacCool   199

▶ Hotels and Restaurants   201

▶ Essential Information   213

▶ Index   222

Introduction to Ireland

An Irishman was once asked if there was an an equivalent Irish word to mañana. "Oh no," he replied, "we have nothing with that sense of urgency!"

Feature: A Way with Words **12**

Feature: Saints and
    Scholars **15**

Feature: "And All Their Songs
    are Sad" **17**

Feature: Ireland in a Festive
    Mood **19**

Timeline **22**

Survival Guide **24**

St. Mary's Abbey at Trim silhouetted against the dappled evening sky

Ireland

Capturing the essence of Ireland in mere words is a daunting task. In 1842, William Thackeray wrote to an English friend: "I am beginning to find out now that a man ought to be 40 years in this country, and then he wouldn't be able to write about it!" Many a visitor would agree with him when struggling to reduce to words the emotional overload of Ireland's unique mix of scenic wonders and a people who are irrepressibly romantic and brushed with a hint of magic. A varied and most welcoming country awaits you.

The Emerald Isle

The real Ireland only begins to come alive as you watch the delicate play of light and shade on the mountains from Glengarriff in County Cork to Kenmare

The Mountains of Mourne sweep down to meet green pastures

in County Kerry, or pass through the lush greenness of County Waterford byways, or gaze in awe at the mystical moonscape of County Clare's Burren, or see a grassy hillside change from the brightest hue of green to silver-gray in the changing light, or view a cloud-studded sky so enormous it makes eternity seem small, or stand on the rocky shore at Ventry on the Dingle Peninsula (Corca Dhuibhne), where legend says the "King of the World" went down to defeat at the hands of Fionn MacCumhaill (Finn MacCool, see page 199) and his Fianna warrior band. But most of all, it is the people who live among those scenic wonders and more than half-believe those ancient legends who defy description. Around every bend, that luminous, ever-changing landscape and the unique charm of the Irish cry out for the poet. Many a poet has answered its call but fallen short of the mark. Poor Thackeray – no wonder he was so frustrated!

Geographically Speaking

To get the statistics out of the way: Ireland covers 32,524 square miles (about the size of New Hampshire, Vermont and Massachusetts combined), 302 miles at its longest point and 189 miles at its widest. It's the "last parish before America," the most westerly island of Europe, and its bowl-shaped contours are formed by a great limestone plain surrounded by mountains (Kerry's Carrantuohill is the highest at 3,414 feet). The many jagged peninsulas create a dramatic coastline that measures more than 3,000 miles and encircles 9,000 miles of rivers (the 230-mile Shannon is the longest) and some 800 lakes, the largest of which is Lough Neagh (153 square miles).

From its early history, Ireland's 32 counties have been divided into the four provinces of Leinster, Munster, Connacht and Ulster (those "Four Green Fields" of song and story). Since 1921, Ulster has been divided into the six counties that form Northern Ireland – Londonderry, Antrim, Armagh, Down, Fermanagh and Tyrone, and three that lie in the Republic – Donegal, Monaghan and Cavan.

All That Rain

You certainly wouldn't come to Ireland for a suntan. However, the Gulf Stream's

Locals and tourists enjoy the sunshine and friendly atmosphere in Kinvarra

warming currents create a friendly climate that deals in moderation rather than extremes – seldom more than 65 degrees in July, 40 degrees in January. That famous (or infamous) rainfall is heaviest and most frequent in the mountains of the west, and frequent enough in the rest of the country to keep at least 40 shades of green glowing. Of course, the country would not be called the "Emerald Isle" were it not for the rain. However, for more sun than rain,

May is good just about everywhere except in the midlands and southeast; June is apt to be sunnier.

About Those Stereotypes

Remember all those "stage Irish" jokes about the innocent-but-dopey Irish? They are nothing like the real Irish people you will meet. The only place you'll find them on their native turf is the comedy stage. Unless, that is, some canny Irishman, tempted by your listening and, most of all, friendly. There's a certain panache about the Irish that so charms the visitor. True, the Irish will seldom bowl you over with all that charm – if there's anything they're not, it's intrusive. But ask the first question, make the first comment, and you're off and running. Your American accent invites instant interest in where you live, where you're going and what you think of their country.

"The English gave us their language," the Irish will tell you with a sly grin, "then we showed them how to use it." There's truth in that – they have turned out a staggering number of extraordinary writers, and even average Irish men and women tend to embellish everyday conversation with colorful phrases that would make any writer weep with envy. And they string them together in yarns that may be wildly fanciful, but are never dull, with words delivered in the most melodic, lilting rendition of the English language. As for the celebrated Irish wit, more often than not it is directed at themselves, with a subtle blend of artful wording and a liberal dash of mischief.

There's more to the Irish, of course, than talk. There's the strong religious influence that passed from Celtic to Catholic rites without a hitch. And the fascinating mix of Celt, Viking, Norman and Saxon blood that has melded into an Irish race of stunning brunettes, blonds and redheads.

expectation of finding those stereotypes, decides to play the complete buffoon and act out a scenario in gleeful anticipation of an entertaining tale for the lads in the local pub.

A Complex People

If it's hard to find words for Ireland itself, it's nearly impossible to capture the complexities of the Irish personality. Complex they most certainly are – warm-hearted, witty, sometimes argumentative, often talkative, great at

When Irish monks began their laborious transcribing in the sixth century, they drew on a bardic oral storytelling tradition that reached back into prehistory. Their first recorded stories came from the glorious tales of fierce battles, passionate love affairs and heroic deeds that had been passed from generation to generation in both prose and poetry. *Tain Bo Cuailgne (The Cattle Raid of Cooley), Lebor na Huidre (The Dun Cow)* and *Lebor Laigen (The Book of Leinster)* preserve the exploits, triumphs and tragedies of such legendary figures as Finn MacCool (see page 199), Cuchulainn, Oisin and the beautiful Deirdre.

Oscar Wilde (1854–1900)

A Way with Words

Brian Merriman's *Cuirt an Mhean Oiche (The Midnight Court)* is a masterful satire on the attitudes of Irish men to marriage, while the *Annals of the Four Masters,* written by Franciscan monks, and Geoffrey Keating's *Foras Feasa ar Eirinn (History of Ireland)* deal with Irish history. Those early works were written in Irish, as was most of Irish literature until the 17th century. During that same period, works on a much lighter note came from the witty poet Raftery and the roguish Owen Roe O'Sullivan.

By the end of the 17th century, the Anglo-Irish literary movement was well established. Irish writers Oliver Goldsmith and Richard Brinsley Sheridan penned English-style drawing-room comedies and English manners novels, while Jonathan Swift, then dean of St. Patrick's Cathedral in Dublin, was verbally flaying the English with his knife-edged satires.

Maria Edgeworth joined the ranks of outstanding Anglo-Irish writers in the 1800s, along with Thomas Moore, Gerald Griffin, William Carleton and Oscar Wilde. Toward the end of that century, dramatist George Bernard Shaw and novelist George Moore began brilliant careers that were to spill over into the next, as did poet William Butler Yeats and playwright John Millington Synge. Edith Somerville and her cousin Violet Martin were busy turning out comic sketches of Protestant life in rural Ireland, and novelist Bram Stoker's Dracula was let loose on the literary public.

The 20th century brought about a veritable explosion of Irish literary talent, whose vitality never flagged, despite the oppressive Censorship Act that drove many Irish writers to foreign publishers. Sean O'Casey's controversial plays put him in the forefront of Irish dramatists; Samuel Beckett was awarded the Nobel Prize while living in exile; James Joyce wrote knowingly of life in Dublin (and is considered by many to be the greatest Irish writer of the 20th century); and Brendan Behan enjoyed an all-too-short burst of literary fame.

Other writers who loom large on the Irish literary scene include playwrights Hugh Leonard, Brian Friel, Bernard Farrell and John B. Keane; novelists and short-story writers Ben Kiely, James Plunkett, Mary Lavin, John Banville, Edna O'Brien, Dermot Bolger and Elizabeth Bowen; and poets Patrick Kavanagh, Thomas Kinsella, John Montague and Seamus Heaney (also a Nobel Prize winner). As impressive as that long list is, it is by no means complete.

Today, scores of talented Irish writers are hard at work, most to an extraordinarily high standard. So, browse the bookshops, pick up any and many titles you find intriguing, and who knows – you may well discover the next famous Irish writer.

An abandoned cottage in fields near Rosmuck, County Galway

About the Past

The landscape of Ireland is haunted by its history. Its ghosts lurk along every road, around every bend, behind every bush. Relics are sprinkled across the land, some left in ruins, others authentically restored. Visit the reconstructed crannog at Craggaunowen in County Clare, and Bronze Age men and women will almost materialize before your eyes. Great monastic crosses and ruined abbeys speak of early Christians, while Norman spirits inhabit ruined castles that squat along riverbanks, atop lofty cliffs and stand proud in lonely fields.

In the Beginning

The earliest inhabitants to have left traces of their existence in Ireland probably arrived from Scotland in 6000 or 7000 BC. It wasn't until about 2000 BC that Neolithic people arrived, bringing along farming expertise and beginning Ireland's long tradition of farming and cattle raising. They cremated their dead and created communal burial chambers beneath stone cairns or inside earthen, tunnel-filled mounds like those at Newgrange in the Boyne Valley. They were followed by Bronze Age metal workers and artisans, who fashioned the exquisite ornaments that fill today's museums and left a wealth of megalithic stone structures. Believed to be descendants of the fertility goddess Eire (Noble), they transferred her name to this small island country.

In the fourth century BC, tall, fair-skinned, red-haired Celts, a fierce warlike people, arrived bearing iron weapons and military skills that soon established them as rulers of the land. A high king of Ireland ruled from Tara, but the countryside rang with battle cries as regional kings embarked on expansionary expeditions, and the high king of the moment never sat easy on his honorary throne. Nevertheless, there was unity in the strong bonds of a common culture and traditions held together by a common language. Tribes honored traveling bards, above all the Druids, who memorized the legends and performed sacred ceremonies.

St. Patrick Arrives

It was the strange Celtic mixture of barbarous warring and a highly developed culture that greeted the arrival of Patrick in the fifth century AD carrying the message of Christianity. Although the Celts showed faint regard for the edicts of Rome (their Easter fell on a date different from that proclaimed by the Pope, for instance), his reception by the war-loving Celts was surprisingly cordial, and conversions came swiftly. By the time of St. Patrick's death in 461, the new religion was firmly established.

Viking Invaders

Viking raiders came by sea in AD 795, making lightning-fast strikes along the coastline and taking away plunder and captives. Their superior mail battle dress and heavy arms made easy victims of even the most stout-hearted Irish. Their raids moved farther and farther inland, with rich monastic settlements yielding the most valuable prizes. Churchmen retreated from the danger to tall, round towers with the only entrance high above the ground. Today you'll find one of the best preserved at the Rock of Cashel in County Tipperary.

Eventually turning to peaceful trading, the Vikings were soon, in a pattern to be followed by subsequent "conquerors," intermarrying with native Irish folk and becoming as Irish as the Irish themselves. Vestiges of their city walls, gates and fortifications remain to this

day – Reginald's Tower in Waterford Quay is thought to be one of the most perfect examples.

The Normans Enter

In 1014, Irish High King Brian Ború won a decisive victory against the Vikings. Ború ascended into the rarefied stratosphere of Ireland's most revered heroes, but his death was followed by a century and a half of kingly tug-of-war to establish one central authority. Dermot MacMurrough, king of Leinster, committed the grave error of stealing the wife of the king of Breffni, who promptly hounded him out of Leinster. MacMurrough persuaded England's King Henry II to send Norman troops to win back Dermot's lost throne. When Rory O'Connor, the last high king of Ireland (buried at Clonmacnois, County Offaly) was defeated, MacMurrough's power began to rival that of King Henry. Alarmed, Henry elicited vows of fealty from many Irish kings who were anxious to hold onto their territories. For the next 350 years, territorial claims kept Anglo-Norman and Irish lords growling at each other as Normans acquired title to more than half of the country, building most of those sturdy castles in which you'll sightsee, banquet or spend the night during your visit.

To Hell or Connaught

By the time Elizabeth I became queen, the Reformation was firmly entrenched in England and the staunchly Catholic Irish found themselves fighting for their religion with even more fervor than they had fought for their lands. Having lost several long and bloody battles, Irish chieftains went into hiding, their lands now confiscated by the British Crown and resettled by loyal English and Scottish Protestants.

Arriving in 1649 and driven by religious fervor as well as political motives, Puritan Oliver Cromwell's campaign across the country left a trail of destruction. The Irish who escaped

The Romans rampaging in southern Britain never did get around to conquering Ireland, but in the fifth century a conquest of quite another nature took place. A pagan religion that had flourished for centuries surprisingly embraced the doctrines and rites of Christianity that landed on Irish shores with Patrick. Born Patricius in Britain as a Roman Empire citizen, in his youth the budding saint had tended swine in Ulster as a slave. He escaped and went back to the Continent, where he entered religious life before returning to his former captors as a missionary in 432.

A 13-foot stone cross stands outside St. Finghin Church

Saints and Scholars

Retaining just enough pagan customs to avoid hostile resistance, St. Patrick managed to transplant rites and superstitions into Christian soil without a murmur. The healing powers of many Irish "holy wells," for example, are those attributed to them by ancient Celts long before St. Patrick arrived on the scene. His firsthand knowledge of Celtic love of the mystical, especially when applied to the natural world, perhaps inspired him to use the shamrock to symbolize the Holy Trinity and thereby make it Ireland's most enduring national symbol. Irish king after Irish king listened to the missionary and led his subjects into the new religion, although none went so far as to abandon such distinctly Celtic pastimes as intra-kingdom warfare and riotous revelry within his own court.

With the coming of Christianity, Celtic culture took a giant step forward. Already deeply respectful of learning in its higher forms, the Irish devoted themselves to a cloistered life within great monasteries that taught all the learning of their time, both Celtic and Roman. As Europe entered its culturally deprived Dark Ages, Ireland's monastic universities kept the lights of philosophy, theology, astronomy, literature, poetry and science brightly burning. Artistic achievement hit new heights inside their walls, as the exquisitely illustrated *Book of Kells* demonstrates. Up until the end of the eighth century, Ireland's Golden Age was the brightest beacon in the Western world.

Away from these seats of learning, monks also moved out to more remote parts of the country. There they lived austere lives of meditation, building the beehive-shaped stone dwellings still intact today and marvelously engineered little stone churches such as Dingle's Gallarus Oratory (see page 132), constructed entirely without mortar and watertight for the past 1,500 years. The impressive stone Celtic crosses that dot the landscape had their origins in the seventh century.

Eventually, Europe's age of darkness retreated, helped by returning European scholars and Irish monks who left home to carry their teachings into cathedrals, royal courts and universities.

were shipped as slave labor to English plantations in the Sugar Islands (a virtual "hell") or driven to the bleak stony hills of Connaught. To his loyal soldiers, Cromwell awarded vast estates in the fertile counties of the country. In the end, less than one-ninth of Irish soil remained in the hands of natives.

King Billy, the Treaty of Limerick and Penal Laws

Irish spirits rose once more when a Catholic, James II, ascended to the English throne in 1688. Deposed by William of Orange – King Billy – James fled to Ireland in 1689, where the Irish took up arms in his defense. King Billy arrived to lead a resounding victory in the Battle of the Boyne, after which James once more took flight. The Irish fought on until October 1691, when they signed the Treaty of Limerick, which allegedly allowed them to retain both their religion and their land. Parliament, however, instituted a series of measures so oppressive they became known as the Penal Laws. Catholics were subsequently stripped of all civil and political rights and forced to work hard on the estates of absentee, rich English landlords. Irish farmers paid extortionate rents for the mere privilege of building primitive huts and using a small plot of ground to raise the potato crops that kept their families from starving – just.

United Irishmen

Anglo-Irish Protestants gradually came to feel a much stronger allegiance to Ireland than to England and, demanding greater independence, got a token Irish Parliament in 1782. Forming the Society of United Irishmen to work for a totally independent Irish republic, and enlisting military aid from France, revolutionist Wolfe Tone led a full-fledged insurrection in 1798. Disaster on the battlefield became even greater than the disaster happening in the halls of the English Parliament. In 1800 the Act of

Union was passed and Ireland became an extension of British soil. It was Daniel O'Connell (affectionately named "The Liberator") who, on getting elected to Parliament in 1828, restored all Catholic civil rights, accomplished a total repeal of the Penal Laws and embarked on a campaign for repeal of the Act of Union. Just as members of the Young Ireland movement were beginning to be heeded, the terrible agricultural disaster of the potato blight gripped the country and the Irish goal became one of simple survival. By 1849 a population of nearly 9 million people was reduced to little more than 6 million. Those who did not die of starvation and disease escaped on ships and fled to the United States and Canada, but the vessels were so overcrowded and disease infested that, for many, they became little more than floating coffins.

The Land League, Home Rule and Sinn Fein

By 1879 Irish tenant farmers were so frustrated by oppressive land rentals that they eagerly joined with Charles Stewart Parnell's Land League. Farmers organized strikes by "boycott" against any landlord who evicted tenants – so called for Captain Boycott, against whom it was first used. Parnell's energetic campaign for Home Rule also granted limited independence, but it wasn't until the eve of World War I that such a measure was finally adopted by the British.

Outnumbered by Catholics, Unionists in Ulster feared Home Rule would become Rome Rule, and put up a strong armed resistance against the equally determined Irish Republican Army. The IRA is the military arm of Sinn Fein, a republican political party whose name is pronounced "shin fain," and means "ourselves alone". The country was fairly bristling with arms when everything was put on hold by the urgency of World War I and the need to fight a foreign aggressor.

Folk musicians playing traditional instruments at an Irish pub

"And All Their Songs are Sad"

So said G. K. Chesterton about the Irish, having just asserted, "All their wars are merry." He may have been half right, but their songs are most assuredly not all sad. The Irish have celebrated, mourned, exalted, damned and lamented everything in their lives through music. Until the 1690s and the Englishman Oliver Cromwell, songs and ballads were composed entirely in Irish. After that, English was the only legal language, imposed as an attempt to help erase any remaining traces of nationalism. Even the Penal Laws were unable to do that, however, for the wily Irish praised their country under the guise of singing about their sweethearts: *Roisin Dubh* and *Kathleen Huallachain* spoke of loved ones, but every Irishman knew they really were odes to Ireland herself. Those traditional songs and airs are still played frequently today. If you listen closely to modern Irish ballads, you'll notice that a few are still concerned with celebrating or mourning, exalting some facet of Irish life.

Performances can feature a number of instruments: the harp, *uilleann* (elbow) pipes – played sitting down and some say developed to get around English law that forbade the playing of any instrument while standing in order to prevent the pipes from playing troops into battle, the *bodhrán* (a drum made of goatskin stretched tightly over a round wooden frame), the tin whistle, fiddle and accordion. These all mix in a unique harmony that can break your heart or send your spirits soaring.

In Ireland, native music has become trendy in recent years, and pubs often feature "trad" groups aiming in that direction. Even if a pub is not known for music, the lyrical Irish spirit frequently bursts forth in pubs as the evening progresses. You are likely to hear the familiar twang of American country music as often as the impassioned lyrics of Ireland's traditional songs.

Culturlann na hEireann (pronounced "Kultur-arn na-Airan"), based in the Dublin suburb of Monkstown, organizes year-round traditional entertainment including *ceilis* (pronounced "kay-lees," traditional set dancing) in hotels, pubs and at local branch meetings, which are all open to the public. During the last weekend in August, look for the All-Ireland Fleadh, pronounced "flah." It's a three-day traditional music and song festival held each year in a different town. Worldwide music lovers congregate in pubs, hotels, private houses and streets to play, sing and just listen to this special brand of music. The Fleadh Nua on the last weekend in May is one of many other showcases for the best in traditional music.

The Winds of Change

The Irish treasure their cultural heritage, but are nowadays using it as a solid base for swiftly moving changes in manners and mores of this dynamic era. With an economy labeled "The Celtic Tiger" and recognized as the fastest growing in the European Union, the country is awash with signs of prosperity and affluence. Lifestyles are changing at a fast clip, but the winds of change are nothing new for the Irish.

With centuries of flexibility in meeting new circumstances, current changes are a piece of cake! The basic elements of Irishness – courtesy, compassion and the ability to laugh at the absurdities of life – are still very much alive and well, even as high-tech industries invade parts of the country and many young people leave traditional working pursuits for much higher pay and city life.

Until the last decade of the 20th century, hard times in Ireland spawned youthful emigration. In the wake of a hard-won reversal of fortunes, an ever increasing number are returning. This influx of returnees and the dramatic decrease in young people leaving for foreign shores has resulted in a large youthful population. Such a vibrant, well-educated and young work force is luring more and more international companies to use Ireland as their gateway to European markets.

On the social front, Ireland has embraced change with breathtaking speed: politically, male domination is fast disappearing and Ireland now has its second woman president.

Ireland's modernity belies the "quaint" label so often applied and makes for a memorable holiday.

An exhilarating way of exploring County Galway's pristine coastline

The festival season in Ireland runs from mid-March to mid-November, and planning a visit around one of these lively occasions is worth considering. The Irish Tourist Board can give specific dates for the time you're visiting. In addition to those listed here, you may come across others just as intriguing, such as Cape Clear's International Storytelling Festival, Lisdoonvarna's Matchmaking Festival and Galway's International Oyster Festival, as you travel around the country during summer.

Folk dancers performing at Galway's Oyster Festival

Ireland in a Festive Mood

(see page 145). Lots of song and dance. A truly festive affair with an international flavor. Fleadh Cheoil na héireann: The venue for this festival changes each year. Regardless of locality it draws international musicians for a three-day, nonstop outpouring of traditional Irish music, song and dance. Scheduled concerts vie with spontaneous street sessions, and there are exacting competitions for the All-Ireland championships.

March 16–19

St. Patrick's Festival: Ireland's largest festival. While there are celebrations of this saint's special day in cities, towns and villages, none quite match the spirit of Dublin with its street entertainment, music, theater, dance, pageants and spectacular parade (featuring numerous American bands).

July

Galway Arts Festival: A two-week colorful, vibrant eruption of theater, street entertainment, visual arts, music, literary and children's events. Fanciful floats created by Galway's avant-garde street theater troupe, Macnas, are highlights.

August

Kilkenny's Arts Festival: Over 10 days the narrow streets and historic buildings of this medieval city make a perfect setting for classical music (in St. Canice's Cathedral), visual arts (in the ruins of Kells Priory) and outdoor theater.

The Rose of Tralee Festival: Draws "roses" from around the globe for a lively five days

September

International Festival of Light Opera, Waterford: The city is awash with musical talent from around the world throughout the 16 nights of musicals – many of them straight from Broadway. And it's not just light opera – pub-singing competitions are also popular.

Mid-October, early November

Wexford Festival Opera: Presents three major productions and more than 40 smaller events. It is unique in its emphasis on obscure, seldom-performed operas. Tickets must be booked well in advance.

Late October

The Cork Jazz Festival: Now running for more than 25 years, this glorious weekend event has been called "the greatest jazz party in the world." Performances by some of the world's most outstanding musicians pour from pubs and concert halls.

The Belfast Festival: This lights up Belfast's Queen's University venues for two weeks with international theater, dance, film and literary productions, plus jazz and comedy.

Horseracing, one of the great Irish passions, at Curragh

The Sporting Life

For the sports-minded, Ireland is a veritable banquet table. Every spectator sports event draws huge crowds, fanatically enthusiastic in cheering on their county soccer, rugby or Gaelic games teams. For fishermen there are rivers and sea coasts teeming with fish, top-notch golf courses for keen golfers and equestrian facilities for exploring the glorious landscape on horseback.

For the Spectator

Horseracing is dear to the heart of the Irish, and each of the more than 250 race meets per year is a festive affair. It's a thrilling sight to see the famed Irish-bred horses round the last bend of a grass course against a backdrop of mountains. And it becomes even more exciting if you have a bet riding on a horse. Placing that bet is a very Irish experience, a matter of choosing the best odds offered by bookmakers who shout out competitive odds that change momentarily as they vie for punters (bettors). If your horse comes up a winner, you'll be paid from a big satchel at the bookmaker's stand.

Probably the year's most popular race meet with the Irish is the Galway races in late July/early August, but people also flock to the Easter Monday meet at Fairyhouse (near Dublin) and Punchestown Steeplechases. Tourist offices can furnish exact dates of meets around the country, but a "don't miss" for visitors is any race meet at a smaller course, where the atmosphere is not unlike a day at a county fair.

Gaelic Games

Hurling is an ancient game unique to Ireland. Played by two 15-man teams of amateur players, it has a two-level scoring system that can be confusing, with goals and points depending on whether the little leather ball is hit past the goaltender and over the goal line or over the goaltender's head and between the upright goalposts. It is one of the fastest field sports in the world, and the skill and speed of athletes wielding hurleys (a bit like ice hockey sticks) are wondrous to behold. Sunday afternoon matches are regular events all around the country, and it's great fun to mingle with the local fans.

While organized Gaelic football matches date back only about a century, the game undoubtedly evolved from fierce tribal rivalries. None of the fervor of participants or spectators has been lost in the shift. An amateur field game, it is played by two teams of 15 and incorporates elements of both soccer and rugby (some say it's more exciting than either). Weekend local matches are great to watch, and for sheer excitement nothing quite matches that of the All Ireland finals in September as more than 90,000 fans in Dublin's Croke Park roar support for their county teams. "Football" in Ireland often means soccer, as it does in America, and American football is only beginning to take hold in Ireland and mainland Europe.

Hands-on Sports

If there's such a thing as a fisherman's heaven, it must be Ireland! Irish waters are home to such freshwater fish (coarse fishing) as bream, dace, pike, perch and various hybrids in rivers, streams and lakes. Or you may elect to stalk the famous Irish salmon from January through September in coastal rivers, their stillwaters and headwaters. Sea trout and brown trout are among other challenging game fish.

Sea anglers will find plentiful supplies of bass, whiting, mullet, flounder, plaice, pollack and coalfish from shore casting on rocks, piers, beaches and promontories. Deep-sea fishing for shark, skate, dogfish, pollack, ling and conger is yours for incredibly low costs all around the coast, and there are plenty of vessels willing to take you out.

Other water sports include surfing, water skiing and windsurfing. And, of course, there are lovely beaches for swimmers who don't demand summer temperatures much above 70 degrees.

The ancient game of hurling is fast and furious

It is positively rejuvenating to walk along the lengthy stretches of beach when there's not another soul in sight. Seaside resorts can also be fun, from the lively Tramore in County Waterford to the quieter Kilkee in County Clare.

For golf enthusiasts, more than 360 superb golf courses dot the Irish countryside, and a growing number of hotels have a course or access to local courses. Ireland is gaining worldwide renown on the championship golf circuit and visiting golfers are welcome. Caddies can be booked ahead at some of the larger courses. And electric golf carts are not very common, but you will find pull-carts at most courses. Many courses have clubs for rent, but some do not. Irish golfing vacations can be arranged to include accommodations, golf clinics, and special weekends with groups. Tourist offices can provide you with lists of locations and specific information about what's available at each course.

Equestrians of any age or level of expertise will find stables offering riding instruction, as well as trail riding, guided point-to-point treks with overnight accommodations or hunting.

Timeline

circa 3000 BC	Neolithic farmers construct sacred burial chambers at Newgrange and Knowth in the Boyne Valley. Bronze Age metal workers come seeking copper and gold.
600	Celts arrive, bringing iron weapons and the Gaelic language.
AD 456	Patrick begins his Christian conversion of Irish tribes.
circa 795	Vikings plunder monasteries and found the cities of Dublin, Wexford, Waterford, Cork and Limerick.
1014	Brian Ború defeats the Vikings at Battle of Clontarf.
1169	Normans, led by Strongbow, begin England's long domination of Ireland.
1608	Leading Irish chieftains flee in the "Flight of the Earls."
1609	Plantations in Ulster begin as English and Scottish Protestants occupy Irish farms.
1649	Lord Protector Oliver Cromwell sweeps through Ireland to subdue the rebellious Irish.
1690	Catholic defeat at the Battle of the Boyne begins a century of Catholic oppression under the Penal Laws.
1791	Wolfe Tone founds the United Irishmen.
1798	Insurrection led by Tone, Robert Emmet and others squelched by English forces.
1800	The Act of Union is passed, handing direct rule of Ireland over to London Parliament.
1845–51	The Great Potato Famine causes widespread starvation and more than 1 million Irish emigrate, chiefly to America.

A "Terrible Beauty is Born"

On Easter Monday of 1916, the whole question of Irish independence was put right back on the front burner. Leading a scruffy and poorly armed little band of patriots, Padraic Pearse and James Connolly took occupation of Dublin's General Post Office in the name of a provisional government. Pearse read "The Proclamation of the Irish Republic to the People of Ireland," and for the next six days, the Post Office stood embattled under the ancient symbol of Ireland (a golden harp on a pennant of brilliant green) and the Sinn Fein banner of green, white and orange.

In the end the rebels surrendered, and Pearse, Connolly and 14 others were executed by firing squad. Irish loyalties became united behind their new republic and the ideal of Irish independence. It was at that moment – as the executioners' gunsmoke cleared in Kilmainham Gaol's yard – that the poet Yeats proclaimed "A terrible beauty is born."

In 1919 Sinn Fein set up the National Parliament of Ireland in Dublin. Bitter bloodshed followed. The Anglo-Irish Treaty was signed naming 26 counties the Irish Free State. Six counties in Ulster would remain – as they wished – an integral part of Great Britain. In 1948 Ireland was formally declared outside the Commonwealth, and Ireland was made a Republic.

1879	Charles Stewart Parnell and Michael Davitt found the Land League to secure tenant land ownership.
1905–08	Sinn Fein political party evolves, with Irish independence its primary goal.
1912	Home Rule goes into effect; Ulster Volunteers founded by loyalists; Irish Republican Army established as military adjunct of Sinn Fein.
1916	Padraic Pearse, James Connolly and others lead Easter Monday uprising; their execution unites Irish and world public opinion in support of Irish independence.
1921	Dominion status granted to 26 counties as Irish Free State; partition leaves six Ulster counties as part of Great Britain; civil war rages until 1923.
1937	New constitution put forth by Eamon De Valera.
1948	Twenty-six of Ireland's counties become a republic with no constitutional ties to Britain.
1968	Violence breaks out in Northern Ireland when British troops fire on peaceful Catholic civil rights demonstration in Londonderry.
1969	Beginning of "The Troubles" in Northern Ireland when Britain stations military force to protect the peace.
1973	The Republic of Ireland joins the European Economic Community.
1986	Anglo-Irish Agreement gives Republic limited input in Northern Ireland affairs.
1994	IRA declares an end to military operations; Loyalist paramilitaries issue similar cease-fire.
1995	President Clinton makes his historic visit to Ireland.
1996	IRA resumes campaign of violence as peace talks collapse.
1997	IRA declares new cease-fire and enters all-party peace talks chaired by United States Congressman George Mitchell.
1998	Good Friday Agreement affirmed by referenda in the Republic and Northern Ireland paves the way for a Northern Ireland Assembly; sporadic violence continues in Northern Ireland.
2000	Northern Ireland executive committee suspended after meeting only 10 weeks when United Unionist Party demands IRA disarm in advance of Good Friday Agreement deadline of May 2000, but reconvenes when compromise is reached.
2002	Launched in January, the euro becomes the official currency of the Republic of Ireland.
2004	A no-smoking policy is introduced in all public places in the Republic of Ireland.
2007	The Northern Ireland Assembly is re-established at Stormont following elections in March 2007.

Survival Guide

- Consider basing yourself in one location for three or four days. Ireland is a small, compact country and lends itself to day trips from a central regional base. While you'll always be made welcome at any pub in the country, when you return a second night, you'll automatically become a "regular" and the locals will delight in hearing what you've done and seen during the day, as well as having "insider" tips to share for the next day.

- Plan to vary your accommodations between hotels, guesthouses and bed-and-breakfast homes. Ireland has an incredible array of high-quality places to stay. Accommodations with kitchens are also an attractive alternative – not only are they money-savers when it comes to meals, but trips to local grocery stores for essentials will add another dimension to your Irish experience.

- If you're traveling with children or if you exult in the glories of country life, book into a farmhouse for a few days. Hospitality seems to take on an even keener edge out in the country, and most hosts will delight in showing you around a working farm. Children especially respond to close-up contact with farm animals.

- Keep your daytime activities flexible enough to stop and spend some time if you come across a street fair, cattle mart or horse fair. County Waterford's annual horse fair in Tallow is a great opportunity to watch such age-old practices as rural people bargaining for horses and sealing a deal with a handshake. Remember, in Ireland time is made for you, not you for time!

- Be sure to bring a raincoat, not only for Ireland's magical rain but also for the flutuating temperatures. It will also be useful as an improvised robe when accommodations have the bathroom down the hall.

- Plan at least one picnic. The Irish landscape beckons to picnickers to spread a lunch on a deserted beach, under a tree on the edge of a field, on a picnic table at a scenic overlook or any place looking out to mountains.

- Make your main meal a large lunch; lunch in even the most expensive restaurants costs a fraction of the same meal in the evening. Most pubs serve hot plates heaped with home-cooked meats and vegetables, as well as excellent cold salad plates of ham or chicken.

- Be sure to inquire about discounts at sightseeing attractions for families, senior citizens and students. They're not always posted and can amount to a considerable saving. Any identification will be helpful.

- Ireland's highways and secondary roads are improving, but especially in the west drivers should be on the lookout for potholes. When off the main roads, expect to encounter

Gaelic Place-Name Spellings

On March 28th, 2005 a legal bill was passed to change the spellings of many place-names in Ireland from English to Gaelic. Most of the changes occur in areas of Ireland known as Gaeltacht, mostly in the west of the country, where the celtic tongue is widely spoken and written. Road signs now show Gaelic spellings only, most prevalent in the counties of Galway, Kerry, Cork, Donegal, Waterford, Mayo and Meath. This process is ongoing and many more Gaelic spellings will be introduced over the coming years (see page 221 for the list of place-names that are already in use).

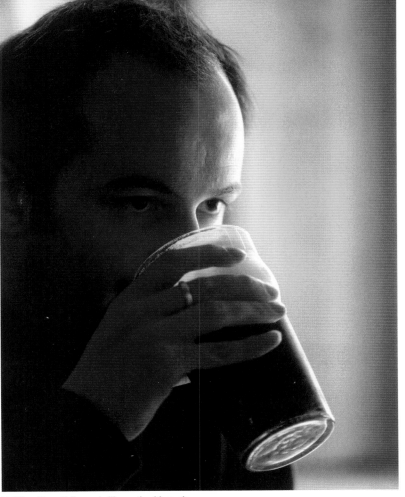

Dublin with no Guinness is like earth with no air

farmers driving cattle or sheep to and from fields in the early morning and late afternoon – just stop the car and wait for the animals to pass.

- The plethora of Irish "roundabouts" (traffic circles) seems to present all sorts of difficulties for American drivers. The cardinal rule is: The driver on the right has the right of way. If you miss your exit, just go around again and be sure you're in the correct lane to exit.

- A few conversation tips: Politics and religion are both very serious subjects in Ireland, and it is best to avoid any discussion of either. The status of Northern Ireland is also a sensitive and complex subject. Be careful in expressing any judgment to people you meet in Ireland.

- Resist swimming off the beach when there's no one else around, especially swimming off the Atlantic beaches in the west, where tides can often be strong and currents can be treacherous. Always swim at more populated beaches.

- Be aware that some conveniences you're accustomed to at home will not be on hand everywhere in Ireland, and some Irish customs are going to differ from those with which you are familiar. Just relax and enjoy the differences.

Connacht

Connacht probably comes closer to the popular perception of Ireland. Its bleak, stony Atlantic landscape has a stark beauty, blending softly with the green and fertile inland counties.

Introduction and Map **28**

Galway **32**

Introduction and Map **32**

Essential Information **34**

Galway Sights **35**

Walk: Stroll Back in Time **37**

Regional Sights **38**

Feature: Journey Through Silence –

Connemara **44**

Drive: Yeats Country **50**

Drive: Achill Island and County

Mayo **55**

Brightly painted boats rest on the shores of Lough Conn

Connacht

► Connacht's counties – Galway, Leitrim, Mayo, Roscommon, Sligo – form a large portion of Ireland's West, a region of which Irish author James Joyce's poet-surgeon friend Oliver St. John Gogarty wrote,

*There's something sleeping in my breast
That wakens only in the West;
There's something in the core of me
That needs the West to set it free.*

That "something" undoubtedly springs from a long history of hardships stoically endured and rebelliously resisted.

Within the boundaries of counties Galway and Mayo lie such distinct geographic divisions as Connemara, the Aran Islands (Oileáin Árann) and Achill Island (Oiléan Acla). Galway's landscape in the east is made up of flat, fertile plains that reach from Lough Derg and the Shannon Valley north to County Roscommon, while to the northwest, lumpy mountains push the mainland into a great elbow bent against the Atlantic. Connemara's stony landscape is bounded by a coastline dotted with wonderful, uncrowded beaches. Lough Corrib stretches its 27 miles along an invisible line that marks the change. Some 30 miles offshore, the Aran Islands are an outpost of rugged, self-sufficient fishermen and their families. These people have kept alive many aspects of

In the heart of Connemara – the peaks of Twelve Pins seen from Roundstone Bay

A mural decorates a storefront in the small town of Kinvarra, Galway

their ancient culture even as they move into easier lifestyles of modern Ireland. Pre-Christian stone forts rub shoulders with early Christian round towers, oratories and churches. The musical Gaelic language of their ancestors is that of today's islanders. Menfolk still fish the sea as they have done over the ages, while their womenfolk spin and weave and knit the clothing that is so distinctly theirs, all the while welcoming and providing for a steady stream of visitors who come by steamer or small aircraft. Eastern County Mayo is flat. It was near Cong, on the Plain of Southern Moytura, that a prehistoric battle raged between Tuatha De Danann and the Firbolgs, ending in the first defeat of the Firbolgs, who declined in power until they were crushed forever seven years later in Sligo. Northeast of Cong is the village of Knock, a shrine to the many reported visions and a place of pilgrimage for thousands of Christians. A circular church, seating several thousands, was built here in 1876, and pilgrims gather on the last Sunday in July each year to walk barefoot in the steps of St. Patrick. Their path takes them to Croagh Patrick on Clew Bay's southern shore.

The dock at Leenane village on the inner reaches of Killary Harbour

Connected to the Irish mainland by a causeway, Achill Island (Oiléan Acla) presents a mountainous face to the sea, its feet surrounded by golden sandy strands. Along the western part of County Sligo are the heathery slopes of the Ox Mountains; the north holds high, flat-topped limestone hills like Yeats' beloved Benbulben. Farther north, the narrow finger of Killary Harbour marks the border line of the County Mayo border.

Out of season, most of Connacht is quiet and many of it's tourist attractions are closed. If you don't want to drive, the best place to base yourself is in Galway city, which has plenty of year-round attractions and opportunities for excursions. These can be arranged by your hotel or the tourist office.

Galway

Galway may have begun its life as a small village that grew from a fishing camp at the only possible ford of the River Corrib, but over the centuries it has blossomed into a thriving, lively city that breathes new life into the entire region. It has become a center for the arts, drama, music and all manner of creative activities that draw visitors from around the world, many of whom elect to stay on as permanent residents in an environment that nurtures talent.

Galway owes its existence to the grief of Breasail, an ancient Celtic chieftain. After his daughter drowned in the River Corrib, he established a permanent riverbank camp that grew into the tiny fishing village of the Claddagh (see page 33). When the Normans arrived, they recognized the potential of the excellent harbor, developed a thriving maritime trade between Galway, Spain and France, and eventually enclosed the fine medieval town with stone walls. The 14 "Tribes of Galway" were composed of

the town's most prosperous merchant families. At the height of the Great Famine in the mid-1800s, the city was filled with starving men, women and children who fought to board the infamous "coffin ships" in a desperate attempt to escape to America and to try and begin a new life.

Today Ireland's fourth largest city is still a prosperous commercial center, a delightful and interesting blend of ancient and modern that welcomes all visitors with open arms. Traces of the city's history abound, with the oldest parts clustering around the harbor and riverside quays: the Spanish Arch, a gateway of the old city walls; Lynch's Castle, a 14th-century town house that is now a branch of the Allied Irish Bank; tiny cobblestone streets and narrow lanes; the Long Walk along the banks of the Corrib, a much-loved waterside promenade for all ages over the centuries; and Galway's version of Paris's "Left Bank" (the High Street and Quay Street quarter of old buildings has been given a new life these days).

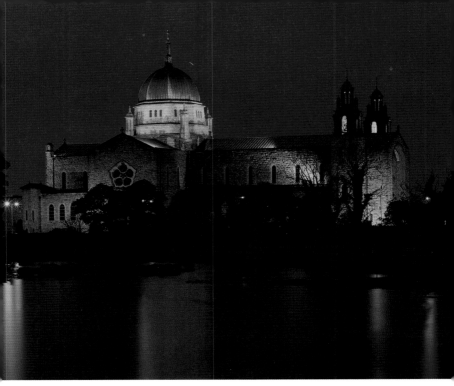

Galway's modern St. Nicholas's Cathedral

While all that ancient history is revered by Galway natives, they are busily creating a modern history that embraces the arts in all forms. Gaelic drama flourishes at the Taibhdhearc Theatre, while the Town Hall Theatre features avant-garde, new Irish and Anglo-Irish classic theater. Galway pubs ring with the sounds of traditional Irish music one night, rock 'n' roll the next, and aspiring (sometimes quite professional) musicians provide street entertainment aplenty.

And then there are the festivals. Galway's Arts Festival rages for 12 entertainment-filled days in July, with all sorts of stage plays, concerts and street entertainment, as well as a massive, offbeat parade that's a highlight.

At the end of July and the beginning of August, the six-day Galway Race Week draws the cream of the local and international horsey sets. When not at the track, horse owners, trainers and "punters" (the betting folk) are never idle – private parties warmly welcome complete strangers, and the track grounds are lined with food stalls and street entertainers. Meanwhile, Galway's pubs are at their liveliest.

In mid-August (weather permitting) there's the Blessing of the Sea, when a

Claddagh Rings

The design of these silver or gold rings originated in the Claddagh. Once a Gaelic-speaking fishing community outside Galway's old city walls by the western mouth of the river, it is now a neat suburb. Claddagh rings depict two hands holding a heart surmounted by a crown, symbolizing a promise, or a hope, of eternal love and friendship. The precious heirlooms were handed down through the family's female line and, depending which way around the ring was worn, showed whether a girl was engaged or still on the marriage market.

procession of fishing boats sail out to sea led by a priest-filled boat whose ecclesiastical passengers implore heavenly powers to grant safe and profitable voyages as the much-awaited herring season opens.

Hordes of Irish people from around the country descend on Galway in September to take part in the Oyster Festival, which they consider to be the festival to end all festivals. The Lord Mayor of Galway opens and eats the first oyster of the season, inaugurating a weekend of sheer, unashamed gluttony. Oyster-openers from around the world gather for lively competitions in opening the most oysters in the shortest time, and although some wash the bivalves down with champagne, the overwhelming drink of preference is "the black stuff" (Guinness).

Galway is an upbeat, vivacious and enjoyable city that is good for shopping, especially if you're hooked on secondhand books and classy crafts. Besides its own variety of attractions, the city is a convenient base for exploring many local areas – Connemara, Lough Corrib, the beautiful Aran Islands and the Burren in County Clare.

Essential Information

Tourist information
Ireland West Tourism (serving counties Galway, Mayo and Roscommon), Áras Fáilte, Forster Street ☎ 091 537 700; fax 091 537 733; www.irelandwest.ie
The office will make reservations for accommodations, excursions, ferry services and bicycle and car rentals.
A tip: be sure to get a city map – it may well save your sanity as you wander this ancient city's narrow, winding streets, which often change names every few blocks.

Urban Transportation
Galway's local bus service, running from the Bus Eireann Travel Centre, Ceannt Station (☎ 091 562 000; www.buseireann.ie) just off Eyre Square, reaches most suburbs, including Salthill and other neighborhoods. From here there are good connections to almost anywhere in the country. Bus Eireann runs several worthwhile day tours from Galway and Salthill: Clew Bay and Killary Harbour; the Maam Valley and Cong. Some are half-day trips; others last the entire day. All are moderately priced, and you can book a tour at the tourist office in Galway or the railroad station.
The most central taxi stand is at Eyre Square. You can also call to order a taxi from Galway Taxi Co-op ☎ 091 561 111.
The first thing to be said about driving in Galway city is don't. The network of tiny lanes, alleyways and medieval passageways make city driving a nightmare. Parking can also be a problem – street parking operates on the disk system, and the few multistory parking garages are expensive and often fill up early in the day. It's best to leave your car at your hotel, take a bus into the center, and walk – the little streets are a joy to wander along.
There's a direct rail service between Galway and Dublin. While there are connecting services to other major destinations around the country, they often involve time-consuming, multi-change schedules. In Galway, trains arrive and depart from Ceannt Station (☎ 091 561 444) just off Eyre Square (down from the Great Southern Hotel).
Several ferry companies operate regular services to the outlying Aran Islands, departing from Galway docks, a 90-minute voyage, or Rossaveal (20 miles west of Galway city on R336, the Barna road, with shuttle service to the ferry from the city), which takes 40 minutes. Make reservations at the tourist office the day before your visit.

Airport Information
Daily Aer Lingus flights between Dublin and Galway use Galway Airport (☎ 091 755 569; www.aerlingus.com) in Carnmore, about 6.5 miles east of Galway city. Aer Arann flies from Connemara Airport (on the Monivea road 4 miles from Galway) to Kilronan, Inis Mór's main port town.

Climate: Average highs and lows

Jan.	Feb.	Mar.	Apr.	May	Jun.	Jul.	Aug.	Sep.	Oct.	Nov.	Dec.
8°C	8°C	10°C	12°C	14°C	16°C	17°C	17°C	16°C	14°C	11°C	9°C
46°F	46°F	50°F	54°F	57°F	61°F	63°F	63°F	61°F	57°F	52°F	48°F
4°C	4°C	5°C	6°C	8°C	10°C	12°C	12°C	11°C	8°C	6°C	5°C
39°F	39°F	41°F	43°F	46°F	50°F	54°F	54°F	52°F	46°F	43°F	41°F

Galway Sights

Key to symbols

✚ map coordinates refer to the Galway map on page 32; sights below are highlighted in yellow on the map
✉ address or location ☎ telephone number
◷ opening times 🚌 nearest bus route 🍴 restaurant on site or nearby 💷 admission charge: $$$ more than €6, $$ €4 to €6, $ less than €4 ℹ information

Cathedral of Our Lady Assumed into Heaven and St. Nicholas

This Roman Catholic cathedral is a striking city landmark. Its tall spire visible from almost any point in the city, the cathedral is often used by residents as a designated meeting place. Set beside the Salmon Weir Bridge on the River Corrib and constructed from native limestone with Connemara marble flooring, the Renaissance-style building topped by a copper dome is a showcase for mosaics, statues and stained-glass windows created by contemporary Irish artisans. It was completed in 1965 after seven years of construction.

Shoals of salmon leap the falls by the Salmon Weir Bridge as they swim upstream to spawn from mid-April to early July.

✚ B2 ✉ University and Gaol roads ☎ 091 563 577 ◷ Daily 8:30–6:30; phone for additional evening opening 🍴 Restaurant 🚌 2, 4, 5 💷 Free (donations welcome)

Galway Arts Centre

This was once the townhouse of Lady Augusta Gregory (1859–1932), a wealthy widow who nurtured a generation of Irish writers and poets, and who founded the Abbey Theatre in Dublin (see page 66). Later, Galway Corporation took it over for office space. These days, it once more nurtures Irish figures such as Fiona Murray and Charles Lamb, as well as presenting international artists through concerts, literary readings and on-going exhibitions.

✚ B1 ✉ 47 Dominick Street ☎ 091 565 886; www.galwayartscentre.ie ◷ Mon.–Sat. 10–6 🚌 2, 4, 5 💷 Concerts: $$$; exhibits: free

Intricate stained glass in Galway's cathedral

Galway Atlantiquaria

One of Galway's top attractions for children and adults alike, the aquarium is located on the Salthill Promenade. It is an amazing insight into the aquatic world off the west of Ireland with an extensive and diverse collection of marine life. This is an all-weather attraction where you can have an underwater adventure without getting wet.

✚ Off map at A1 ✉ Toft Park, Salthill ☎ 091 585 100 ◷ Mon.–Fri. 9–5, Sat.–Sun. 9–6 mid-Mar. through Oct. 31, Wed.–Sun. 10–5, rest of year 🍴 Restaurant 🚌 1 from city center or 15 min. walk 💷 $$$

Galway City Museum

Occupying what was once a private house, this most striking museum has exhibition and information panels on three floors. Displays on the first floor trace Galway's history from medieval times to the present day, including one on the second floor devoted to a post-famine Claddagh village. Frequent art shows are staged. The ground floor exhibitions concentrate on contemporary Galway with an emphasis on arts in the city. There are great views to be had of the city and the river.

✚ C1 ✉ Spanish Arch ☎ 091 532 460; 091 532 467 ◷ Mon.–Sun. 10–5 Jun.–Sep. 30; Tue.–Sat. 10–5 Oct.–May 31 🍴 Coffee Shop

Leisureland

Give the kids – and yourself – a break from
sightseeing by reserving purely recreational
time at Leisureland. There's a heated indoor
pool, a tropical beach pool and treasure cove.
Most popular of all is the 200-foot waterslide.
Many other diversions, such as crazy golf and
an amusement park, will keep you and your
youngsters occupied.

➕ A1 ✉ Salthill ☎ 091 521 455; www.leisureland.ie
🕐 Daily 9:30–10, Apr.–Oct.; 12:30–2, 5:45–7:15 and
8–10, rest of year 🍴 Poolside restaurant 🚻 1 💷 $$$

Nora Barnacle House

This tiny cottage was the girlhood home of
James Joyce's lady love, later his wife and life-
long inspiration, "rousse auburn" haired
Nora Barnacle. The tiniest museum in
Ireland, it can be found in a quiet street close
to the city center and was built in the 19th
century. Norah lived here with her family,
however, around the turn of the century until
she left for Dublin in 1903.

Literary enthusiasts will enjoy perusing
an interesting and enlightening collection of
photographs and other exhibits pertaining to
the Joyce's connections with Galway (the
Joyces were one of the ancient tribes that
founded the city).

➕ B2 ✉ 8 Bowling Green ☎ 091 564 743
🕐 Mon.–Sat. 10–5, mid-May to mid-Sep.
🚇 City Centre 💷 $

Royal Tara China Visitor Centre

You can take a tour of the Royal Tara China
factory and watch master craftspeople busy at
work creating fine bone china as each piece
passes through no less than 10 stages of
production. Set in Tara Hall, a lovely Queen
Anne-Georgian style mansion, the center has
a wide variety including exclusive hand-
painted pieces and a barrelmen collection
that will evoke a smile. There is a
replacement service for discontinued lines
and for price savings take a look at the
slightly imperfect pieces.

➕ C2 ✉ Tara Hall, Mervue ☎ 091 705 602;
fax 091 757 574 🕐 Mon.–Sat. 10–5:30, Sun. 10–5
🍴 Coffee shop 🚌 Half-hourly buses from Eyre
Square to Mervue 💷 Free

Festivities in Eyre Square, Galway, a popular
place to gather and relax

St. Nicholas Collegiate Church

Tradition has it that Christopher Columbus
worshipped here in 1477 during a stopover
on his way to discover the New World.
That would be quite appropriate, since this
church is dedicated to St. Nicholas of Myra,
the patron saint of all travelers.

Built in 1320 on the site of an earlier
chapel, this is Ireland's largest medieval
church that is still in constant use. The
unique shape of the church came about when
extensions were made during the 16th
century. Cromwellian forces headquartered in
the church in 1652 destroyed many of its
features. Still intact, however, are tombstones
from the 12th to 20th centuries, including
that of a Norman crusader's tomb from the
12th or 13th century. Other outstanding
relics are the unique free-standing holy water
holder (benitier) and a carved font from the
16th or 17th century.

In September 2002, the Collegiate Church
attracted controversy by carrying out the first
same-sex "marriage", or Avowing Friendship
ceremony within its walls. There have been
no more such ceremonies since.

➕ B1 ✉ Market Street ☎ 091 563 081
🕐 Daily 10–5; check for services 🚇 City Centre
💷 Free (donations welcome)

Walk: **Stroll Back in Time**

Refer to route marked on city map on page 32.

There's hardly a street or lane in Galway center that doesn't hark back to facets of the city's history. Allow 1 to 2 hours.

Leaving the tourist office, head along Forster Street to Eyre Square.
At the far end of the square on the left side, the Bank of Ireland dates to 1836, but the site reaches back to 1312 or earlier when the priory of the Knights Templars sat there. Inside, a silver civic sword and mace are on display. The sword was made in Galway in 1610 and the mace in Dublin, 100 years later.

Leave the bank, cross the street and walk into busy Eyre Square.
This is the setting for all kinds of street entertainment. Originally called the Fair Green, it was presented to the town in 1710 by Mayor Edward Eyre. President John F. Kennedy spoke to the crowd here in 1963, and its name was officially changed to John F. Kennedy Park, although it's referred to locally as Eyre Square.

The rusting sails of the fountain symbolize the dark brown sails of the Galway Hookers (fishing boats) and Púcáns of the Claddagh fishing fleet. Look for Brown's Doorway, removed from an old mansion in Lower Abbeygate Street, dating from 1627.

Turn left at the top corner of the square and continue down Williams Street to Shop Street.
Lynch's Castle stands on the corner of Shop and Abbeygate streets, its stone facade bearing coats of arms (including those of the Earl of Kildare and King Henry VII), gargoyles and exotic escutcheons.

Continue down Shop Street to Abbeygate Street, turn right down the street and left onto Market Street.
Around the corner, look for the Lynch Memorial Window, a marble plaque over a Gothic doorway commemorating a legend that historians dispute but others defend as

the true origin of the expression "Lynch law." This is where, in 1493, Mayor James Lynch carried out "stern and unbending justice" when he condemned his 19-year-old son, Walter, to death after he pleaded guilty to murder. Walter was held in such high esteem, however, that the town executioner refused to carry out the execution. The sorrowing elder Lynch embraced his son and did the deed himself. Hence, some say, the entry of justice by "Lynch law" into common use.

Just across the street, No. 8 Bowling Green is the Nora Barnacle House (see page 36).

Go back across Market Street and turn right.
On Market Street, look for "marriage stones" set into house walls, which display the coats of arms of two families united in marriage. Also look for the main gates of the St. Nicholas Collegiate Church (see page 36).

Turn left into Churchyard Street and cross the intersection of Shop and Mainguard streets to High Street.
On your left you'll see the King's Head Pub. An ideal stop for refreshment and a look at the magnificently carved 1612 chimneypiece. Some say that the pub is haunted by King Charles I's restless spirit.

Continue down High Street to Cross Street, turn right, then take a short left into Kirwan's Lane. At the bottom of the lane turn right into Quay Street.
Continuing right, you enter the area known as Spanish Parade in memory of the Spanish merchant ships that once docked here. The air in the Fishmarket across the road once rang with the sound of Claddagh women selling their wares.

By the river, a sculpture commemorates Christopher Columbus' landing in 1477. Farther along is the Spanish Arch, a fine example of medieval walling. Across Wolfe Tone Bridge is the Claddagh (see page 33), much changed since its beginnings as a tiny village. The refurbished Galway City Museum, with three floors of exhibits, is next door to the Spanish Arch through which you can reach the pleasant quayside Long Walk.

Walk to the end of Merchant's Road, turn left and first right. Continue to Forster Street to return to the tourist office.

Connacht

Regional Sights

Key to symbols

⊞ map coordinates refer to the region map on page 29; sights below are highlighted in yellow on the map

⊠ address or location ☎ telephone number

◷ opening times 🍴 restaurant on site or nearby

💶 admission charge: $$$ more than €6, $$ €4 to €6, $ less than €4 ⓘ information

Aran Islands (Oileáin Árann)

Lying some 29 miles offshore, almost directly across the mouth of Galway Bay, the three inhabited Aran Islands are Inisheer (Inis Óirr, or eastern island), the smallest and nearest to the mainland (6 miles from Doolin, County, Clare); Inishmaan (Inis Meáin, or middle island); and Inishmore (Inis Mór, or big island), 7 miles from the Connemara coast. Ferries dock at Kilronan (Cill Rónan), the only safe harbor. Bleak and virtually treeless and with no significant hills or mountains, these three remote islands are linked geologically with the Burren in County Clare. The sheets of gray rock are reminiscent of a moonscape (see page 134).

The cracked limestone islands are steeped in tales of the hardy fishermen and farmers who developed a culture of self-sufficiency that reaches back before recorded history. Traces of the past remain in one of the most dramatic stone forts in western Europe, Dún Aengus, while early Christians left tiny churches. Here you'll also still hear Gaelic.

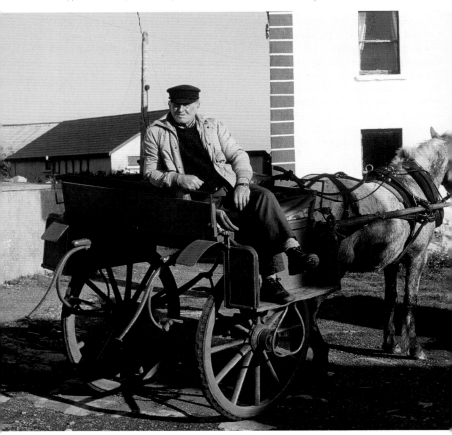

A traditional alternative to modern transportation in Kilronan, the capital of Inishmore

Mere survival was an everyday challenge for those early inhabitants: for generations, fishermen braved the seas in frail wood-and-canvas curraghs (keel-less rowing boats), while those who stayed at home laboriously collected seaweed and sand to enrich the rocky soil and support enough produce to keep body and soul intact. They also built stout stone walls as protection from the strong Atlantic winds.

With the advent of electricity, modern plumbing and improved travel to and from the mainland, the centuries-old isolation of the islands has lifted and everyday life is easier. Day-to-day necessities arrive daily instead of monthly; larger, safer fishing vessels now augment catches of curraghs that still sail to sea, but in more limited numbers. And the traditional dress of the islanders is reserved for special occasions. Probably the most important attack on isolation has been the arrival of tourism, with the consequent opening of island homes and restaurants to accommodate visitors.

Upon arrival at Kilronan (Cill Róngin) pier on Inishmore (Inis Mór), you'll be greeted by cars and minibuses for hire to explore the island with delightful and informative narratives by your driver-guide. There are bikes for rent as well. And although Gaelic is the everyday language, the courteous islanders will speak to you in English.

If you're a walker, this is the place for it, with stops to chat a bit with an old man smoking his pipe in an open doorway or a housewife hurrying along to the village. The Aran Way comprises three separate walks on each of the three islands: the Inis Mor Way (21 miles), the Inis Meain Way (5 miles) and the Inis Oirr Way (6.5 miles). The highest point is Baile na mBrocht at 400 feet.

No matter how you choose to explore the island, don't miss the islands chief attraction, Dún Aengus. Dramatically perched some 300 feet above the sea, this 11-acre cliff-top stone fort inhabits one of the most peaceful spots in Ireland. Don't miss the cluster of ecclesiastical ruins known as the Seven Churches, and you can also visit Aran's Heritage Centre to see Robert Flaherty's 1934

The Aran Islands – at the edge of Western Europe

Man from Aran film, which vividly depicts the harsh life of islanders in the past.

If you have a yen to visit Inishere (Inis Óirr) or Inishmaan (Inis Meáin) ask any of the fishermen at the Kilronan pier and they'll arrange to take you over by curragh or another small boat. Both islands have fortresses, churches and folk museums. And if you're really taken with the islands, the tourist office in Galway lists several good accommodations. Occasionally you might see someone in traditional Aran dress, but it is a rare sight nowadays.

Several ferry companies serve the islands from Galway, Rossaveal and Doolin. Aer Arann fly small aircraft to all three islands. All transportation services may be affected by weather and it is best to check schedules before your visit.

✚ A1

Tourist information ☎ Inishmore 099 61263; Inishmaan 099 73010; Inisheer 099 75008; www.visitaranislands.com

Aer Arann ✉ Connemara Regional Airport, Inverin, Co. Galway ☎ 091 593 034; fax 091 593 238

Doolin Ferries ✉ Doolin, County Clare ☎ 065 707 5555; fax 065 707 4417

Island Ferries ✉ 4 Forster Street, Galway ☎ 091 568 903

Aran Direct ☎ 091 566 535

Twelfth-century remains of the Cistercian abbey at Boyle

Boyle

The Cistercian abbey that stands beside the rushing River Boyle in the heart of Boyle is the main reason to visit this quiet town. Dating from the late 12th century, it was founded as a daughter-house of Mellifont Abbey (see pages 94–5). Unsuccessful in their efforts to keep the world's violence at bay, the they abbey's monks were slaughtered and its walls torn down, leaving these ruins to tell their story. The nave, with its Romanesque and Gothic arches, as well as the choir and transepts are in good condition, and the restored 16th- to 17th-century gatehouse houses an interpretive center.

In the beautifully restored King House, with its delightful setting overlooking the River Boyle, historical exhibitions give the 18th-century mansion, home of the Earls of Kingston, a hands-on museum quality. Historical events from 1603 to 1957 are explained by the King family in one exhibit. In another you get to beat a regimental drum as you hear the exploits of the Connaught Rangers army regiment billeted here. In yet another, try your hand at building a brick vault. You can see how difficult or easy it is to write with quill and ink, as well as join a clan feast in still another.

A short distance east of Boyle is Lough Key Forest and Activity Park, a lovely mixed woodland of 850 acres. Especially interesting is the bog garden, with heathers and other small peat-growing plants, and the dozen or so islands in the lake: Trinity Island holds the ruins of a McDermott castle and a medieval priory, and Church Island also holds the remains of a medieval priory. Wildlife thrives in the park's varied habitats.

A major redevelopment has brought new attractions to the park, with the Lough Key Experience, the Adventure Play Kingdom and the Boda Borg Challenge for older children. Lovers of traditional music may want to make a pilgrimage to Keadue village (4 miles northeast of Lough Key). The blind harpist Turlough O'Carolan lies in Kilronan Abbey cemetery just west of the village. On the cemetery's arched gateway is inscribed: "Within this churchyard lie the remains of Carolan, the last of the Irish bards who departed this life 25th March, 1738. R.I.P."

Nearby Tullyboy Farm is a marvelous treat for children. Centered around an

Lough Key, a naturalist's paradise northeast of Boyle

18th-century farmhouse, this family-run working farm has the usual animals plus exotic breeds such as llamas, Jacob sheep, ostriches and Angora and Anglo Nubian goats. Soda bread is baked on the open hearth of the kitchen, and there's a vintage threshing mill for oats. As well as learning some history there are pony rides, a playground and a picnic area to keep youngsters occupied. ➕ C2

Tourist information ✉ The Courthouse, Market Street Boyle ☎ 071 96 62145 ⏰ Mon.–Sat. 10–5:30, May–Sep.

Boyle Abbey ✉ N4 to Garrick ☎ 071 96 62604 ⏰ Daily 10–6, Easter–Oct. 31 💰 $

King House ✉ Main Street ☎ 071 96 63242; fax 071 96 63243; www.kinghouse.ie ⏰ Daily 10–6, Apr.–Oct.; pre-booked groups rest of year 🍴 Coffee shop 💰 $$$ ℹ Children's activities and crafts shop

Lough Key Forest Park and Activity Park ✉ N4, just east of Boyle ☎ 071 967 3122; www.loughkey.ie ⏰ Daily 10–6, Apr.–Oct.; Fri.–Sun. 12–4, rest of year 🍴 Tearooms overlook the lake 💰 $$$ Borda Borg; $$$ Lough Key Experience; $$ Adventure Play

Kingdom; $$ parking ℹ Combined ticket available **Kilronan Abbey** ✉ 4 miles northeast of Lough Key **Tullyboy Animal Farm** ✉ Tullyboy, 2 miles south of Boyle on N61, Boyle-Roscommon road ☎ 071 96 68031; fax 071 96 68031; www.tullyboyfarm.ie ⏰ Mon.–Fri. 10:30–6, Sat.–Sun. noon–6, Easter–Sep. 🍴 Café 💰 $$$

Castlebar

Castlebar is the county town of County Mayo; its most notable attraction is the Museum of Country Life. In a carefully renovated 18th-century house, along with extensions, this is the first branch of the National Museum to be located outside Dublin. Innovative displays, utilizing 50,000 items – crafts, household utensils, tools and clothing – reflect the everyday lives of Ireland's people and brilliantly illustrate the country's history over the past 200 years. ➕ B2

Museum of Country Life ✉ Turlough Park House ☎ 094 903 1755; www.museum.ie ⏰ Tue.–Sat. 10–5, Sun. 2–5 🍴 Restaurant 💰 Free

The attractive grounds of Ashford Castle are a match for its exuberant architecture

Castlerea

Lying in the west of County Roscommon, Castlerea is the second biggest town in the county. The most impressive site here is Clonalis House, the home of the O'Conor Don, chieftain of the Clan O'Conor, one-time high kings of Ireland, traditional kings of Connaught and Europe's oldest family. Their ancestors can be traced back through 60 generations to 1100 BC. Built in 1878, the house is largely furnished with Sheraton and Louis XV pieces, and has a collection of artifacts including the harp of the bard Turlough O'Carolan (1670–1738), rare glass and china, paintings, the ancient O'Conor inauguration stone and Gaelic manuscripts.
✚ B2

Clonalis House ✉ On the Roscommon–Castlebar road (N60) just west of Castlerea ☎ 094 96 20014; www.clonalis.com ⏰ Mon.–Sat. 11–4, Jun.–Sep. ✋ $$$

Cong

Successive generations of Americans have loved Ireland as a direct result of the antics of John Wayne, Maureen O'Hara and Barry Fitzgerald as they romped through "The Quiet Man," the epic 1952 film that went on to become a classic. The main village street scenes took place near the cross in the market square of Cong, and the nearby general store was transformed into Cohan's Bar to play its part in the film. Many of the exterior shots were taken on the grounds of Ashford Castle – including the woodlands, the church, Squire Danaher's house and the salmon river with its arched bridge.

In the town now, the Heritage Centre has re-created a typical working Irish cottage and life there in the 1920s. Clever exhibitions in the Archaeological and Historical Interpretative Centre detail the plethora of relics in the Cong area.

Enter Cong's Augustinian abbey through this impressive stone doorway

The marvelous, fairyland architectural concoction that is Ashford Castle makes a superb luxury hotel much favored by international celebrities (President and Mrs. Reagan stayed here during their 1984 visit). No less marvelous are its grounds, with beautifully landscaped lawns sloping down to the island-dotted lake. The castle was originally built by the de Burgoes in 1228, and since then a French chateau-style mansion of the early 1700s and Sir Benjamin Guinness' additions in the mid-1800s have been incorporated – somewhat eccentric, to say the least.

At the edge of this picturesque little village is the Royal Abbey of Cong. This was built in 1120 by Turlough Mor O'Conor, high king of Ireland, and is the final resting place of Rory O'Conor, last high king, who died in 1198. Situated on the site of an earlier seventh-century St. Fechin community, this was an important ecclesiastical center for

more than 700 years, and as many as 3,000 people once lived here.

Immediately east of Cong toward Cross lies the Plain of Moytura, where you'll find the Ballymagibbon Cairn. Dating from about 3,000 BC, the 60-foot-high, 287-foot-circumference cairn was erected to commemorate a fierce prehistoric battle between the Firbolg and de Danann tribes. It seems that the Firbolgs carried the day during the early fighting, and each warrior presented a stone and the head of a Danann to his king, who used the stones to build the cairn in honor of the grisly tribute.

On a happier note, nearby Moytura House (privately owned and not open to the public) was once the home of Sir William Wilde and his wife Speranza, parents of Oscar Wilde.

🚭 B2

Tourist information ✉ Abbey Street, Cong ☎ 094 95 46542 🕐 Daily 10–6, Mar. to mid-Nov.

Quiet Man Heritage Cottage and Archaeological Historical Centre ✉ Circular Road, Cong ☎ 094 95 46089; fax 094 95 46448 🕐 Daily 10–5, Jun.–Oct.; otherwise by appointment 💷 $$

Ashford Castle ✉ Cong, 0.5 miles outside Cong on the right of the Galway Road ☎ 094 95 46003; fax 094 95 46260 🕐 Daily 10–5; hours vary based on hotel occupancy 💷 $$

Grand Tudor Gothic architecture at Kylemore Abbey

Journey Through Silence – Connemara

To travel through Connemara is to journey through largely unpopulated spaces. The landscape is constantly changed by shifting light and shade that generations of artists have struggled to capture on canvas. Rock-strewn fields contrast with glimpses of sandy strands at the sea's edge.

Natural Country Rhythms

Life is simple in Connemara. Keep your eyes open for turf being cut and dried in the boglands April through June. Especially along the coastal road you may see donkeys with loaded creels transporting the dried turf to be stacked against the winter's cold. Sheep-shearing is done by hand in June and July, often within the roofless walls of ruined cottages. Washed-up seaweed is traditionally harvested from the shore at the time of full and new moons. Thatchers are usually at work in September and October, and the biggest concentration of thatched cottages is between Ballyconneely and Roundstone and between Cleggan and the Clifden road by way of Claddaghduff.

At Roundstone and Cleggan, small trawlers fish year-round, with open lobster boats and curraghs setting out only in summer months. You may want to allow time to stroll two beautiful nearby beaches, Goirtin and Dog's Bay. If you're lucky, you'll happen upon a curragh race in one of the coastal villages – be sure to stop and join in the conviviality.

Roundstone is also the home of master *bodhrán* maker Malachy Kearnes, whose workshop is in the IDA Craft Centre. The *bodhrán* is a one-sided goatskin drum, and Malachy's artist wife, Anne, decorates the finished *bodhráns* with colorful Celtic designs. The store here also sells crafts, CDs and musical instruments.

Clifden

The August Connemara Pony Show is in Clifden, where the spirited bidding for the sturdy little animals takes on an air of ritual in a country-fair atmosphere. This is a great family day of eating, drinking and visiting with like-minded horse lovers. Summer evenings also bring traditional music in many of Clifden's hotel bars and pubs; check with the tourist office or the hotel's front desk. One thing you won't want to miss in Clifden is the spectacular Sky Drive, a cliff road that forms a 9-mile circle around a peninsula and opens up vast seascapes. It's well signposted from Clifden. Boats are also available (through most accommodations) for deep-sea fishing expeditions for mackerel, blue shark, conger, cod, ling and many other varieties.

North of Clifden, Cleggan is the mainland departure point for Inishbofin Island, a place of great tranquility, wide beaches and stunning views.

You can learn all about the shaping of Connemara from prehistoric times to the present from an excellent audiovisual presentation at the Connemara Heritage and History Centre at Lettershea, 4 miles east of Clifden. There is a most spectacular view of a 5,000-year-old burial site, a reconstruction of a crannóg (lake dwelling), ring fort and early Christian oratory.

Mountains and Moors

Stretching south near the 19th-century Quaker village of Letterfrack is the 4,942-acre Connemara National Park, encompassing mountains, bogs, heaths and grasslands, and crisscrossed by nature walks through beautiful woodlands and surrounding hills. Irish red deer and herds of Connemara ponies roam these same grounds, and birdwatchers will delight in the variety of winged species. Allow time to visit the park's visitor center, with its informative audiovisual presentation and exhibition, and perhaps walk one of its shorter nature trails.

To the east of Letterfrack is magnificent Kylemore Abbey in a picturesque setting of woodlands on the banks of Pollacappal Lough, the impressive neo-Gothic facade reflected in the lake's mirror surface. The stone mansion dates from the 19th century, when it was built as a private residence. It is now home to an order of Benedictine nuns who have for many years conducted an international girls' school, a thriving pottery industry and craft shop.

Not to be missed is the beautifully restored Gothic chapel, reached by a footpath beside the delightful lakeside. Their beautifully restored walled Victorian garden is the largest in Ireland and is accessed through a marvelous woodland walk.

Coastal Views and Butterflies

Letterfrack's Ocean and Country Museum brings alive the Connemara coastal oceans, most vividly through scenic and wildlife coastal cruises aboard the *Queen of Connemara*, sealife exhibits and an aquarium. On the grounds are sandy coves, picnic areas, children's play areas and a craft shop. And on Sunday afternoons, there are children's plays and Irish music sessions.

Tourist information ✉ Galway Road, Clifden ☎ 095 21163; fax 095 21887 🕐 Mon.–Sat 10–5, Jun.–Aug.
Roundstone Musical Instruments ✉ IDA Craft Centre, Roundstone ☎ 095 35808; fax 095 35980 🕐 Mon.–Sat. 9:30–5:30 🍴 Café
Connemara National Park ✉ Letterfrack, Clifden–Westport Road (N59) ☎ 095 41054 🕐 Park: open all year; visitor center: daily 9:30–6, Jul.–Aug.; 10–5:30, Jun., Sep. to mid-Oct., Apr.–May 🍴 Tearoom 💲$
Kylemore Abbey and Garden ✉ Connemara, near Letterfrack ☎ 095 41146; fax 095 41440; www.kylemoreabbey.com 🕐 Abbey: daily 9–5. Gardens: daily 10–4:30, Easter–Oct. 31 Closed Good Friday and Dec. 25–31 🍴 Restaurant, 💲$$$
Ocean and Country Museum ✉ Renvyle Peninsula, Connemara ☎ 095 43473; fax 095 43911 🕐 Daily 10–6, Mar. 1 to mid-Oct. 🍴 Café 💲$$$

The 16th-century tower house of Thoor Ballylee

Gort

Gort is surrounded by history, which includes the seventh-century monastic settlement of Kilmacduagh, and five castles within a 5-mile radius. The poet William Butler Yeats bought Thoor Ballylee, a 16th-century castle keep, for just £35 ($56) in 1917 when it was not much more than a ruin. After restoring it to a habitable state, he summered here until 1929. Poems written about or at Thoor Ballylee are included in his book of poems *The Tower*. His life and times are vividly portrayed in an audiovisual presentation.

The town is much associated with Yeats' contemporary, Lady Augusta Gregory (Dame Isabella Augusta neé Persse, born the 12th child in a family of 16 children), whose house at Coole was demolished in the 1940s. There must always have been creative inspiration in this tranquil setting, for this patron of the arts and founder of the Abbey Theatre in Dublin attracted many of Ireland's illustrious literary figures – writers W. B. Yeats, George Bernard Shaw and Sean O'Casey all drew encouragement from stimulating and appreciative conversations while visiting Coole House. Sadly, only ruins mark the place where the house once stood – the grounds are now a nature reserve. You can, however, take a look at the famous "Autograph Tree" for carved names of literary guests.

Such literati also had links with Dunguaire Castle. In the early 1900s it was a country retreat for Irish writer Oliver St. John Gogarty, who held regular literary gatherings. Furnishings of the castle reflect its medieval beginnings, and the banquet and literary evening attractions are much more intimate than those at Bunratty and Knappogue. The entertainment reflects Ireland's bardic tradition and celebrates the richness of this country's literary and musical past.

➕ B1

Tourist information ✉ Thoor Baliyee, Gort ☎ 091 631 436 🕐 Mon.–Sat.10–6, May–Sep.

Yeats Tower (Thoor Ballylee) ✉ Signposted near Gort, half a mile off N18 (Galway–Limerick road) and half a mile off N66 (Gort–Loughrea road) ☎ 091 631 436 May–Sep., 091 537 700 rest of year; fax 091 537 733 🕐 Mon.–Sat. 9:30–5, May–Sep. 🚻 $$ 🅸 Picnic area, tourist office and exchange bureau

Coole Park ✉ 2 miles north of Gort, due west of N18 ☎ 091 631 804; www.coolepark.ie 🕐 Vistors center: daily 10–6, Jun.–Aug.; 10–5 Sep.; Tue.–Sun. 10–5, Apr.–May. Grounds open all year 🚻 Visitors' center: $$; grounds: free

Dunguaire Castle ✉ Kinvarra 10 miles northwest of Gort on the N18 Galway road ☎ 061 360 788; fax 061 361 020 🕐 Daily 9:30–5 (last admission at 4:30), mid-Apr. through Oct. 31 🚻 Castle: $$

Read the runes inscribed on Sligo's monument to the poet W. B. Yeats

Sligo

Sligo (Sligeach, Shelly Place) grew up around a ford of the River Garavogue, which rises in Lough Gill and tumbles over swift rapids as it approaches its estuary. The town's strategic position gave it early prominence as a seaport, and as a fine religious center, it is the cathedral town of both a Catholic and Protestant diocese. While many come to Sligo for the sights associated with the poet William Butler Yeats, it would be a mistake not to see the hightlights of the old town itself.

Its streets are filled with quaint old storefronts and 19th-century buildings. The ruins of the Dominican Abbey on Abbey Street represent the town's only surviving medieval building. Kings and princes of Sligo were brought for burial here, and the abbey often suffered raids, eventually closing in 1641. The altar here is one of the few surviving medieval altars in Ireland. On Adelaide Street, the Cathedral of the Immaculate Conception is a massive limestone structure of Renaissance Romanesque style. St. John's Church on John Street dates from the mid-1700s and was designed by the same architect as Leinster House (see page 80), the seat of the Irish government in Dublin.

The Town Hall on Quay Street dates from 1865 – a graceful Italian Renaissance building that legend says stands on the site of a 17th-century Cromwellian fort. At Teeling and Chapel streets, the Courthouse incorporates part of an earlier courthouse. In 1832, when cholera swept over Sligo, the building housed coffin builders. You can't miss the impressive Pollexfen Ships Building at the corner of Adelaide and Wine streets; the large stone building originally belonged to the owners of the largest shipping company in Sligo. It was Yeats' grandfather who, on owning the building, added the tower as a lookout point for his ships returning to port.

There's no shortage of nighttime entertainment in Sligo. The Hawks Well Theatre was the first purpose-built theater in western Ireland, and it places a strong emphasis on Irish playwrights. Productions are performed by leading Irish theater companies, with an occasional evening of poetry, musical concerts and traditional song, dance, drama and comedy. It's fairly easy to find traditional music and ballads in Sligo pubs. However, since the schedule for such happenings is often a non-schedule, be sure

© Govt of Ireland

to check with the tourist office for information about pubs that are likely to have musical entertainment.

For Yeats' devotees, it comes as no surprise that Sligo offers much information and memorabilia: For two weeks in late July or early August, Sligo breathes, eats and sleeps the incomparable poet as the Yeats International Summer School presents seminars, lectures, workshops, readings and dramas that draw throngs of scholars from around the world. However, the ultimate source of information on W. B. Yeats can be found at the Yeats Society, headquartered in the red-brick 1895 Yeats Memorial Building on Hyde Bridge. Inside, the Sligo Art Gallery's plethora of exhibits relating to the poet include his complete works in first editions and his 1923 Nobel Prize for Literature.

Sligo has intrigued painters as much as writers, and Yeats had no family monopoly on fascination with this countryside – his painter brother, Jack Yeats, sought to capture it on canvas, and there's an extensive collection of his paintings and drawings.

County Sligo encompasses some of Ireland's most wondrous scenery – the sort of sea and mountains and far-flung vistas that shaped Yeats' life and work. From boyhood stays in Magheraboy with his grandparents to the end of his life when he was laid to rest in Drumcliff churchyard, Yeats' imagination was fired by legends of ancient heroes who lived out their sagas in this part of Ireland and left the countryside strewn with mementos of their passing; cairns, dolmens, passage graves and prehistoric relics continue to bear silent witness to the lives that so engaged him.

Places associated with Yeats are marked by simple signposts inscribed with appropriate verses, but before rambling through Yeats Country, go by the tourist office or a Sligo bookshop and pick up the excellent booklet *The Yeats Country*, which tells you which poems were written about which places. The Yeats Country drive on pages 50–52 also takes you to some of these spots: beautiful Lough Gill, where you'll find his Lake Isle of Inisfree; the cairn at Knocknarea's summit where according to Yeats "passionate Maeve is stony-still." His

The graceful Italian Renaissance tower of Sligo Courthouse

words about this mystical, magical part of Ireland cannot be bettered, and you will find yourself recalling them again and again.

Scattered over the face of the county are traces of the prehistoric races who lived here during three periods: Late Stone Age (Neolithic, 2500–2000 BC);, the Bronze Age (2000–500 BC); and the Early Iron Age (500 BC to AD 500). The tourist office has a detailed leaflet, "Archaeology in County Sligo," that tells you where to find the most important court cairns, portal dolmens, passage graves, ring forts and gallery graves. In the immediate vicinity of Sligo town is Carrowmore (south near Ballysadare), Ireland's largest and most impressive group of megalithic tombs.

✚ C3 (regional map on page 29)

Tourist information ✚ B1 ✉ Temple Street ☎ 071 91 61202; fax 071 91 60360 🕐 Daily 9–5:30, Apr.–Oct.; Mon–Fri 9–5, rest of year

Sligo Art Gallery ✚ B2 ✉ Yeats Memorial Building, Hyde Bridge ☎ 071 91 45847; www.sligoartgallery.com 🕐 Mon.–Sat. 10–5:30 💷 Free

Hawks Well Theatre ✚ B1 ✉ Temple Street ☎ 071 91 61518 🕐 Box office: Mon.–Fri. 10–5:30, Sat. 3–6 (8 on performance days)

Drive: Yeats Country

Duration: 1–2 days

Steeped in echoes of the poet William Butler Yeats and prehistory, you'll find in this corner of Ireland a happy unison of wooded lakes, bare mountaintops and Atlantic seascapes. This 98-mile tour starts from the tourist office on Temple Street in Sligo.

Take the N15 for 5 miles to Drumcliff.

> Under bare Ben Bulben's head
> In Drumcliff churchyard Yeats is laid
> An ancestor was rector there
> Long years ago; a church stands near,
> By the road an ancient cross,
> No marble, no conventional phrase;
> On limestone quarried near the spot,
> By his command these words are cut:
> Cast a cold eye
> On life, on death,
> Horseman, pass by!

Yeats' poem describes Drumcliff completely, and his grave can be found easily in the Protestant churchyard. Yeats died in 1939 in the south of France and was buried in a cemetery overlooking the Mediterranean Sea. His remains were brought home to his beloved Sligo in 1948 and placed here, as

he wished, in the shadow of Benbulben. The road runs through a monastic site to the church where the poet's grandfather was rector.

Continue on the N15 and almost immediately take a turn left for 4 miles to Lissadell.

Yeats was a regular visitor to the Greek-revival style Lissadell House. The slightly forbidding classical facade hides the romance captured in his poem in memory of the Gore-Booth sisters, Eva (of whom he was particularly fond) and Constance, which begins thus:

> The light of evening, Lissadell,
> Great windows open to the south,
> Two girls in silk kimonos, both
> Beautiful, one a gazelle.

Constance became the Countess Markievicz, a leader in the Easter Rising of 1916 and the first woman to be elected to Westminster, although she never took her seat. The 1830s limestone mansion has a charming music room and a dining room with intriguing murals. The striking two-story entrance hall is lined with Doric columns and features a beautiful double staircase. Among the multitude of family documents are diaries of Robert Gore-Booth, whose charity to the poor during famine years forced him to mortgage the estate. The house is set in fine parkland near the sea and seals can be spotted basking on the sandbanks.

Drive through the parkland, rejoin the road and turn left, then right at the fork. Soon after that, turn right and continue to the village of Grange. Turn left to rejoin the N15 for Bundoran.

Contrasting with the placid towns and coastal villages of the northwest, the busy seaside resort of Bundoran offers many attractions, a good beach and cliff walks. Southwest of Bundoran, at Streedagh, a small park commemorates the place where three vessels of the Spanish Armada foundered in 1588. Members of the crew who struggled ashore from the overladen ships found little help on land.

Take the R280 for 3 miles to Kinlough. This attractive village is at the north end of Lough Melvin and is good for coarse and salmon fishing. On the shore is the ruin of Rossclogher Abbey, and on an artificial island are the remains of the MacClancy Castle (known as Rossclogher Castle), where nine survivors of the Armada were given refuge.

Follow the R281 along the Lough Melvin shore for 8 miles, then turn right onto the R282 for Manorhamilton. This unassuming village in County Leitrim stands in an area of untouched mountain valleys with lofty peaks, lush fertile slopes, steep clefts and gray cliff walls. It's overlooked by a ruined castle that was built at the meeting of four mountain valleys by the Scottish 17th-century planter Sir Frederick Hamilton, who gave his name to the village.

Take the N16 for Sligo. After 7 miles turn right onto an unclassified road for Glencar Lake. Glencar is a beautiful lake; the steep valley slopes are clothed with mixed woodland, a profusion of rare plants and luxuriously heathered mountaintops. Glencar waterfall, white with spray, cascades down from a rocky headland and is immortalized by Yeats in his poem "The Stolen Child."

At the end of the lakeside road, turn right toward Sligo on the N16, then left to Parke's Castle Visitor Centre on the R286. Although its name comes from the English family who moved in during the 1620

Glencar waterfall tumbles down through the trees and rocks

plantation of this part of Ireland, the beautifully restored Parke's Castle is a fortified manor house that was originally the home of the O'Rourke clan, rulers of the kingdom of Breffni. The audiovisual show not only tells this story (including how the Parke family unashamedly dismantled a neighboring castle for materials to use in their own), but also includes a wealth of information on other points of interest in the area. From Parke's Castle, there is a superb view of Lough Gill, and to the southwest is the Isle of Innisfree for which Yeats yearned – "where peace comes dropping slow" – and to which you can take a cruise from Parke's Castle (including one at sunset). If you explore the lake, you'll find a sweat-house, medieval Ireland's answer to the sauna.

Continue on the R286, then turn right onto the R288 for Dromahair or Carrick-on-Shannon, then turn right on the R287 for Sligo. After 2.5 miles turn right again, following the R287 past the sign for Innisfree to Dooney Rock Forest, before rejoining the N4. This corner of Lough Gill reveals forests and paths to satisfy any enthusiastic walker and great views of the lough. Dooney Rock Forest bears the vestiges of a once important oak

The Georgian Lissadell House, built in 1834 by Sir Robert Gore-Booth

forest. Here you can see the "twining branches," two linked oaks. Yeats wrote of "The Fiddler of Dooney," who made folk "dance like the waves of the sea." The poem has inspired a Fiddler of Dooney competition for the champion fiddler of Ireland. It's held in Sligo in July.

Cairns Hill Forest Park marks the two cairns on Belvoir and Cairns peaks. A legend holds that these cairns are the burial places of the warriors Omra and Romra. Omra fell in love with Romra's daughter Gille (meaning beauty). When a mortal battle ensued after the lovers were discovered by Romra, Gille drowned herself, and Lough Gill was formed from the tears of her nursemaid.

Travel south on the N4, then turn right on the R292 for Rathcarrick and Strandhill.
Great Atlantic breakers crash onto the beach at Strandhill – a favored place for surfing championships. If you prefer calmer waters drive to Culleenamoret. The town nestles beneath the cairn-capped Knocknarea mountain. This is the great Misgaun Maeve, an unopened cairn about 200 feet in diameter and 80 feet high that archeologists believe covers a vast passage grave, but legend insists

is the burial monument to Maeve, the warrior queen of Connacht. If you climb to the summit of Knocknarea, Sligo tradition suggests that you add a stone to the cairn as a protection against the fairies.

Among the fields below Knocknarea at Carrowmore is one of Europe's largest concentrations of megalithic tombs. Visitors are inevitably quite moved at the sight of this sacred burial place of more than 100 passage graves. The earliest tombs are said to predate the famous passage grave at Newgrange by about 700 years. It's best to wear shoes suitable to walking on uneven terrain.

Take the R292 for 5 miles back to Sligo.
Lissadell House ✉ Drumcliff, off N15 (main Sligo–Donegal road) 8 miles north of Sligo ☎ 071 91 63150; www.lissadellhouse.com ⏰ Daily 10:30–6, mid-Mar. through Oct. 31 🅿 $$
Parke's Castle ✉ Fivemile Bourne, Co. Leitrim, on the north shore of Lough Gill ☎ 071 91 64149 ⏰ Daily 10–6, Mar.–Oct. 🍴 Tearoom 🅿 $
Carrowmore Megalithic Cemetery ✉ Carrowmore Visitors Centre. Signposted on N15 from Sligo, N4 from the south ☎ 071 91 61534 ⏰ Daily 10–6, May–Oct.; open to groups on request during winter months 🅿 $

Strokestown and Roscommon

Many Irish towns and villages reveal their Georgian origins in wide streets, but Strokestown, said to have the widest main street in Ireland, is exceptional in that it was originally modeled on Vienna's Ringstrasse. The town is little more than an adjunct to Strokestown Park House, one of Ireland's finest great houses, which lies beyond the Gothic triple arch on this main street. Dating from the early 1700s, the 45-room Palladian house incorporates parts of an earlier tower house. The reception rooms, galleried kitchen and some bedrooms and nurseries are furnished in its original style. The restored walled "pleasure garden" invites a stroll. Elaborate vaulted stables in the south wing of the house hold the fascinating Irish Famine Museum.

Roscommon Castle ruins date to 1269

Strokestown Park was the family seat of the Pakenham Mahon family from the 1600s to 1979, and family archives that were purchased with the house shed light on the heart-wrenching plight of the Irish poor during the devastating years of the potato famine. They also form an authentic platform for the museum's critical view of contemporary world poverty and hunger.

South of Strokestown, the county town of Roscommon also lies to the west of Lough Ree and has many fine old buildings, including several churches, the Old Military Barracks, the Court House and the Old Jail, which had an 18th-century female executioner called "Lady Betty." Condemned to death herself, allegedly for murdering her son, she volunteered to step into the breach when the hangman was ill on condition that her life be spared. She was subsequently appointed for the job with a salary and accommodation at the jail where she remained for about 30 years. She drew charcoal portraits of some of her clients, whom she dispatched from a hinged board outside her third-floor window.

Overlooking the town, ruins of drum towers are all that remain of the 13th-century castle that once stood here. After changing hands between the O'Kelly and O'Conor clans over the centuries, it finally fell into those of Cromwellian troops, who left behind the destruction of all but the towers. The remains of Félim O'Conor, 13th-century king of Connacht, rest in the ruins of a Dominican priory in a tomb decorated with effigies of gallowglasses (soldiers of fortune).

Three miles southwest of Roscommon, the ruins of Fuerty, a Franciscan church, mark the setting for the slaughter of 100 priests by a local tyrant. Among the interesting headstones in the graveyard is that of a blacksmith, with carvings depicting an anvil, bellows and tongs, and that of a shepherd with his crook and sheep.

✚ C2

Tourist information ✉ John Harrison Memorial Hall, Roscommon ☎ 090 66 26342 🕐 Mon.–Sat.10–6, Jun.–Sep.

Strokestown Park House, Garden and Irish Famine Museum ✉ Strokestown, on N5 (Dublin–Castlebar road) ☎ 071 96 33013; fax 071 96 33712; www.strokestownpark.ie 🕐 Daily 11–5:30, mid-Mar. through Oct. 31 🍴 Restaurant ✋ $$$

Westport

With an octagonal center and lime trees lining both sides of the river, Clew Bay at its feet and a wealth of grand Georgian buildings, Westport is one of western Ireland's most charming market towns and is designated a Heritage Town of Ireland. The Thursday morning market at the Octagon brings the farmers into town, and there is a frenzy of buying and selling clothes, produce and novelties. It's even more lively when the

An attractive 18th-century corner of Westport

annual arts festival takes place in late September, with live music, visual arts, theater and lots more.

Westport's main sight is Westport House, a lovely old Georgian mansion set in fine parkland near the quay. It dates back to 1731, but sits on the grounds of an earlier O'Malley castle, the dungeons of which are now visited by children who are happily "terrified" by horrors installed for their entertainment. Lord and Lady Altamont are in residence here, and over the years they have turned their estate into a stylish virtual museum of Irish memorabilia and craftsmanship, with a magnificent drawing room, two dining rooms, a long gallery and grand entrance hall. Up the marble staircase, four bedrooms hold such treasures as state robes and coronets and 200-year-old Chinese wallpaper. On the grounds there's an animal park, rides and amusements – including a log flume ride – and opportunities for boating and fishing on the lake and river.

Between Louisburgh and Westport, Clew Bay opens before you as the road passes through stony, barren hillsides and touches the bay at several points. The 16th-century pirate queen Grace O'Malley (Granuaile) roamed these waters freely, darting in and out of the bay to attack merchant ships that sailed coastal waters. When summoned to London by Queen Elizabeth I in 1575, she refused to bow in submission, proudly proclaiming herself "Queen of Clew Bay." The square tower near the harbor on Clare Island was her refuge and stronghold, and splendid views of Clew Bay and the mountains of Connemara and Mayo undoubtedly explain her deep love of the island, which also holds a 15th-century abbey and an ancient promontory fort on its southern cliffs. Regular mailboat sailings from Roonagh Pier (4 miles west of Louisburgh) carry present-day visitors to Clare Island year-round.

Five miles west of Westport, Croagh Patrick, Ireland's holy mountain, rises to 2,510 feet. St. Patrick is believed to have fasted at the summit for 40 days. Each year pilgrims climb the stony paths, some in their bare feet, on the last Sunday in July for a four o'clock morning Mass at its top.

✚ A2

Tourist information ✉ James Street ☎ 098 25711; fax 098 26709 ◷ Daily 9–6, Jul.–Aug.; Mon.–Fri. 9–6, Sat. 10–6, Mar.–Jun., Sep.–Oct.; Mon.–Fri. 9–5:45, Sat. 10–1, rest of year

Westport House ✉ Westport ☎ 098 25430 or 098 27766; fax 098 25206 ◷ Daily 11:30–5:30, Apr.–Sep.; Sat.–Sun. 11:30–5:30 in Oct. 🍴 Tearoom 💷 $$$

Drive: **Achill Island and County Mayo**

Duration: 2 days

The ghost of pirate queen Grace O'Malley will follow you on this 207-mile tour that travels to Achill Island, Ireland's most scenic island and home to one of O'Malley's many strongholds.

Starting from Westport's tourist office on The Mall, take the N59 north for 8 miles to Newport.
Picturesque little Newport, which dates from the 17th century, faces Clew Bay and is sheltered by mountains. Its neo-Romanesque Catholic church was built in 1914 and features a superb stained-glass window of the Last Judgment designed by Harry Clarke. Four miles west, Rockfleet Castle, sometimes called Carrigahowley Castle, is one of Grace O'Malley's strongholds, where the indomitable pirate queen came to live permanently after her second husband died in 1583.

Follow the N59 west to Mulrany, then the R319 to Achill Island, 28 miles.
Connected to the mainland by a bridge, Achill Island is the largest of Ireland's islands. Only 15 miles long and 12 miles wide, it is a scenic mix of soaring cliffs, golden beaches, heathery boglands and tiny villages. Fishing for shark and other big-game fish is excellent, and you'll find boats and guides for hire. The Atlantic Drive is spectacular, climbing from gently rolling mountain foothills, past stretches of sandy beaches, and through charming villages with excellent views of the sea, Clew Bay and the mainland. Yes, it's easy to see why Grace O'Malley fell in love with Achill's unspoiled wildness and profound peacefulness. Beside Kildownet Castle are the ruins of a small 12th-century church. At the center of holiday activities is Keel, which has a fine sandy beach and a small harbor with fishing and sightseeing boats for rent. Viewed from a boat, the sea-carved rocks below the Menawn cliffs at the eastern end of the beach take on fanciful shapes. At Doogort, nestled at the foot of Slievemore, the fascinating Seal Caves cut far into the cliffs of Slievemore.

Fishing in the River Moy at Ballina

Take the R319 back to Mulrany, then turn north on the N59 for the drive to Crossmolina, passing through Ballycroy and Bangor Erris (where the N59 turns sharply east).

At Crossmolina, on the shores of Lough Conn, you'll find the huge genealogical data bank of the North Mayo Family Heritage Centre, where ancestors can be traced by searching through church registers, wills, leases and even school rollbooks. The Heritage Centre displays a collection of farm implements and household items from rural life of long ago.

Northward via the R315 to Ballycastle is Céide Fields. More than 5,000 years old, it's the oldest enclosed farm system in the world revealed virtually intact underneath the bogs. The 12-square-mile site holds relics of Stone Age rural life and includes stone walls that surrounded the ancient community and megalithic tombs. A 20-minute presentation in the visitor center precedes a guided tour.

Continue on the N59 to Ballina.

Founded in 1730 on the River Moy, Ballina is County Mayo's largest town. An important fishing center, it celebrates its week-long festival each July. Beside the 1892 Cathedral of St. Muiredach, with its fine stained-glass window, are the ruins of an Augustinian abbey built about 1427. Eight miles north of Ballina via the R314 is Killala, which has a wealth of antiquities, inluding one of the finest round towers in the country. On the east side of Killala Bay is the pleasant 3-mile beach resort of Enniscrone (N59 northeast then turn left onto the R297), whose most noted attractions are bath houses that specialize in curative submersions in hot, seaweed-enriched soakings.

Take the N26 south to Foxford.

Foxford is famous for its woolen mills, set up by a forward-looking nun in 1892 as a means of providing work for the many unemployed in the area. Since then, it has grown into one of the country's leading mills, producing world-renowned blankets, tweeds and rugs. View the visitor center's multimedia presentation of the mill's history, then go on the industrial tour.

Continue on the N26 through Foxford on to Swinford. Follow the R320 south to Kiltimagh, then turn southeast on the R323 for 5 miles to reach Knock.

The little church in the village of Knock has become a shrine, for it was here in 1879 that an apparition of Our Lady was seen at the Church of St. John the Baptist. Now officially designated a Marian Shrine, the magnificent basilica built on the grounds has welcomed visitors from around the world, including Pope John Paul II and Mother Teresa of Calcutta. More than 1.5 million pilgrims visit the shrine annually to attend one of the seven daily Masses. The 32 pillars in the ambulatory were contributed by all counties in the country and the four medieval-style windows represent the four provinces of Ireland. On the south side of the basilica, the Knock Folk Museum portrays life in rural Ireland at the end of the 19th century.

Take the N17 south to Tuam.

A thriving commercial and agricultural center under James I's charter of 1613, Tuam was altered to include a diamond-shaped town "square" on which all roads converged. Tuam claims Ireland's first industrial museum, the Mill Museum – an operational corn mill with mill wheel and other industrial exhibits. St. Mary's Cathedral, founded in 1130 and rebuilt in the 19th century, is a fine example

Interior of the 20th-century giant hexagonal church at Knock

of Gothic-revival architecture and incorporates a 12th-century chancel with magnificent windows. The town's well-adorned but incomplete 12th-century high cross stands in its grounds.

> Leave Tuam on the N17 southwest. After 3 miles, turn west on the R333 for 9 miles to reach Headford. Take the R334 northwest for just over 6 miles, then turn left to Cong via the R346.

The little town of Cong was the setting for the popular 1950s film "The Quiet Man." That, however, is the least of its claims to fame. More notable are the ruins of the Royal Abbey of Cong and the impressive Ashford Castle (see page 43).

> At Cong take the R345 northeast to the R334 and turn left for Ballinrobe. Take the N84 north to Castlebar.

Partry lies between Cong and Castlebar, and 4 miles north you will find the restored Ballintubber Abbey. This is the only church in the English-speaking world with a history of uninterrupted services since the seventh century. What makes this all the more remarkable is that Catholic Mass has been celebrated within its walls since 1216 despite years of religious suppression, two burnings and the assault of Cromwellian troops.

During these times, suppliants sometimes had to kneel before the altar in secret, and under open skies when there was no roof.

> Take the N5 road southwest, back to Westport.

North Mayo Family Heritage Centre ✉ Enniscoe, Castlehill, Ballina, about 2 miles south of Crossmolina (off R315) on Lough Conn ☎ 096 31809; fax 096 31885 🕐 Museum, shop and tearoom: daily 9–6, Apr.–end Oct.. Genealogical center: Mon.–Fri. 9–4 🎟 Museum: $$; genealogical center: free

Céide Fields ✉ About 22 miles west of Ballina, 5 miles northwest of Ballycastle on the R314 ☎ 096 43325; fax 096 43261 🕐 Daily 10–6, Jun.–Sep.; 10–5, mid-Mar. through May 30, and Oct. 🎟 $$

Foxford Woollen Mills ✉ St. Joseph's Place, Foxford, about 20 miles north of Castlebar en route to Ballina ☎ 094 92 56104 🕐 Mon.–Fri. 9:30–6, Sat. 10–6, Sun. noon–6. Some weekend closures in winter, phone to check 🍴 Restaurant 🎟 $$$ 🛍 Shop, art gallery, tourist office

Knock Shrine and Knock Folk Museum
✉ Knock ☎ 094 93 88100; fax 094 93 88295; www.knock-shrine.ie 🕐 Basilica: daily 24 hours; museum: daily 10–6, May–Oct.; daily noon–4, rest of year 🎟 Basilica: free; museum: $$

Ballintubber Abbey ✉ Claremorris, on N84 Cong–Castlebar road ☎ 094 90 30934; fax 094 90 30018 🕐 Daily 9 a.m.–midnight 🎟 Free (donations are always welcome)

Leinster

The gentle landscape of Leinster is one of green fields, rolling hills laced with beautiful valleys and deserted beaches, framed by the soft slopes of the Wicklow Mountains.

Introduction and Map **60**

Dublin **64**

Introduction and Map **64**

Essential Information **69**

Dublin Sights **70**

Feature: Dublin Specials **75**

Feature: Enjoy Exploring **78**

Walk: South of the Liffey **86**

Feature: Dublin's Literary

   Greats **88**

Regional Sights **90**

Drive: Boyne Valley **94**

Drive: Witches and Castles **100**

Feature: A Long Tradition of

   Spectacular Gardens **106**

The mighty headland of the Howth peninsula, north of Dublin Bay

Leinster

▶ The 12 diverse counties that make up the Leinster region – Carlow, Dublin, Kildare, Kilkenny, Laois, Longford, Louth, Meath, Offaly, Westmeath, Wexford and Wicklow – have collectively borne witness to most of the complex historical events that have shaped modern-day Ireland. And at its center is cosmopolitan Dublin, which has now entered the world stage as a major capital city. It is the largest city in the country and a favored destination for many.

Long before Norsemen arrived in AD 840 to found Dubh-Linn (Black Pool) on the banks of the Liffey as an important trading port, prehistoric and pre-Christian settlers set up whole communities along glacial folds that edged ancient lakes. Over the centuries, lakes became bogland and nature brushed rolling hills and miles of tilled fields with all of Ireland's famed "forty shades of green" as they merged softly into the marshy browns of the bogs. The resultant landscape is pockmarked with the remains of ancient burial sites, religious buildings, castles and other tangible records of each wave of early invaders who stayed on to become inhabitants. It was, in fact, from the fearsome iron-bladed spears (*laighens*) of invading Celts that Leinster took its name.

Leinster might well be called the "Royal Province" of Ireland. It has been a seat of power from the days of the prehistoric clans who constructed the great burial mound at Newgrange to the high kings of Ireland who held court on the Hill of Tara, and from the warring days of the Celtic, Viking and Norman conquerors to appointees of English kings and queens.

In such a setting, it is little wonder that a legacy of myths and legends endure to this day, legends that blend magically with this region's long factual history, and that have been passed from generation to generation by bardic poets and storytelling *seanashai*. Tales still abound of gods, goddesses and the heroic deeds of Finn MacCool (see page 199) and his valiant band of Fianna warriors, as well as the military and romantic exploits of the high kings.

It was just northeast of Dublin at Clontarf that the Vikings were finally defeated in 1014 by BrianBorú, some say the greatest of Ireland's high kings. Englishman Oliver Cromwell arrived in 1649 and proceeded to cut a swath of slaughter from Dublin to Drogheda that claimed thousands of men, women and

Looking across from Lacken to the Wicklow Mountains

The remains of the old monastery of Clonmacnois beside the River Shannon in County Offaly

children as victims. And the long-lasting effects of William of Orange's overwhelming victory at the 1690 Battle of the Boyne, which so profoundly changed the course of Irish history, are echoed in headlines of today.

Set amid County Wicklow's most beautiful mountain scenery, Glendalough and its twin lakes reflect the tranquility of its ecclesiastical past. To the south of The Pale's fortifications, County Wexford already bore the scars of Viking occupation when Cromwell's

rampaging forces passed this way. The arrival of Normans in 1169 and the disastrous uprising of 1798 also left their imprint on that beleaguered county. Normans gravitated to the lush countryside of counties Carlow and Kilkenny, founding a town that for a time outdid Dublin as an administrative center and appropriating the most scenic locations for their distinctive castles.

Legend has it that County Kildare's Hill of Allen hosted Finn MacCool and his followers during winter months. Today

Away from the coast, vestiges remain of Athlone's military might when it stood guard over County Westmeath's lake-dotted landscape and Ireland's most important waterway, the River Shannon. Neighboring County Longford has nurtured writer Oliver Goldsmith and several other literary figures. Clonmacnois on the banks of the Shannon in County Offaly is still an impressive place of pilgrimage for thousands of visitors who come to glimpse the splendor of its ecclesiastical heyday, when its monastic community (founded in 548) presided over one of Europe's most important centers of learning. These remains are remarkably well-preserved.

The vast flatness of Ireland's great central plain is interrupted only by the Slieve Bloom Mountains rising in the northwest corner of County Laois.

While Leinster is a repository of history, it is it is the international set who flock year-round to its horse stud farms, which consistently turn out winners on international racetracks as well as Kildare's own Curragh track. Counties Louth and Meath still wear the mantle of royalty, from the little town of Kells, birthplace of the magnificent *Book of Kells*, to the stirring Hill of Tara, to Mellifont Abbey (Ireland's first Cistercian monastery, founded in 1142), to Newgrange's enigmatic burial mound that predates the Egyptian pyramids and Britain's Stonehenge. also acknowledged to be Ireland's most progressive and rapidly changing region. In the last decade, Dublin has grown by leaps and bounds, not only in size and as a primary tourism destination, but as an important European financial center and leading commercial port. Its problems of traffic and housing spring from the swiftness of its growth and a pace of life that belies its easy-going, gentle landscape, which serves as a backdrop to the thousands of residents who commute daily from surrounding Leinster counties to the capital city.

Dublin

Dublin might rightly be called the birthplace of the celebrated Celtic Tiger that has brought such prosperity to Ireland in an amazingly brief period. On an international front, Ireland has attracted investments from leading industrial, commercial and financial firms, with a concentration in and around Dublin that has swelled the capital city's numbers to roughly one-third of the country's population of more than 4 million.

As fast-moving as Dublin's growth and social change have been, the city has managed to hold onto and value the treasures of its past. Side by side with its modern developments, Dublin still reflects the blemishes and beauty spots left by its colorful history. Over the centuries, the ancient city has been called many things. Baile Atha Cliath (Town of the Ford of the Hurdles) is its Irish name (a wicker bridge – the hurdles – once spanned the river). Norsemen called it Dubh-Linn (Dark Pool) when they founded the present city on the banks of the Liffey in 840. By any name, Dublin is one of Europe's loveliest capital cities, with proud old Georgian buildings (a style that harks back to the early 1700s to the mid-1800s, during the reigns of George I to George IV), elegantly groomed squares of greenery (Fitzwilliam, Parnell, Merrion), and acres of shaded leisure space (St. Stephen's Green and Phoenix Park). Its heart beats to the rhythm of the Liffey, and its horizons extend to craggy Howth Head to the north, around the softly curving shores of Dublin Bay, to the brooding slopes of the Wicklow Mountains to the south.

Little remains of medieval Dublin, but it's easy to trace its outlines and see how the modern city has grown around it. To

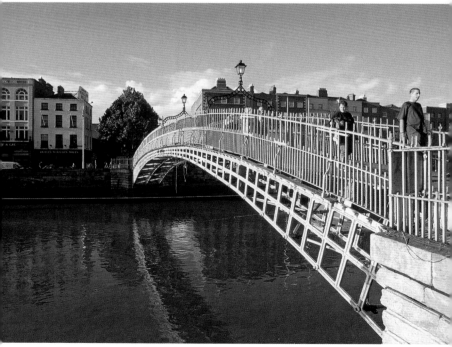

The elegant cast-iron arch of the Ha'penny Bridge crossing the Liffey north of Temple Bar

the south of the Liffey, you'll see Christ Church Cathedral's square tower – almost the exact center of the original city. To the east, Grattan Bridge stands near the "black pool" that marked its eastern boundary and served as a Viking trading port. Little Ship Street follows the course of the River Poddle (now underground), once a city boundary on the river's south bank, and the quays along the north bank marked another outpost of the original city.

There were few changes in Dublin until the magnificent Georgian buildings began to appear in the 18th century. The Victorian age arrived in the mid-1800s, leaving traces in railway stations, banks, pubs, markets and hospitals. From 1916 to 1922 Dublin was scarred by the ravages of uprising, but careful rebuilding has erased most of the damage.

In the 1960s came the first "office revolution," when, in a fit of progressive zeal, the grand old city came close to demolishing many of her finest legacies. Citizens halted this destruction at an early stage, so you may walk through both past and modern structures.

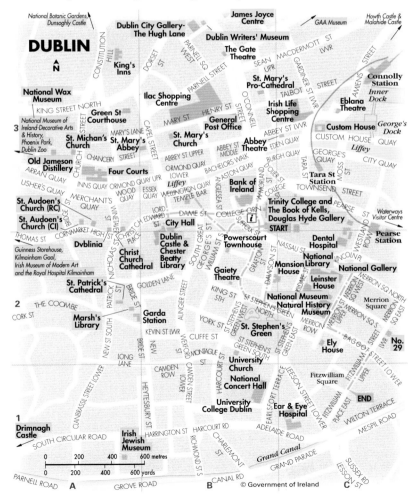

DUBLIN

© Government of Ireland

The Liffey, which flows from west to east, divides the mile-long city center into "northside" (to Parnell Square at the northern end of O'Connell Street) and "southside" (to Stephen's Green at Grafton Street's southern end).

Of the Liffey's 15 bridges, O'Connell Bridge is the primary link between north and south. North of the river, O'Connell Street is an extension of the bridge and the location of landmarks such as the historic General Post Office, statues of Parnell, Father Matthew and Daniel O'Connell and a monument, the Spire, erected in 2002, as well as a leading hotel, Clery's (one of Dublin's oldest department stores) and a jumble of fast-food eateries. Once the center of social life in the city, O'Connell Street had deteriorated badly over the years, but it has now undergone a massive cleanup and redevelopment to restore its charms. It is still advisable, however, to exercise big-city caution when walking there after dark.

To the south of O'Connell Bridge, Westmoreland Street extends for only one block before becoming College Green, a broad intersection fronting on the entrance to Trinity College. College Green then quickly becomes Grafton Street, Dublin's most fashionable shopping street. It is reserved for pedestrian traffic only and features good (and some not-so-good) street entertainment. At the southern end of Grafton Street is the cool, green oasis of beautiful St. Stephen's Green, a peaceful refuge from city streets.

The Liberties (so named in medieval times because its residents were exempt from the long arm of the law) is one of Dublin's oldest neighborhoods. It has been home to some of the city's most colorful and strongly independent characters, as well as a distinctive, easily recognized accent. Its boundaries lie west of Upper Kevin Street beginning at The Coombe, its main thoroughfare (named for the valley or coomb of the River Poddle), and run west to somewhat indeterminate borders. Nearby are such historic landmarks as St. Patrick's Cathedral, Christ Church Cathedral and Dublin's oldest pub, the Brazen Head (see page 78), which

Theater and the Performing Arts

The Abbey Theatre in Lower Abbey Street was born in 1903 when Augusta Lady Gregory, W. B. Yeats and J. M. Synge determined to perform Irish plays with Irish casts. The theater has provided a voice for such passionate writers as J. M. Synge and Sean O'Casey, even though this has sometimes rattled ultra-conservative Irish audiences. The original Abbey was quite small. When it burned in 1951, it was 15 years before its modern, functional replacement was completed.

The National Concert Hall is an intimate venue for presentations that range from jazz and folk music to classical concerts by the National Symphony Orchestra, the Irish Chamber Orchestra and a host of visiting international luminaries.

On a much larger scale, The Point, which has undergone a major refurbishment and is due to reopen in late 2008, is well equipped to host leading international rock stars, classical ballet companies and full-scale musical stage shows.

The Gaiety Theatre on South King Street is the venue for the two-performance seasons of the Opera Ireland repertory company. International opera companies sometimes perform at The Point.

🛈 You can pick up most concert and theater tickets at the Ticketmaster desk in the tourism center on Suffolk Street or go online at www.ticketmaster.ie

O'Connell Street at night taking traffic from O'Connell Bridge to north Dublin

witnessed much United Irishmen activity in the 18th century.

You will find some of the best examples of Dublin's famed Georgian architecture, a legacy of 18th-century residents, clustered around Merrion and Fitzwilliam squares and adjacent streets. Doorways whose fanlights are embellished with ornate wrought-iron decorations, cast-iron foot scrapers, doorway lamps, knockers and railings give each red-brick townhouse its own distinction. South of the Grand Canal, only a short walk from the city center, Ballsbridge is Dublin's most upscale residential section and the setting for several smart hotels and restaurants. So many embassies, including that of the United States, are located in this area that it has been dubbed by locals as "Embassy Row."

Temple Bar, Dublin's lively center of popular culture and entertainment, is the result of a massively funded and carefully planned development of a city-center section where narrow lanes and alleys had at one time become glaring examples of neglect and urban decay. Named for the river walkway (once known as a "bar") of Sir William

Temple, whose family owned much of this site from 1554 to 1628, this area is bordered by Essex, Wellington and Aston quays to the north, Lord Edward Street and Dame Street to the south, Westmoreland Street to the east and Fishamble Street to the west. With its narrow lanes recobbled and ancient buildings restored, Temple Bar is Dublin's 21st-century bohemia. Its eclectic collection of street entertainment, avant-garde boutiques, art galleries, trendy pubs and trendier restaurants gives this area a vibrant, youthful air. The development of Temple Bar has continued into Cow's Lane.

"Dubs" ("jackeens" in the vernacular) are a breed, or rather, several breeds apart, with an increasingly cosmopolitan population mix. True Dubs will tell you, however, that unless you're born and bred in the city, you remain a *culchie* (country person) no matter how long you make the city your home. Arrogant? Not really – the tags are applied with good humor and a dollop of sharp wit, and are as often directed at themselves as at those other "blow-ins." Proud? Without doubt. Dubliners are happily convinced their city is not only the centerpiece of Leinster, but of Ireland and the entire universe as well.

Still, anything even remotely connected with reverence – including their own claims to their beloved city – is simply nonexistent in their makeup. Take, for example, when the Dubs christened a fountain – whose reclining female figure was meant to represent Anna Livia, Joyce's poetic name for the Liffey river – "The Floozie in the Jacuzzi." Or the wonderfully realistic figures of two housewife shoppers at the north end of the Ha'penny Bridge tagged "Hags with the Bags." Or the statue of Sweet Molly Malone at Nassau and Grafton streets, now universally known as "The Tart with the Cart." Any new statue or monument erected by the city fathers is certain to fall prey to this brand of Dublin wit.

It's sometimes hard to hear Irish music as it pours from the irrepressible Irish spirit finding its voice in its own environment. With a very few exceptions, that's something you almost

always have to stumble onto when the music and song are totally unplanned. In Dublin, however, that spontaneous spirit in all its passionate glory is alive and well at the headquarters of Cultúrlann na hÉireann in Monkstown (☎01 280 0295). There's traditional entertainment here most nights of the week, but to hear some of the best musicians, go on Friday or Saturday. Fiddlers fiddle, pipers pipe, whistle players whistle, dancers take to the floor, and singers lift their fine Irish voices in informal musical sessions.

Cabaret in Dublin is served up with distinctly Irish seasonings: "Danny Boy" and "The Rose of Tralee" are favorites of many audiences, both for Irish people and visitors alike. You'll find an Irish comic telling Irish jokes, pretty, fresh-faced colleens dancing, singing and playing the harp, an Irish tenor or baritone, and youngsters stepping a lively jig or reel. It's Irish entertainment on the light side. No purists, these – but they're lots of fun and the performances

Excursions

If time is at a premium, the quickest way to see major attractions is by organized bus tours. Any of the Dublin Tourism centers can furnish details of what's offered during your visit and make tour bookings.

The one-hour, 30-minute open-top bus (covered double-deck bus on rainy days) tour is a delightful way to view the highlights of Dublin's major sightseeing attractions. The tour is a photographer's dream and includes Trinity College, the Guinness Brewery, St. Patrick's and Christ Church cathedrals, elegant Georgian squares, historic Phoenix Park and other points of interest.

With the all-day ticket for Dublin Bus Hop-On, Hop-Off tour, you can stay aboard for the one-hour, 15-minute tour of 20 stops at major

attractions, or you may elect to leave the bus at a stop of special interest and catch a later bus to complete the tour. Buses operate frequently, so you won't have a long wait for ongoing segments of the tour.

Dublin Bus also operates a 3-hour North Coast and Castle tour that visits the 12th-century Malahide Castle along a scenic coastal drive to the village of Howth, and on to Howth Head for great views of Dublin Bay. The South Coast and Gardens Tour, lasting 4.5 hours, takes you through scenery sometimes called Dublin's Riviera. The route includes Dun Laoghaire's yacht-filled harbor, Joyce's Tower at Sandycove, Killiney Bay, Bray and Greystones before turning inland to visit the Wicklow Mountains, Enniskerry and Powerscourt.

are usually well above average. Most performances are held in hotels, and you can opt for dinner and the show or come for the show alone. The most popular cabaret is at the Burlington Hotel in Ballsbridge, which has been running almost 35 years.

For many Dubliners, the best possible start and finish to a Dublin evening is a visit to their favorite pub. With "Enjoy Exploring" (see page 78) as a guide to pubs, you can opt for your own "local" during your stay or embark on a pub crawl for an entertaining sampling.

Essential Information

ℹ️ Tourist information
● Dublin Tourism ✉️ Suffolk Street
☎️ 01 605 7700 🕐 Mon.–Sat. 9–7, Sun. 10:30–3, Jun.–Sep.; Mon.–Sat. 9–5:30, Sun. 10–3, rest of year

● Dublin Airport ☎️ 01 844 5388 🕐 Daily 8–10 p.m.
● Ferry Terminal, Dun Laoghaire ☎️ 01 280 6600 🕐 Mon.–Sat. 10–6
● Failte Ireland, Baggot Street Bridge ☎️ 01 602 4000 🕐 Mon.–Fri. 9:30–5
● Upper O' Connell Street (walk-in office only) 🕐 Mon.–Sat. 9–5

🏧 A Dublin Tourism's money-saving Dublin Pass Card can cut charges to more than 30 major attractions. The Dublin Tourism website is a useful source of information for many aspects of your visit: www.visitdublin.com.

🚌 Urban Transportation
Dublin Bus services the city and outlying areas, making it easy to seek accommodations beyond the center. The main bus station, "Busáras," is on Amiens Street. Buses marked "An Lar" will be headed for the city center. Buses run from 6 a.m. to 11:30 p.m. There is a limited Nitelink bus service Monday to Saturday; confirm times with Dublin Bus. For more information, call Dublin Bus ✉️ 59 Upper O'Connell Street ☎️ 01 873 4222; www.dublinbus.ie.

The electric train suburban service that runs from Howth to Greystones stops at some 30 stations en route. Called the Dublin Area Rapid Transit (DART), the service is fast, silent and convenient, since departures are every five minutes during peak hours, every 15 minutes other times. Service begins at 6:30 a.m. and ends at about 11:30 p.m. Some 19 feeder bus lines link up with the DART. Timetables can be obtained at most of these stations. For information, contact DART, Pearse Street Station, Dublin 2 ☎️ 01 703 3504.

Opened in 2004, the fast and efficient Luas tram system operates two lines from Dublin center out to the suburbs.

Taxis cannot be hailed from the street, but may be called by telephone, and they operate from stands at all bus and train stations and many city-center locations, including Grafton Street, Lower O'Connell Street, College Green and St. Stephen's Green. They're listed in the telephone directory under "Taxi-cab ranks." Rates are set by law, and all taxis are metered, with a small extra charge for each additional passenger and each piece of luggage. There's also a small additional charge between the hours of 8 p.m. and 8 a.m.

Driving is best avoided. Public transportation is efficient and frequent. Parking can be difficult. Remember, once you reach the city center, most places are going to be within walking distance.

Dublin's two ferry terminals are Dun Laoghaire Ferryport (☎️ Stena Line 01 204 7700) and Dublin Ferryport (☎️ 0818 300 40; www.irishferries.com), with bus and taxi services meeting ferries at both.

✈️ Airport Information
Dublin International Airport is located some 7.5 miles north of the city center.

The Airlink bus goes to and from the airport from Busáras, the central bus station on Store Street, north of the Liffey. An alternative is the Aircoach, which makes several stops in the city. Taxis are readily available at the airport.

Climate: Average highs and lows

Jan.	Feb.	Mar.	Apr.	May	Jun.	Jul.	Aug.	Sep.	Oct.	Nov.	Dec.
8°C	8°C	10°C	12°C	14°C	17°C	19°C	19°C	17°C	14°C	10°C	8°C
46°F	46°F	50°F	54°F	57°F	63°F	66°F	66°F	63°F	57°F	50°F	46°F
3°C	3°C	4°C	5°C	7°C	10°C	11°C	12°C	10°C	8°C	5°C	4°C
37°F	38°F	39°F	41°F	45°F	50°F	52°F	54°F	50°F	46°F	41°F	39°F

A figure in the Chester Beatty Oriental collection

Dublin Sights

Key to symbols

⊞ map coordinates refer to the Dublin map on page 65; sights below are highlighted in yellow on the map

⊠ address or location ☎ telephone number

⊘ opening times ⊞ restaurant on site or nearby

⊟ nearest bus or train station ⊞ admission charge: $$$ more than €6, $$ €4 to €6, $ less than €4

⊞ information

Bank of Ireland

This magnificent semicircular building facing onto College Green was built in 1729. It was the highlight of Ireland's wonderful years of freedom at the end of the 18th century, when Dublin reached the peak of its architectural achievement. Architect Edward Lovett Pearce designed the recessed south-facing "piazza" of Ionic columns (*circa* 1729–39) and the rooms behind it. James Gandon added the curving, windowless screen and the east-facing Corinthian portico between 1785 and 1789, and a corresponding portico was added to the west side years later.

The structure started life as the seat of the Irish Parliament, which gained its legislative independence in 1782. When the Act of

Union was passed in 1800, Henry Grattan (whose statue stands across the way), although quite ill, rose to bid an eloquent farewell to the independent parliament. After the parliament was dissolved, the building was acquired by the Bank of Ireland in 1802 on the condition that the lower house be demolished to avoid any possible coup d'etat. The House of Lords is still intact, resplendent with two fine 18th-century tapestries by Jan van Beaver – one that portrays King James II at the 1689 Siege of Londonderry and the other that shows King William of Orange at the 1690 Battle of the Boyne – topped by a 1788 crystal chandelier made up from 1,233 intricate crystal pieces.

⊞ B3 ⊠ 2 College Green ☎ 01 677 6801 ⊘ House of Lords: Mon.–Fri. 10–4 ⊟ All city center (An Lar) buses ⊞ Free ⊞ House of Lords tours on Tue. (except public holidays) at 10:30, 11:30 and 1:45

Chester Beatty Library and Gallery of Oriental Art

There are more than 22,000 cultural items in this extraordinary collection, given to the Irish nation by American-Irish engineer Sir Alfred Chester Beatty (1875–1968) in 1956. Biblical materials include papyri dating from the second to fourth centuries, and the Islamic collection contains more than 270 copies of the Koran. Rare books, illuminated manuscripts and miniature paintings originate from an impressive range of ethnic groups.

⊞ B2 ⊠ Clock Tower, Dublin Castle, Dame Street ☎ 01 407 0750; fax 01 407 0760; www.cbl.ie ⊘ Mon.–Fri. 10–5, Sat. 11–5, Sun. 1–5; closed Mon., Oct.–Apr. ⊟ 50, 51B, 54A, 77A, 123 (from Eden Quay) ⊞ Free

Christ Church Cathedral

Christ Church Cathedral dates back to 1038 when King Sitric erected a wooden structure, which was replaced with stone following the Norman invasion in 1169. Anglo-Norman leader Strongbow lies here, with a memorial in the cathedral nave. King Richard II came in 1394 to knight four Irish kings after they pledged allegiance to the British Crown. James II prayed here in 1689 before the Battle of the Boyne, and King Billy came back to

The Georgian Custom House is considered Dublin's finest piece of architecture

offer thanks for his victory in that battle. The south transept, the oldest part of the upper church (1180), contains many examples of late Norman and early Gothic architecture, and there are fine 16th- to 19th-century sculptures. You'll find statues of English kings, medieval carvings and oddities such as a mummified cat and rat, thought to have become trapped during a chase through organ pipes. Linked to the cathedral by a covered stone bridge is Synod Hall, which holds the Dvblinia exhibition (see page 74).

🚻 A3 ✉ Christchurch Place ☎ 01 677 8099; fax 01 679 8991; www.cccdub.ie 🕓 Daily 9–6, Jun.–Aug.; 9:45–5, rest of year 🚌 78A (Aston Quay) or 50, 51B, 65, 90 (Eden Quay) ✋ $$ ℹ Prayers for peace in Ireland noon Mon.–Sat.; Eucharist and sermon 11 a.m. every Sun.; call for times of other services

Custom House

Designed by James Gandon, the Custom House is an outstanding example of Georgian architecture. Its facade is made up of arched arcades with a Doric portico at its center, topped by a green copper dome with a statue of Commerce crowning the dome. Above the center the frieze has a series of allegorical heads which represent the 13 rivers of Ireland and the Atlantic Ocean. After dark, floodlights that illuminate the gracious 1791 Customs House provide one of Dublin's most impressive nighttime sights, especially when viewed from the opposite bank of the Liffey.

🚻 C3 ✉ Custom House Quay ☎ 01 888 2000 🕓 Not open to the public ℹ Five-minute walk from O'Connell Bridge

Douglas Hyde Gallery

Opened just under 30 years ago, and funded by Trinity College and the Arts Council of Ireland, this purpose-built space over two floors is one of Ireland's leading contemporary art galleries. The diverse collection of temporary exhibitions displays thought-provoking art that embraces both emerging and well-established Irish and international artists. There are tours and lectures available.

🚻 B3 ✉ Trinity College (Nassau Street entrance) ☎ 01 608 1116; www.douglashydegallery.com 🕓 Mon.–Fri. 11–6, Thu. 11–7, Sat. 11–4:45 🚌 Any city center (An Lar) bus ✋ Free

Drimnagh Castle

Surrounded by a flooded moat, this is Ireland's last surviving medieval castle. Restored to their original style, its great hall, undercroft and battlement tower with a lookout post create a real feeling for that

The Record Tower at Dublin Castle, one of the few remaining parts of the original building

long-gone time in history. The 17th-century formal garden features box hedges, yew trees and a shaded walkway with hornbean trees.
✚ A1 ✉ Long Mile Road, Drimnagh ☎ 01 450 2530; fax 01 450 8927 ⏰ Wed. noon–5, Sun. 2–5, or by appointment 🚌 18, 56A, 77, 77A (from Eden Quay); Drimnagh Luas 💷 $$

Dublin Castle

Dublin Castle is built on the site of an earlier Danish fortress. The only remaining portions of the original castle (built between 1208 and 1220) are a bit of a curtain wall and two towers. You can get a pretty good idea of the original outline from the upper castle yard (dubbed "The Devil's Half Acre" by Dubliners when this was the nerve center for repressive British rule for centuries). British viceroys resided in the opulent state apartments (now restored). It was from here that the injured James Connolly, patriot leader of the 1916 uprising, was taken by stretcher to Kilmainham Gaol to be executed.

Sumptuous furnishings, huge Waterford crystal chandeliers, tapestries, hand-tufted Donegal carpets mirroring the ceiling plasterwork and Robert Adam fireplaces abound, revealing the palatial lifestyle led by the viceroys. One of the most impressive rooms, St. Patrick's Hall, is cluttered with banners and coats of arms beneath an ornately painted ceiling and is now used for the inauguration of Ireland's presidents. The throne room contains a massive throne believed to have been brought to Dublin by William of Orange after his victory at Boyne.

Other points of interest are the Church of the Most Holy Trinity (formerly the Chapel Royal), the 13th-century Record Tower and the memorial outside the main gate honoring those Irish killed here during Easter Week of 1916, standing on the spot where heads of Irish kings once were displayed publicly on high spikes. In addition, the complex houses the Chester Beatty Library (see page 70).
✚ B2 ✉ Dame Street ☎ 01 677 7129; fax 01 679 7831; www.dublincastle.ie ⏰ Mon.–Fri. 10–4:45, Sat.–Sun. 2–4:45 🍴 Café/Restaurant 🚌 49, 56A, 77, 77A (from Eden Quay) 💷 $$ ℹ Apartments may be closed for functions

Dublin City Hall

One of Dublin's finest neoclassical buildings, which dates from 1779, contains a

fax 01 872 2231; www.writersmuseum.com
🕐 Mon.–Fri. 10–6, Sat. 10–5, Sun. 11–5, Jun.–Aug.;
Mon.–Sat. 10–5, Sun. 11–5, rest of year 🍴 Restaurant
and coffee shop 🚌 10, 11, 13, 16A, 19A; 10-minute
walk from DART Connolly Station 💷 $$$
ℹ️ Extensive bookshop with a mail-order service.
Self-guiding audio tour also available

multimedia exhibition tracing the evolution
of the city from 1170 to the present day. The
story is told through displays of civic regalia,
including the Great City Sword and other
treasures, with computer interactives, archive
films, models and costumes.
➕ B3 ✉️ Cork Hill ☎️ 01 222 2204; fax 01 222 2620
🕐 Mon.–Sat. 10–5:15, Sun. 2–5 🍴 Coffee shop 🚌 50,
51B, 54A, 77, 77A, (from Eden Quay) 💷 $$

Dublin Writers' Museum

Ireland's wealth of internationally recognized
literary talent (including four Nobel prize
winners) is celebrated in this superbly
restored Georgian house that holds books,
letters, portraits and personal belongings for
the likes of Shaw, Wilde, Yeats, Swift, Joyce
and Beckett. There are examples of
magnificent stucco in this late 18th-century
building, especially on the first floor. The
colonnaded main salon, now the Gallery of
Writers, has busts and paintings of famous
names, a decorative ceiling and boisterous
friezes. Children's literature is allotted its own
room, and there are frequent visiting
exhibitions and readings. Next door, the Irish
Writers' Centre nurtures contemporary
writers by providing meeting and work space.
➕ B3 ✉️ 18 Parnell Square North ☎️ 01 872 2077;

Dublin Zoo and Phoenix Park

Established in 1830, Dublin Zoo
encompasses 60 acres on the grounds of
Phoenix Park. The zoo is noted for breeding
lions and other large cats, having bred the
first lion cubs in captivity in 1857.
Picturesque landscaping and gardens
surround two natural lakes (alive
with pelicans, flamingos and scores of
ornamental ducks and geese) and there are
spacious outdoor enclosures. Monkey islands
in the "World of Primates," the antics of
polar bears in "Fringes of the Arctic" and
lions, jaguars and snow leopards in the
"World of Cats" are among the most popular
attractions. Check out "The African Plains"
and take a "safari" tour. Youngsters will
delight in the small Children's Pets Zoo.

Beautiful Phoenix Park, with its main
entrance on Parkgate Street, is always
referred to by Dubliners as "The" Phoenix
Park. It is Europe's largest enclosed city park,
and within its 1,652 acres are the residences
of Ireland's president as well as that of the
American ambassador. In addition to Dublin
Zoo, the lofty trees shade humans during the
day and a free-roaming herd of deer after
dark. Walkways lace the grounds, where
ornamental gardens are joined by plantings
of indigenous shrubs and trees. The 205-foot
obelisk erected in 1817 commemorates the
Duke of Wellington, a Dublin native and the
beautiful Papal Cross marks Pope John
Paul II's 1979 visit to Dublin.
➕ A3 ✉️ Phoenix Park ☎️ Zoo: 01 474 8900;
www.dublinzoo.ie. Park Visitor Centre: 01 677 0095
🕐 Zoo: Mon.–Sat. 9:30–6, Sun. 10:30–6, Mar.–Sep.;
Mon.–Sat. 9:30–dusk, Sun 10:30–dusk, rest of year.
Park Visitor Centre: Daily 10–6, mid-Mar. to Oct.; 10–5,
rest of year 🍴 Several eateries 🚌 10 (from
O'Connell Street), 25, 26, 66, 67, 68, 69 (from Middle
Abbey Street); Heuston Luas 💷 $$$ ℹ️ Play area, pet
care area, discovery center

Making friends at Dublin Zoo

Dunsoghly Castle

Dating from the 15th century, this ruined castle has been designated a National Monument. The original oak roof beams are still intact, as is the square tower with its rectangular turrets.

➕ A3 ✉ 3 miles north of Finglas on N2

Dvblinia and The Viking World

Across the footbridge from Christ Church Cathedral you walk into a medieval setting that re-creates Dublin life from the time the Anglo-Normans arrived in 1170. The exhbition is housed in the beautifully preserved former Synod Hall. An audio headset guides you on a "Journey Through Time" among lifesize reconstructions of scenes from those long-ago times. Merchants' stalls in the "All the Fun of the Fayre" section spill over with wares such as medicines, clothes, foods and spices, bringing a real-life atmosphere to the street. A exhibition includes a reconstruction of Viking Dublin and shows life on a Viking warship.

➕ A2 ✉ St. Michael's Hill, Christ Church ☎ 01 679 4611; fax 01 679 7116; www.dublinia.ie 🕐 Daily 10–5, Apr.–Sep.; Mon.–Sat. 11–4, Sun. 10–4, rest of year. Closed Dec. 24–26 🚌 50 (from Eden Quay), 78A (from Aston Quay), Luas: Four Courts 💲 $$$

Four Courts

The Chancery, King's Bench, Exchequer and Common Pleas are the four courts for which James Gandon designed this unique building in 1785. Political turmoil delayed its opening until 1796, and it was finally completed in 1802. Scars can still be seen on portico columns as a result of a heavy bombardment in 1922 during Ireland's civil war, when anti-treaty forces occupied the building. A massive explosion destroyed irreplaceable historical records and left the building a burned-out shell. Beautifully restored, this massive Georgian edifice confronting the Liffey now functions as originally planned. The courts radiate from a circular central hall; at lunchtime you can witness bewigged lawyers fraternizing with their clients.

➕ A3 ✉ Inns Quay ☎ 01 872 5555 🕐 Mon.–Fri. 10–1 and 2–4 when courts are in session 🚌 Any city center (An Lar) bus; Four Courts Luas 💲 Free

During special events, the entire city enters into the festive spirit. You should check with the Irish Tourist Board about specific dates during your visit. Advance inner-city accommodations reservations are vital, and prices may become a little inflated.

St. Patrick's Festival

For generations, celebrations of Ireland's patron saint were confined to March 17, but since 1996 Dublin's festival has been running over a four-day period. A theme is selected each year, and with more than 5,000 performers (including U.S. marching bands), it has grown into Ireland's largest annual celebration. The undisputed highlight is the Festival Parade, but each day is filled with street events that include a Monster Ceilí in St. Stephen's Green, colorful carnival events along the quays, amusements, magic, comedy and puppet performances, and mini-parades and boisterous festivities wind up with spectacular fireworks.

🔲 For full details on future festivals, contact St. Patrick's Festival, St. Stephen's Green House, Earlsfort Terrace, Dublin 2, or visit their website at www.stpatricksday.ie

Bloomsday

For many visitors, Bloomsday, which commemorates the June 16, 1904 setting of James Joyce's *Ulysses*, is reason enough to come to Dublin. At least a week before June 16 each year, Joyce scholars – as well as just plain fans – are busily attending readings, lectures and dramatic performances. The day itself, however, is anything but a serious, head-scratching analysis of the book: streets are thronged with people in period costumes reenacting events recounted in the classic

Laughter and music in the Dublin streets

Dublin Specials

tale. Pubs visited by the novel's central character Leopold Bloom go all out with special meals and readings. And there's a general air of revelry as Dubliners celebrate turn-of-the-20th-century life in their beloved city and accord the writer a celebrity that simply eluded him during his lifetime.

Dublin Horse Show

This is the social highlight of the year. For a week in August, the showgrounds of the Dublin Royal Society are packed with sophisticated international visitors who mingle happily with Irish horse-lovers. In some of the finest jumping enclosures in the world, virtually nonstop jumping competitions are a backdrop for auctions that net enormous sales figures for horses with impeccable pedigrees. The Aga Khan Trophy competition is Friday's main event. And on Saturday, the International Grand Prix of Ireland ends the week. Festivities include army band concerts, a Ladies' Day fashion competition, floral displays and art exhibits (www.dublinhorseshow.com).

Dublin Theatre Festival

Two weeks at the end of September and the beginning of October are devoted to the Dublin Theatre Festival (www.dublintheatrefestival.com). Every theater in the city, as well as university campuses and community halls, are filled with a series of first nights of innovative Irish drama and major overseas theater and dance companies. The festival provides a lively platform for Irish playwrights, many new plays are performed and theatergoers have a rare opportunity to meet actors and directors in the Festival Club.

Bronze statue of the dying Cuchulain, in the central hall of the General Post Office

GAA Museum

The Gaelic Athletic Association is Ireland's largest sporting organization. This museum, at the home of Ireland's national games of hurling and football, explores an integral part of Irish life and heritage. Touch-screen technology and high-definition interactives bring the games to life.

➕ Off map ✉ Cusack Stand, Croke Park ☎ 01 819 2323; fax 01 819 2324; www.gaa.ie ◉ Mon.–Sat. 9:30–5, Sun. noon–5 (Jul.–Aug. 9:30–6) 🚌 3, 11, 11A, 16, 16A ♿ $$

General Post Office

The imposing General Post Office, with its Ionic portico and fluted pillars, was built in 1814. In 1916 its classical entrance provided a dramatic platform from which Padraic Pearse hoisted the Irish tricolor for the first time and proclaimed to his fellow Irish citizens and the world at large that Ireland would from that date on claim its independence (see page 22). After intense shelling, the building was set afire and its interior gutted. Now completely restored, its central hall holds a statue of Ireland's ancient mythical warrior hero, Cuchulain, a memorial to the men who fought here. On the marble base is inscribed Pearse's proclamation. Across the road is the striking 394-foot-high steel Spire monument, unveiled in 2002.

➕ B3 ✉ O'Connell Street ☎ 01 705 7000 ◉ Mon.–Sat. 8–8, Sun. 10:30–6 🚌 Any city center (An Lar) bus ♿ Free

Guinness Storehouse

The sprawling Guinness Brewery, set on some 60 acres south of the Liffey, is the largest brewery in Europe. From its home, Guinness exports more beer than any other company in the world. The rich, dark stout it has produced since 1759 is truly the "wine of Ireland." As you enter the Storehouse, an escalator whisks you to the heart of the building into what is described as a large glass pint. Within the structure you journey through the production process of a pint of Guinness. Old machinery is utilized to present entertaining displays and audiovisuals give an insight into the history, manufacturing and advertising of Dublin's

Contemporary art in The Hugh Lane Gallery

famous product. You end your visit in the rooftop Gravity bar, which has excellent views, to try a free glass of the "black stuff." ✚ A2 ✉ St. James's Gate ☎ 01 404 4800; fax 01 408 4965; www.guinnessstorehouse.com 🕓 Daily 9:30–7, Jul.–Aug.; 9:30–5, rest of year 🍴 Café, bar 🚌 51B, 78A (from Aston Quay), 123 (from O'Connell Street); James Street Luas 💵 $$$ ✚ Free parking

The Hugh Lane (Dublin City Gallery)

Occupying one of Dublin's finest Georgian mansions, the Hugh Lane Gallery is the permanent home for Sir Hugh Lane's art collection, which was donated to the gallery in 1908. There's an extensive collection of 20th-century Irish art, French Impressionists Manet, Monet, Renoir and Degas, and ever-changing temporary exhibitions of works by international contemporary artists. The re-creation of Francis Bacon's studio contains some 7,500 examples of the artist's work. ✚ B3 ✉ Charlemont House, Parnell Square North ☎ 01 222 5550; fax 01 872 2182; www.hughlane.ie 🕓 Tue.–Thu. 10–6, Fri.–Sat. 10–5, Sun. 11–5 🍴 Café 🚌 3, 10, 11, 13, 16, 19, 46A 💵 Free ✚ Guided tours by reservation

Irish Jewish Museum

The former Dublin synagogue now houses a fascinating museum, yet the upstairs in this building is virtually unchanged and could be used to conduct a service without much delay. Irish and Jewish documents, photographs and relics of Jews in Ireland for the past 500 years are displayed here. Belfast-born and Dublin-educated Chaim Herzog opened the museum in 1985 when he was president of Israel. ✚ A1 ✉ 3–4 Walworth Road, off Victoria Street, South Circular Road, Portobello ☎ 01 490 1857 🕓 Tue., Thu. and Sun. 11–3:30, May–Sep.; Sun. 10:30–2:30, rest of year 🚌 16, 16A, 19, 19A, 122 💵 Free (donations welcome)

Irish Museum of Modern Art and the Royal Hospital Kilmainham

Built in 1684 as a home for retired soldiers, the Royal Hospital in Kilmainham is one of Ireland's finest 17th-century buildings. These days it houses the Museum of Modern Art, which includes more than 1,200 woodcuts, etchings and engravings by Irish and international artists, such as French Impressionists Manet, Degas and Renoir, and old masters Rembrandt, Hogarth and Goya. ✚ A2 ✉ Royal Hospital, Military Road, Kilmainham ☎ 01 612 9900; fax 01 612 9999; www.imma.ie 🕓 Tue.–Sat. 10–5:30 (except Wed. 10:30–5:30), Sun. noon–5:30 🍴 Coffee shop 🚌 51B, 78A (from Aston Quay), 123 (from O'Connell Street); Museum Luas 💵 Free ✚ Prebooked tours Tue.–Fri. 10, 11:45, 2:30, 4

There are more than 1,000 pubs in Dublin, each with its own personality, each specializing in conversation, music or "the best pulled pint in Dublin" (a hotly debated accolade throughout the city's pubs). Those listed here are among the most interesting, but don't confine yourself to these – drop into the nearest establishment anytime you're overcome with a terrible thirst, and you'll likely go home raving about your own favorites. Nondrinkers will be pleased to know that, as centers of sociability, Irish pubs are quite happy to serve soda (minerals) as well as the hard stuff. It's the craic (an Irish word that sums up conversation and the ambience of an evening) that matters most and is a national art. Pub hours are from 10:30 a.m. to 11:30 p.m. Monday to Thursday and until 12:30 a.m. on Friday and Saturday; Sundays are 12:30–11:30.

Enjoy Exploring

Dubliners in its 130 years of dispensing drink. Mirrored partitions along the bar and ceilings add to the setting and provide drinking "snugs" (enclosed nooks). Journalists, politicians, artists and just plain people often fill bars to over-flowing, and there's always a flow of lively and stimulating conversation.

The Stag's Head

Another long-standing favorite of Dubliners is the Stag's Head, tucked away in Dame Court. Getting there is a bit complicated, but worth the effort. The Stag's Head has been here since 1770, wearing its age with grace, its stained-glass windows and skylights, gleaming wood and mounted stag's head reflecting the soft patina of time. Regulars, from executive types to shop clerks, gather here and mingle happily with tourists. Along with its "best-pulled pint" credentials, the Stag's Head serves an excellent pub lunch.

The Brazen Head

The southside is pub country. The Brazen Head, the oldest drinking place in Ireland, may have been licensed by Charles II in 1666, but it drew its name from a beautiful redhead who couldn't contain her curiosity during a civil disturbance, stuck her head out of a window, and promptly lost it to an English sword. The entrance is tucked away at the back of a courtyard down an arched alleyway on the west side of Bridge Street. It's dimly lit inside with low ceilings, brass lanterns and uneven wooden floors. Patriots Robert Emmet, Wolfe Tone and Daniel O'Connell often came here to drink.

Doheny and Nesbitt

This is the place for people-watching. Doheny and Nesbitt, 5 Lower Baggot Street, has earned a special place in the affections of

Mulligan's

This is as much a conversation pub today as it was when it was favored by James Joyce and other Dublin notables. Mulligan's on Poolbeg Street has been a Dublin institution since 1782, and the 19th-century gas lights are among its original trappings. Said to serve the best pint of Guinness in town.

Davy Byrnes

For James Joyce fans, Davy Byrnes, 21 Duke Street, still draws those who come looking for the "moral pub" described in *Ulysses*. True, the 1890s wall murals are still here, but the atmosphere these days is likely to be more that of a modern-day cocktail lounge than what Leopold Bloom encountered, with orders for exotically named mixed drinks outnumbering calls for the pint.

McDaids

Brendan Behan staked out a spot for himself, his pint and his typewriter in McDaids, 3 Harry Street, a dark, high-ceilinged pub that became his second home. Literary luminaries such as Patrick Kavanagh and Flann O'Brien also drank here, and many current wordsmiths have followed suit. Who knows, in such an ambience, they may become the great writers of the future.

The Old Stand

Patronized by what sometimes seems to be at least half of Ireland's rugby team, as well as other athletes, The Old Stand at 37 Exchequer Street is a center for sports conversation. All those sports figures mingle with a mixed clientele. A favorite lunch and after-work drinking spot for office workers.

Share in the gossip and hospitality of the city pubs

Ryan's

Northside pubs are traditional and popular with locals. Ryan's, 28 Parkgate Street, is a real gem. Located in the Phoenix Park area, it had been in the Ryan family since 1920 until recently. Ryan's is worth a visit just for the decor: superb antique mirrors, four brass lamp fittings mounted on the bar counter and a magnificent old oak and mahogany central bar with a unique double-faced mechanical clock and partitions of ornate, beveled-mirrored dividers. Heads of state and celebrities from the movie and theater worlds regularly mingle with natives to enjoy the great atmosphere.

Kavanagh's

Adjacent to what was once the main gate to Glasnevin Cemetery, Kavanagh's, 1 Prospect Square, is now run by its eighth-generation Kavanagh proprietor. The pub has been here for over a century-and-a-half and during that time has accumulated an inexhaustible fund of stories about gravediggers who would bang stones against the pub's wall and then wait for drinks to be passed through an opening and placed on their waiting shovels.

Kavanagh's remains today a plain, unadorned working-man's pub, with sawdust on the floor, worn wooden booths and cubbyholes, and a dart game or two.

Pubs with Music

In recent years, there has been an expansion of the kind of music performed in pubs, from traditional to jazz, blues, country, rock and even Cajun. You can check in local newspapers if you're in search of a musical evening. Oliver St. John Gogarty in Temple Bar is considered one of the city's best music pubs and features traditional Irish music nightly most of the year, which can go on well into the early hours.

You won't find a better ballad club in all of Ireland than the Abbey Tavern out in Howth, nine miles north of Dublin. The bar and restaurant is low-ceilinged, candlelit and has a fire glowing on cool nights, making it an informal, cozy place to eat. Shows in the big hall run through a host of ballads including some you'll never hear anywhere except on Irish soil. You can opt for a dinner and show package, or go for the show only. It is essential to reserve ahead. There's a good bus and train service to Howth.

O'Donoghue's, 15 Merrion Row, is an attraction for young and not-so-young musicians who flock here bearing guitars, uilleann pipes, bones and spoons and just about any musical instrument they have to hand. Music is spontaneous and lively and although it's always packed to the gills, it remains a popular gathering place.

Exhibits at Kilmainham Gaol evoke the bleak reality of a term of imprisonment

James Joyce Centre

Of all the literati to grace the Dublin scene during the 20th century, James Joyce has earned the greatest reputation, so it is fitting that this lovely 18th-century Georgian house is devoted to the writer and his work. Take time to browse in the extensive library and gaze at the portraits of those featured in the master's work. You can see the original doorway rescued from the now demolished No. 7 Eccles Street, the imagined residence of the *Ulysses* hero, Leopold Bloom. The center is also a starting point for an 80- to 90-minute walking tour of the Joycean sites.

➕ B3 ✉ 35 North Great George Street ☎ 01 878 8547; www.jamesjoyce.ie 🕐 Tue.–Sat. 10–7 🍴 Café 🚌 3. 10, 11, 13, 16, 19 ♿ $$

Kilmainham Gaol

In the years between its opening in 1796 and its closure in 1924, Kilmainham Gaol has held political leaders of rebellions in 1798, 1803, 1848, 1867 and 1916. President Eamon de Valera was confined within its walls in 1916 and again in 1923 and was its final prisoner. Though the cells hold no prisoners these days, corridors evoke a strong sense of patriots held here such as Robert Emmet, Charles Parnell, volunteers involved in the Easter Week Rebellion of 1916, and James Connolly and the 14 people executed with him in May 1916. As a museum documenting the Irish struggle for independence, a visit to Kilmainham Gaol is a profoundly moving experience not easily forgotten. Access by guided tour only.

➕ A2 ✉ Inchicore Road, Kilmainham ☎ 01 453 5984; fax 01 453 2037 🕐 Daily 9:30–5, Apr.–Sep.; Mon.–Sat. 9:30–4, Sun. 10–5, rest of year 🍴 Tearoom 🚌 51B, 79; Suir Road or Heuston Luas ♿ $$

Leinster House

Since 1925, this 1745 mansion has been the home of Ireland's Parliament (Oireachtas na hÉireann), composed of the Dáil (the lower house) and the Seanad (the senate). Look for the memorial on Leinster Lawn that commemorates Arthur Griffith, Kevin O'Higgins and Michael Collins, all among the founders of the Republic of Ireland. Leinster House is flanked on each side by the National Gallery and the Natural History Museum.

➕ C2 ✉ Kildare Street ☎ 01 618 3781 🕐 Check for visiting hours when Parliament is not in session; otherwise, admittance is only as an invited guest of a member of Parliament 🚌 Any city center (An Lar) bus

Marsh's Library

Jonathan Swift and James Joyce are among Dubliners who have made great use of the

Georgian Leinster House, Ireland's parliament building

25,000-volume literary collections housed in Marsh's Library, the first public library in Ireland. Built beside St. Patrick's Cathedral in 1701 by Archbishop Narcissus Marsh, its beautiful interior remains unchanged since it opened, with dark oak bookcases and unique wire cages in which readers were locked when studying rare books. Some books were actually chained to the shelves. The four collections cover a wide range of subjects (theology, ancient history, music, law, travel and medicine) and include about 300 manuscripts, including "The Lives of the Irish Saints," which dates to 1400.

➕ A2 ✉ St. Patrick's Close ☎ 01 454 3511; www.marshlibrary.ie 🕐 Mon. and Wed.–Fri. 10–1, 2–5, Sat. 10:30–1 🚌 50, 54A, 56A (from Eden Quay) 👆 $

National Gallery

In his youth, George Bernard Shaw spent many inspirational hours in the National Gallery and expressed his appreciation and gratitude by bequeathing royalties from his plays for its upkeep. Its doors first opened in 1864 with only 125 paintings, a collection that has grown to include some 2,500. There's a major collection of works by Irish artists, and European masters such as Rubens and Rembrandt are well represented.

A fascinating collection of Irish portraits lines the grand staircase, culminating in the fiery Countess Markiewicz, who was furious at being pardoned for her part in the Easter 1916 Uprising. Representing works up to the 19th century, the gallery has excellent computer facilities for obtaining information about its paintings. The Millennium Wing, opened in 2002, houses a center for the study of Irish art, temporary exhibition galleries and an archive dedicated to Jack B. Yeats.

➕ C2 ✉ Merrion Square West ☎ 01 661 5133; www.nationalgallery.ie 🕐 Mon.–Sat. 9:30–5:30, Thu. 9:30–8:30, Sun. noon–5:30; closed Good Friday and Dec. 24–26 🍴 Two restaurants 🚌 Any city center (An Lar) bus 👆 Free ℹ Tours Sat. at 3 and Sun. at 2, 3 and 4

National Library of Ireland

Those with an interest in Irish studies or for tracing Irish ancestry will find the National Library an invaluable resource. Opened in 1890, the library now holds thousands of volumes, many of them first editions, and works of Irish writers. James Joyce fans will recognize the library as the Chapter Nine setting in *Ulysses*.

➕ C2 ✉ Kildare Street ☎ 01 603 0200; www.nli.ie 🕐 Mon.–Wed. 9:30–9, Thu.–Fri. 9:30–5, Sat. 9:30–1 🚌 Any city center (An Lar) bus 👆 Free

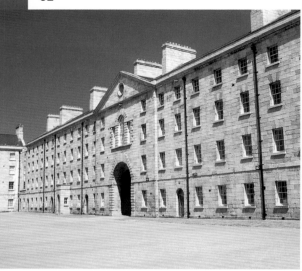

The imposing granite facade of the National Museum of Ireland – Decorative Arts and History, housed in Collins Barracks

that time is among the wealth of items on display.
🔟 Off the map ✉ Benburb Street
☎ 01 677 7444; www.museum.ie
🕐 Tue.–Sat. 10–5, Sun. 2–5
🍴 Café 🚌 25, 25A, 66, 67, 90;
Museum Luas 💶 Free
ℹ Audiovisual room and community education room

Number Twenty-Nine

So perfectly has this four-story townhouse been restored to its late 18th-century comfort and elegance that you may feel you're an invited guest of the middle-class family who occupied it back then. From top to bottom, every item is authentic to the period, whether genuine antique or a meticulous reproduction by Irish artisans. The living rooms are the epitome of respectability, and the upper-floor bedrooms, especially the nursery – where you can admire an enormous dolls' house – exude charm.
🔟 C2 ✉ Lower Fitzwilliam Street (entrance on corner of Upper Mount Street) ☎ 01 702 6165; fax 01 702 7796 🕐 Tue.–Sat. 10–5, Sun. 1–5; closed Dec. 11–25 🍴 Tearoom 🚌 7, 10, 45 (from city center) 💶 $$

National Museum of Ireland – Archaelology and History

Opened in 1890, the museum's collections include artifacts spanning the centuries from 2000 BC to the 20th century. The archeological section has relics from the Iron Age to the 15th century. Prehistoric and Viking Ireland, Ireland's Gold and Ancient Egypt collections breathe life into each era. "The Road to Independence" is a study of Ireland from 1916 to 1921.
🔟 C2 ✉ Kildare Street ☎ 01 677 7444;
www.museum.ie 🕐 Tue.–Sat. 10–5, Sun. 2–5 🍴 Café
🚌 Any city center (An Lar) bus 💶 Free

National Museum of Ireland – Decorative Arts and History

Collins Barracks, which occupy 18 acres north of the Liffey, are the oldest military barracks in Europe, built in 1701. When the National Museum purchased the large, rather austere building in 1994, its decorative arts, weapons, furniture, costumes, silver, ceramics and glassware collections were moved from their Kildare Street home and installed in these more spacious rooms. The radical Protestant barrister Wolfe Tone, who set up the United Irishmen in Belfast, was held prisoner here, and his pocketbook from

Old Jameson Distillery

Back in the sixth century, *uisce beatha* (pronounced "ish-ke ba-ha") which translates to "the water of life," was the name given to Ireland's blended whiskey. It was anglicized to "fuisce" before evolving into "whiskey."

The Jameson Distillery, housed in an old warehouse that once used to mature whiskey, features an audiovisual history of the making of Irish whiskey, an interesting museum that includes a copper-pot still, distillery model and other implements of the trade. With any luck, you'll be chosen as one of four tasters to sample various brands. Luck or no luck, everyone gets a sample at the end of the tour, in the Jameson bar. A reminder: when you bend an elbow, don't forget to turn to your neighbor and raise your glass in the traditional Irish toast, *slainte* (pronounced "slawn-che") – it means "good health."

➕ A3 ✉ Bow Street, Smithfield ☎ 01 807 2355; fax 01 807 2369; www.oldjamesondistillery.com
🕐 Daily 9:30–6 🍴 Café 🚌 68, 69, 79, 90; Smithfield Luas 🚃 $$$

Oscar Wilde House

In the northwest corner of Merrion Square resides the wonderful statue of Oscar Wilde languishing on a rock. Dressed in a velvet smoking jacket, Wilde appears incredibly lifelike and is especially haunting when illuminated at night. Across the road the house, with its exceptional cornices and architraves, he lived in between 1855 and 1876 is a fine example of the Georgian architecture so typical of this part of Dublin. Now owned by the American College Dublin, the house is only open to groups.

➕ C2 ✉ 1 Merrion Square ☎ 662 0281 🕐 Open for groups of a minimum of 25 only (on a tour), advance booking necessary, call for information 🚌 Cross-city buses 🚃 $$

St. Audoen's Church of Ireland and Roman Catholic Church

The Celtic Church of St. Columcille stood on this site before the Normans replaced it in 1190, dedicating it to St. Ouen (eventually corrupted to its present spelling). The three bells in its tower are reputed to be the oldest still in Ireland (1423), and there's a pre-1309 Christian gravestone known as the "Lucky Stone," which supposedly possesses strange powers. Of note is the 1190 west doorway and the 13th-century nave. The churchyard park is bordered by part of the old city walls, and steps descend to St. Audoen's Arch, the only surviving gateway of the old city.

The Roman Catholic church situated next door is a much younger building, dating from 1847, and very much more intact than its neighbor. The fine interior is accessible by a side door. The two giant clam shells, relics of a Pacific Ocean voyage, are used as holy water containers.

➕ A3 ✉ Cornmarket, High Street ☎ 01 677 0088
🕐 Daily 9:30–5:30, May–Sep./Oct. Renovation work due to start Sep. 2008 🚌 21A, 78A, 78B 🚃 Free

Interior of a grand bedroom in the museum of Number Twenty-Nine

St. Michan's Church

St. Michan's Church dates to the 17th century, but its square tower is that of a 1095 Danish church that stood on this site. Through some strange process not fully understood, elements from the soil and the air in the crypt combine to perfectly preserve bodies that have lain here for centuries. Mummified bodies, which include those of a 15th-century nun and the Sheare Brothers (patriots executed for treason during the 1798 rebellion), can be viewed through a small hatch. Their co-conspirator in that rebellion, Robert Emmet, was comforted by St. Michan's rector in the last hours of his life, and his remains are reputed to be buried in the churchyard.

➕ A3 ✉ Church Street ☎ 01 872 4154 🕐 Mon.–Fri. 10–12:45 and 2–4:45, Sat. 10–12:45, Mar.–Oct.; Mon.–Fri. 12:30–3:30, rest of year 🚌 34; Smithfield Luas 🚃 $

St. Patrick's Cathedral

St. Patrick is said to have baptized Christians on this site, and there's been a church here since AD 450. The present building, the largest church in the country, replaced the earlier structure in 1191. From 1320 to 1520, this was Ireland's first university, and, in the

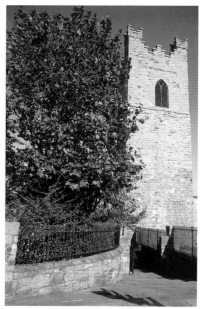

The Anglo-Normans founded Dublin's parish church of St. Audoen's

of city streets. It is beautifully landscaped with mature plantings, a lovely artificial lake and a network of pathways threading their way through colorful flower beds. There are numerous statues and busts of famous Irish men and women dotted about, including impressions of James Joyce, Robert Emmet, Wolfe Tone and Sir Arthur Guinness. The park is also surrounded by some of the finest buildings in Dublin, dating back to the city's Georgian prime. Architectural gems include the fashionable Shelbourne Hotel, with statues of Nubian princesses and their ankle-fettered slaves decorating the front, and the neo-Byzantine interior of the atmospheric Roman Catholic University Church. Dublin office and shop workers often head for the Green for a picnic lunch, and visitors also gravitate to its peaceful tranquility in the very heart of the city.

B2 Mon.–Sat. 8–dusk, Sun. 10–dusk

Any city center (An Lar) bus; St. Stephen's Green Luas

Trinity College and The *Book of Kells*

Trinity College was founded by Queen Elizabeth I in 1592 on a 40-acre site in the heart of the city, ostensibly "to civilize Ireland with both learning and the Protestant religion." Catholics were allowed entry – as well as free education – provided they converted to Protestantism. The roll of honor is impressive: Edmund Burke, Jonathan Swift, Oliver Goldsmith, Bram Stoker, Wolfe Tone, William Congreve, J. M. Synge and Samuel Beckett have all passed through these hallowed portals.

Walk through its gates and you're in a world of cobbled squares and red-brick buildings from the early 1700s called the Rubrics, the college's oldest surviving structures. The lofty vaulted Long Room – where the ghosts of many literati stalk – and Colonnades Gallery in the Old Library hold some of Ireland's most important antiquities, including the magnificently illustrated *Book of Kells* (created circa AD 800). The richness of color and design throughout this four-volume, handwritten, Latin transcript of the four gospels is absolutely stunning.

17th century, Englishman Oliver Cromwell's troops used it as a stable. Huguenots worshipped here from 1666 to 1816, and reminders of its long history bombard your view on all sides, from Celtic gravestones to centuries-old proud Irish regimental banners to different memorials for some of Ireland's most famous citizens, including Carolan, last practitioner of the Irish bardic tradition. The tomb of the cathedral's best-known dean (1713 to 1745), Jonathan Swift (author of *Gulliver's Travels* and a plethora of witty, satiric essays), can be found in the south aisle near that of his beloved "Stella." Christians of all denominations are welcome at all church services.

A2 St. Patrick's Street 01 453 9472; fax 01 454 6374; www.stpatrickscathedral.ie Mon.–Sat. 9–5, Sun. 9–11, 12:45–3 and 4:15–6, Mar.–Oct.; Mon.–Sat. 9–5, Sun. 10–11 and 12:45–3, rest of year 50, 54A, 56A (from Eden Quay) SS

St. Stephen's Green

Since 1690, peaceful St. Stephen's Green, at the foot of Grafton Street, has been preserved as a bucolic respite from the hustle and bustle

Old Library Hall, Trinity College

"The Book of Kells, Turning Darkness into Light" is a major exhibition in the Old Library that explains the context of the book and highlights the rare manuscript. Also on display are the beautiful ancient books of Durrow and Armagh.

Since 1801 Trinity College has had the historic right under copyright law to claim a free copy of all British and Irish publications and now houses a vast collection of nearly three million volumes in eight buildings. Even on a stringent selection basis, nearly half a mile of new shelving is required each year to house newly acquired publications, which are now kept off-site.

✠ B3 ✉ College Green ☎ 01 896 1661; www.tcd.ie/library ⊕ Old Library: Mon.–Sat. 9:30–5, Sun. 9:30–4:30 (Sun. noon–4:30, Oct.–Apr.); closed 10 days over Christmas and New Year 🚌 Any city center (An Lar) bus 💲 Campus: free; Old Library: $$$

Walk: **South of the Liffey**

Refer to route marked on city map on page 65.

Dublin is a small, vibrant city that's a delight to explore on foot. From broad O'Connell Street on the northside to the leafy green spaces of St. Stephen's Green on the southside and the tiny lanes of Temple Bar, you can soak up the atmosphere of a city steeped in history, yet firmly in step with today and looking forward to tomorrow. Allow about three hours for this walk.

Begin at the tourist office on Suffolk Street, turn left onto Andrews Street, then down Trinity Street to Dame Street. Cross Dame Street to the Central Bank Plaza and Cope Street into Crown Alley (behind the bank) to reach Temple Bar.
Chances are that something will be going on in Temple Bar. Allow time to wander the maze of tiny 18th-century cobblestone streets that only a few years ago were lined with ancient, dilapidated warehouses. Urban renewal has brought an amazing cultural vibrancy to this area, with street entertainment that includes jazz, ethnic and rock concerts, street theater, art exhibits and The Ark, an arts center and theater for children. Look for the Temple Bar Gallery and Studios and some of Dublin's most interesting shops, quirky boutiques and equally interesting restaurants, cafés and pubs (see page 67). Crown Alley takes you to Temple Bar Square (site of many open-air entertainments and sidewalk artists) and Merchants Arch, through which you will see the rejuvenated, cream-colored Ha'penny Bridge (see page 64), which exacted a half-penny toll from pedestrians from 1816 to 1919.

Take Temple Bar Street to Parliament Street, turn left and walk to the City Hall.
The Corinthian-style City Hall was built between 1769 and 1777 as the Royal Exchange, and it is now the venue for meetings of Dublin City Council. Its impressive entrance rotunda displays statues of Daniel O'Connell and other Irish leaders, and the corporation's coat of arms and motto are represented in the floor mosaic. During the 1780s, this was a meeting point for volunteer rallies, and during the 1798 rebellion it was used by government troops as barracks and torture chambers. The roadway outside City Hall was once the entrance to the medieval city through the Dame Gate.

Turn left up Cork Hill (between City Hall and Newcomen's Bank) and walk to the Upper Castle Yard gate.
Dublin Castle (see page 72) really doesn't look much like a castle these days. That's because of drastic 18th-century renovations that left intact only a few of the original towers (1204) and no trace of the curtain wall's massive towers, drawbridge or portcullis. Surviving today are the record tower and the Bermingham tower (from the 14th century). Dubliners will point out with a wry smile that Van Nost's statue of justice atop the upper castle yard gate was placed with its back to the city's citizens. The elegant state apartments are open to the public, as are 10th-century Viking defenses, which were exposed by renovation work in 1990, and the impressive Chester Beatty Library and Gallery of Oriental Art (see page 70).

Walk east to Dame Street, continue east on Dame Street to meet College Green.
The Bank of Ireland, a magnificent Georgian structure, only became a bank in 1800 after the Irish Parliament legislated its own death when it passed the detested Act of Union. The elegant former House of Lords is open to the public during banking hours (see page 70). Opposite the bank is Trinity College (see page 84) and you'll find the beautifully decorated *Book of Kells* in the Colonnades. While Catholics were barred from attending Trinity College unless they obtained special dispensation or converted to Protestantism until 1966, women (non-Catholics, of course) were admitted as early as 1903. On the corner of Grafton Street, the Provost's House is a superb Georgian mansion.

Powerscourt – a maze of fascinating shops, market stalls, cafés and restaurants

From College Green, walk south on Grafton Street, a pedestrian avenue lined with fashionable shops. The lovely bronze statue near the corner of Nassau and Grafton streets depicts Molly Malone of the "Dublin's Fair City" song. The figure has been irreverently (but affectionately) dubbed the "Tart With the Cart." Turn right at Johnson's Court, a narrow lane, and proceed to the Powerscourt shopping center.

Set in a 1774 townhouse built by Lord Powerscourt, this shopping center is a far cry from its modern counterparts. Both the house itself and the courtyard have been only slightly modified to accommodate a wide variety of small stores and restaurants.

Return to Grafton Street and walk south. At the foot of Grafton Street, St. Stephen's Green is a beautifully landscaped oasis of greenery and calm in the heart of the city and is a favorite sunning and lunching spot for Dubliners. Once known as "Beaux Walk," the north side of the Green now houses some of Dublin's most prestigious private clubs.

Turn left on St. Stephen's Green North, then left onto Dawson Street for Mansion House.

In January 1919 the first assembly of Dáil Éireann (the Irish Parliament) met in this beautiful 1710 mansion, now the official residence of the Lord Mayor of Dublin. It is used mainly for receptions and exhibitions and is not open to the public.

Return to St. Stephen's Green North and turn left onto Kildare Street. Leinster House (see page 80) is on your right. From the north end of Kildare Street, turn right onto Nassau Street, which becomes Leinster Street, then Clare Street before reaching Merrion Square.

Take a look at the blue plaques on many of the Georgian houses that line this square, one of Dublin's finest. They commemorate notable former residents such as W. B. Yeats and Daniel O'Connell.

Continue south along the west side of the square, which becomes Merrion Street, then turn left onto Lower Baggot Street. Turn right onto Fitzwilliam Street and on your right is Fitzwilliam Square.

A pocket of well-preserved Georgian architecture, this square, although among the city's smallest, is worth browsing to appreciate elegant fanlights above front doors, elaborate iron bootscrapers and other ingenious details such as glass recesses for lamps. The studio of one of Ireland's most famous artists, Jack B. Yeats, was in No. 18.

For such a small country, Ireland has contributed an inordinate number of articulate, sharp-witted writers who have used the well-turned phrase to produce a wealth of words both timeless and universal. Dublin has been home to many of the country's best writers, and while some of the landmarks they left behind have disappeared and others have changed, the following sights will bring you closer to that rich literary legacy.

James Joyce portrait by Jacque Emile Blanche
©ADAGP, Paris and DACS, London 2007

Dublin's Literary Greats

Elizabeth Bowen

Born in Dublin at 15 Herbert Place off Lower Baggot Street in 1900, Elizabeth Bowen studied and lived abroad for much of her life, although her ironic wit enlivens novels, short stories and essays, many of them based on Irish life. Novels such as *Friends and Relations, The Heat of the Day* and *The Death of the Heart* mark her as a master of modern literature. She died in London in 1973.

Samuel Beckett

Born in Cooldrinagh in Foxrock, Dublin in 1906, Samuel Beckett had a brilliant academic background. He moved to Paris and turned to writing novels and short stories before moving into works for the stage. His most memorable play is undoubtedly *Waiting for Godot*, quickly followed by such bleakly horrifying comedies as *End Game*. A prolific poet, novelist and playwright, Beckett produced a body of work considered to be the greatest influence on mid-century European drama. He died in Paris in 1989.

Brendan Behan

With youthful years spent at 14 Russell Street, Brendan Behan was born in Dublin in 1923. He became involved with the IRA by the age of 15 and was sentenced to jail for 14 years in 1942. He was released in a 1946 amnesty and set about chronicling his prison experiences in plays like *The Quare Fellow* and *The Hostage* in a bluntly honest, irreverent style that often angered fellow Dubliners. He died in 1964 and was laid to rest in Glasnevin Cemetery. No doubt his spirit still roams the city streets and bends a ghostly elbow in McDaid's pub, one of his favorites, still reveling in the vagaries of life in Dublin today.

James Joyce

The house at 41 Brighton Square West, Rathgar was the birthplace of James Joyce in 1882. From his self-imposed exile he mapped the face of his native city in unremitting detail. A museum devoted to Joyce memorabilia now occupies the Martello Tower in Sandymount, where he lived for a time in 1904 with Oliver St. John Gogarty. The tourist board has prepared a "Ulysses Map of Dublin," but the meanderings of Joyce's character Leopold Bloom can be traced from the book as unerringly as if Joyce had written a guidebook to the city rather than his *Ulysses* masterpiece. Bloomsday is celebrated every June 16 (see page 75). The James Joyce Centre, 35 North Great George's Street, has a library, book and coffee shop.

Thomas Moore

In 1779 at 12 Aungier Street, Thomas Moore was born and acquired much of his higher learning at Trinity College. Although opinions differed widely during his lifetime as to whether songs from his Irish Melodies were truly Irish or merely "stage-Irish," many however, are still popular today with the Irish and visitors alike. He died in England in 1852, having suffered mental illness for several years.

Iris Murdoch

Born in Dublin to an Anglo-Irish family in 1919, Iris Murdoch wrote a series of distinguished and highly successful intellectual novels. Several deal brilliantly with conflicting loyalties of families such as her own, most notably *The Red and the Green*, published in 1965 and set in the turbulent 1916–23 period of Irish life. She died in England in 1999 after a long illness.

Sean O'Casey

A product of Dublin's northside slums, Sean O'Casey was born in 1884. Self-educated, he was deeply involved with the labor movement and worked closely with James Connolly in the Irish Citizens Army. His first play to be accepted by the Abbey Theatre was *The Shadow of a Gunman*, a highly controversial work that caused consternation among ultra-conservative audiences. Later, *The Plough and the Stars* was to cause the most dramatic row in Ireland for years. When the Abbey refused to produce *The Silver Tassie*, O'Casey left Ireland and remained abroad until his death in 1964.

Cornelius Ryan

You'll know Cornelius Ryan, who was born in 1920 at 33 Heytesburn Street (off the South Circular Road), for his outstanding World War II accounts *The Longest Day* and *A Bridge Too Far*. He died in Washington, D.C. shortly before the latter was published in 1976, after a long battle with cancer.

George Bernard Shaw

Best remembered as the dramatist whose prolific output includes *St. Joan, Man and Superman* and a wealth of other plays, George Bernard Shaw was born at 33 Synge Street in 1856. He continued to write plays, political treatises and autobiographical sketches right until his death in 1950. Shaaw's birthplace has been restored to the way it was when he lived here and is open to the public.

Abraham Stoker

Although Abraham (Bram) Stoker, born in 1847 at 15 Marino Crescent in Clontarf, wrote a dozen novels, his literary immortality is assured by his masterpiece *Dracula*. Quite possibly, it is the most reprinted, translated, filmed, serialized and drawn-in-comic-strips novel of all time, and has moved into the world's folklore. Stoker died in 1912.

Jonathan Swift

The house at 7 Hoey's Court, where Jonathan Swift was born in 1667, stood very near St. Patrick's Cathedral, his last resting place after some 32 years as the cathedral's most famous dean. Trinity College (see page 84), where Swift studied, also echoes with memories of the great irreligious satirist, poet and novelist who penned such masterpieces as *Gulliver's Travels*, and his relationships with "Stella" and "Vanessa" are debated even today. He died in 1745, leaving funds to found St. Patrick's Hospital for Imbeciles, the first institution if this kind in Ireland. His body of work reflects a compelling mixture of compassion and rage at mankind's behavior.

Oscar Wilde

Born at 21 Westland Row in 1856, many critics consider Oscar Wilde's finest work to be *The Ballad of Reading Gaol* (an account of his years in prison on a charge of homosexuality). His brilliance in challenging conventional thinking and espousing sometimes bizarre new ideas shines through such other works as *The Importance of Being Earnest* and his gripping novel *The Picture of Dorian Gray*. He died penniless in Paris in 1900.

W. B. Yeats

The birthplace of W. B. Yeats (1865) was 5 Sandymount Avenue, and from 1928 to 1932 he resided at 42 Fitzwilliam Square. Aside from his poetry and *The Celtic Twilight* about "romantic Ireland," one of Yeats' most important contributions to Irish culture was his involvement in the founding of Dublin's Abbey Theatre (see page 66). He was often seen in Toner's pub on Lower Baggot Street in Dublin. Yeats died in Paris in 1939, but at the end of World War II his remains were returned for burial at Drumcliff near his beloved Thoor Ballylee (see page 46) where his more esoteric writings were produced.

Regional Sights

Key to symbols

✚ map coordinates refer to the region map on page 60; sights below are highlighted in yellow on the map
✉ address or location ☎ telephone number
◉ opening times 🍴 restaurant on site or nearby
🚌 nearest bus or train station 👐 admission charge: $$$ more than €6, $$ €4 to €6, $ less than €4
🅸 information

Athlone and the Shannon

Straddling the River Shannon, the historic town of Athlone is a premier center for cruising and fishing in the heart of Ireland. The river marks a change in character between the two halves of the town, with narrow streets of old buildings grouped around the castle on the west bank and 19th- and 20th-century developments on the east. Athlone has always been an important crossing on the Shannon (*Áth Luain* means the Ford of Luan) and Athlone Castle, dating from 1210, was positioned as a powerful defense of this strategic ford of the river.

During Oliver Cromwell's rampage through Ireland, the castle was the focus of seiges of the town in 1690 and 1691. At the end of the 18th-century, the ruined walls were heavily reconstructed when there was a threat of a Napoleonic invasion. An audiovisual presentation in the visitor center details the seige history, and there are exhibits about the castle, the town and the power resources of the Shannon. The Museum of the Old Athlone Society in the castle keep, includes medieval gravestones and mementos of the great Athlone-born tenor, John McCormack; his birthplace is marked by a bronze plaque in The Bawn, a narrow lane off Mardyke Street.

South of Athlone along the river is one of Ireland's holiest sites, Clonmacnois, where St. Ciaran founded a monastery in 548. It was plundered by Irish chieftains, Vikings and Anglo-Normans, and it finally gave in to its attackers when Cromwell's forces desecrated it beyond restoration. Today you'll find among its ruins a cathedral, eight churches, two round towers, the remains of a castle, more than 200 monumental slabs and three sculptured high crosses. There are guided tours during the summer months, and an excellent presentation at the visitor center.

East of Athlone on the N6 road is Locke's Distillery. Established in 1757, Locke's was one of the first licensed distilleries in the world and operated for nearly 200 years before it closed in 1957. Restored as a museum, it uses the original machinery to demonstrate whiskey-making techniques.

The River Shannon is the longest river in the Ireland. Rising in a humble pool in County Cavan, it carves a ponderous course to Limerick through the brimming flood plains and water meadows of several counties straddling the Leinster-Connacht border. At first the landscape around the river appears monotonous – a shallow saucer of endless unremarkable arable and pasture land broken by lakes, rivers and canals – and there are few memorable vistas.

The smallish watery counties forming the geographical heart of Ireland are often portrayed as places to get through on the way to somewhere more interesting. Busy, dreary main roads blast through on radial routes from Dublin to the west coast of counties Mayo and Galway and facilities for visitors are limited compared with popular western or southeastern spots. However, these lakeland counties offer a less stereotyped picture of Ireland.

The Shannon is not only an important navigable waterway, but also a popular recreational base for fishing and boating activities, scenic interest and wildlife habitats. Visitors are welcomed with true Irish hospitality, with no pressure to buy sweaters or shamrock table linen!

✚ A3

Tourist information ✉ Athlone Castle ☎ 09064 94630 ◉ Mon.–Sat. 9–6, Jul.–Aug.; Mon.–Fri. 9:30–5, May–Jun. and in Sep.

Athlone Castle ✉ St. Peter's Square ☎ 09064 92912 ◉ Daily 10–5:30, May–Oct. 👐 $$

Clonmacnoise and Bog Tour ✉ 4 miles north of Shannonbridge on R357, Co. Offaly ☎ 09096 74195 ◉ Tours only daily 9–7, mid-May to mid-Sep.; 10–5:30, rest of year 🍴 Coffee shop 👐 $$

Locke's Distillery ✉ Main Street, Kilbeggan,

Boats moored at the harbor in Dalkey

Co. Westmeath ☎ 05793 32134; fax 05793 32134
🕐 Daily 9–6, Apr.–Oct.; 10–4, rest of year
🍽 Restaurant ✋ $$$

Avoca

Avoca, a pretty hamlet of neat white cottages
in a wooded setting, is the home of Avoca
Handweavers, Ireland's oldest hand-weaving
mill dating from 1723, whose weaves, colors
and patterns have won worldwide acclaim.
The Avonmore and Avonbeg rivers combine
to become the Avoca River, here inspiring
19th-century poet Thomas Moore's tribute
"Meeting of the Waters." A path leads down
to the river bank and a clearing, which holds
a bust of the poet; the tree stump on which
he sat while composing his famous lines is
marked with a plaque.

Just 4 miles north toward Rathdrum, in
one of County Wicklow's most beautifully
forested areas, is Avondale House. Charles
Stewart Parnell, a heroic and tragic figure
among Ireland's most prominent nationalist
leaders, was born and lived much of his life
in this 1777 mansion. Much of his patriotic
fervor undoubtedly came from his mother,
an American with strong anti-British
leanings. His political career was crowned by
land reforms achieved by his leadership of
the Land League. His popularity, however,

was dealt a death blow when he was named
correspondent in a divorce action against his
long-time mistress Katherine (Kitty) O'Shea,
from which he never recovered politically.
There's a small museum filled with mementos
of his life (1846–91) and an interesting gift
shop. A walk in the adjacent forest park
provides a restful interlude.
➕ C2

Avoca Handweavers ✉ Old Mill, Avoca ☎ 0402
35105 🕐 Daily 9–6, May–Oct.; 9:30–5:30, Nov.–Apr.
🍽 Café ✋ Free

Avondale House and Forest Park ✉ 1 mile south of
Rathdrum ☎ 0404 46111; fax 0404 46333 🕐 Daily
11–5, May–Aug.; Tue.–Sun. 11–5, mid-Mar. through
Apr. 30, and Sep.–Oct. 🍽 Restaurant ✋ $$

Dalkey

Originally a fishing village at the southern
end of Dublin Bay, Dalkey is one of the
Leinster coast's most charming spots. In
recent years it has become a stylish address
for several stars. Nothing new, really – George
Bernard Shaw lived for a time in a cottage on
Dalkey Hill, and writers Flann O'Brien and
Hugh Leonard (still a resident) have also
called Dalkey home.

Off the coast from Collemore Harbour,
22-acre Dalkey Island is inhabited these days
only by a few wild goats, but there is

evidence that people lived here as early as the fourth century BC. It's a wonderful get-away-from-it-all spot, and even better if you bring a picnic. During summer it is possible to rent a boat from Bulloch Harbour to take you to the island. The Heritage Centre is located in restored Dalkey Castle, and its exceptionally helpful staff can steer you to other points of interest in the area and arrange guided tours with advance notice.

Killiney Bay has been likened to the Bay of Naples, and it is best viewed from Victoria Park, which is only a short walk from Dalkey along the Vico Road. A beautiful public beach leads to Killiney Hill and Victoria Park. Panoramic views of the bay add to the tranquility of the park's open green spaces, which are interspersed with rocky outcroppings perfect for hiking up if you want an even better view.

✚ C3

Tourist information ✉ Dublin Tourism, Suffolk Street ☎ 01 605 7700 ⏰ Mon.–Sat., 9–7, Sun. 10:30–3, Jun.–Sep.; Mon.–Sat. 9–5:30, Sun. 10–3, rest of year **Dalkey Castle and Heritage Centre** ✉ Castle Street, Dalkey ☎ 01 285 8366; fax 01 284 3141; www.dalkeycastle.com ⏰ Mon.–Fri. 9:30–5, Sat.–Sun. 11–5 🚌 8, DART Dalkey Station 💷 $$

Drogheda

Drogheda stands at the lowest bridging point of the River Boyne, just a few miles from the site of the famous Battle of the Boyne in 1690. Something of the historic medieval town can still be seen in the hilly streets, though little remains of the old town walls.

To the west of Drogheda lies the Boyne Valley, and while it is filled to overflowing with historical landmarks, none is more significant than this stretch along the Louth and Meath border. It was here that William of Orange defeated James II, changing the course of Irish history dramatically.

The Boyne Valley is strewn with some of Ireland's most important archeological monuments, more than 40 in all, and the Brú Na Bóinne Visitor Centre (Palace of the Boyne) in Donore unfolds their story before you set off to explore this remarkable landscape. It is also the required starting point from which to tour the two most

impressive megalithic tombs, Newgrange and Knowth. The visitor centre operates a minibus service to and from these wonders. The numbers for each tour are strictly limited, but the experience is worth the wait.

Newgrange was probably built by the first settlers who came to Ireland from the European continent more than 5,000 years ago. This makes it possibly 1,000 years older than Stonehenge. We know almost nothing about them or what the ornamental spirals and other decorations at this massive burial mound symbolize. We don't even know for whom the structure was built, whether holy men, chieftains or kings. What we do know is that they were skilled builders, for the corbeled roof above the burial chamber has kept out the dampness of 40 centuries, the 62-foot-long passage still serves quite well as an entry to the 19-foot-high chamber, and the stone at its entrance remains an enduring testament to prehistoric craftsmanship. This amazing 36-foot mound includes 200,000 tons of stone and a six-ton capstone. Stones as large as 16 tons each came from as far away as County Wicklow.

Archeologists are constantly carrying out research at Newgrange in an effort to unravel such mysteries as the reason a roof box above the doorway is so placed that the sun's rays reach the burial chamber only at 8:58 a.m. on the shortest day of the year, and then for exactly 17 minutes!

At busy times you will have to arrive early in the day to ensure admission to Newgrange. Archeological work continues in the Boyne Valley, which means that some sites may be closed. Knowth, about a mile northwest of Newgrange, is still under excavation. Here there are two passage tombs, with another 17 smaller tombs in the immediate vicinity. Like Newgrange's artwork, the enigmatic passage tomb artwork at Knowth is some of the finest in Europe.

Directly west of Newgrange is a traditional 333-acre farm growing barley, wheat and other grains. The cows, bulls, heifers, goats, pigs, ponies, Hampshire Downs sheep (the ones with a "teddy-bear coat"), rabbits, dogs and chickens are the main attraction. Here, one of the farmers will

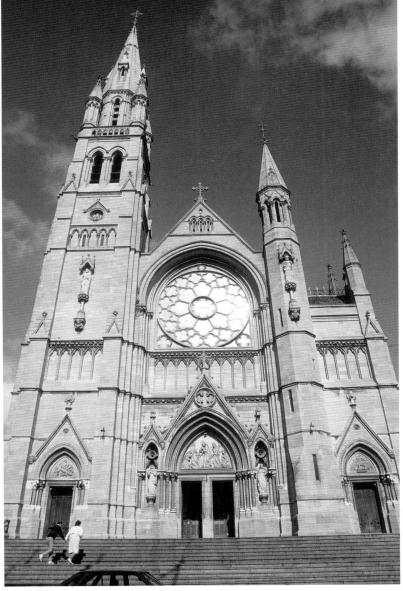

The mid-18th-century Church of St. Peter, Drogheda

lead you through this thriving menagerie, and give a running and informative commentary about how the farm works.

✝ C4

Tourist information ✉ Drogheda Bus Station, Donore Road ☎ 041 983 7070 ◷ Mon.–Sat. 9:30–5:30, Sun. noon–4:30, May–Sep.

Brú Na Boînne Visitor Centre ✉ Donore, Co. Meath (for directions see drive on page 95) ☎ 041 988 0300; fax 041 982 3071 ◷ Daily 9:30–5:30 Mar.–Apr.; 9–7 Jun.

to mid-Sep.; 9–6:30 in May and mid- to end Sep.; 9:30–5:30, Oct.; 9:30–5, rest of year.

Knowth ◷ Daily, May–Oct.; call tourist office for details. Last tour for Knowth and Newgrange departs 1 hour, 45 minutes before closing ◷ Newgrange/ Knowth: $$$; visitor centre: $

Newgrange Farm ✉ Located at Slane village, 7 miles from Drogheda on N51 ☎ 041 982 4119; fax 041 982 4119; www.newgrangefarm.com ◷ Daily 10–6, Easter–Sep. 🍴 Café 🅿 $$$

Leinster

Drive: **Boyne Valley**

Duration: 1–2 days

This historic 84-mile drive through Ireland's past passes through pleasant countryside rich in megalithic and early-Christian monuments.

Starting from the tourist office at Drogheda, take the R312 for Belfast. After 5 miles turn left, following signposts for Boyne Drive, Monasterboice. After half a mile, turn left again.

Monasterboice was once a large monastic community. Pick your way between ancient and modern graves to see two of the finest high crosses in the country. These free-standing carvings in stone were of a quality unparalleled anywhere in Europe at the time they were erected, and yet the very high round tower is a reminder that these remarkable works of art were created in the midst of Viking attacks. The West Cross stands close to the round tower, while the 17-foot-high Cross of Muiredach – so called because of the inscription on the base, "A prayer for Muiredach by whom this cross was made" – is smaller and more perfect. The messages on these crosses follow coherent themes of God's grace to man and the parallels between Old and New Testaments. On Muiredach's Cross, look for stories of Adam and Eve, Cain and Abel, the Last Judgment and the crucifixion of Christ.

An event of religious significance of more recent times was the visit of Pope John Paul II in 1979, and the point where he celebrated Mass is marked on the main Belfast to Dublin road.

Continue past Monasterboice. After a mile, turn right for Mellifont. After a mile, turn left on the Drogheda road, R168, and after another mile, turn right for Mellifont.

The vast passage tomb at Newgrange is faced with sparkling quartzite

To walk in the footsteps of monks who founded Mellifont Abbey here on the banks of the Mattock river in 1142 is to drink in the peacefulness of a setting that invites meditation. The chapter house and ruins of the cloister still remain from the structures built in the 13th century, but only the foundations are left of the original building. An octagonal lavabo once equipped with water jets and basins is the most interesting structure.

> Return to the crossroads and turn right. After 2 miles turn right. Go straight over the intersection, following the signpost to King William's Glen. After 1 mile turn right on to the N51, then 2.5 miles farther on, turn left and follow signs for Newgrange (see page 92).

Irish architecture may have begun in the Boyne Valley in 3000 BC. People who had only stone and wood for tools created the most impressive monuments of their kind in Western Europe. Little is known of these people or of those interred in these prehistoric tombs, but excavations have shown that they cultivated crops and cleared areas of forest.

The mound at Newgrange, constructed with water-rolled pebbles, is retained by a curb of great stone blocks lying end to end, topped by white quartz and granite boulders. The passage is lined with huge stones, and the central cross-shaped chamber is roofed with a vault untouched in 5,000 years. Standing around the mound is an incomplete circle of stones.

At Dowth – where you cannot enter the site but can walk around – a larger passage tomb has two chambers, while Knowth has two passage tombs surrounded by 18 smaller ones. Knowth was used from the Stone Age, and in the early Christian era was a seat of the high kings of Ireland. The significance of the Boyne Valley tombs is that here artwork combines with the engineering feats of the passage tombs of Ireland. Spirals, lozenges, zigzags, sunbursts – figures cut in stone with stone implements – decorate the monuments.

> Return by minor roads to the N51 and turn left for Slane.

Slane occupies an attractive curve on the River Boyne and is overlooked by the Hill of Slane, where St. Patrick is said to have announced Christianity's arrival in Ireland. Legend or fact, the summit of Slane Hill would certainly have been ideal for that purpose, with its sweeping views of the Boyne Valley. From the viewpoint on the hill, the pleasant village of Slane can be seen running steeply down to the banks of the

One of Kells' four high crosses

From the time that pagans worshipped here, Tara has figured in Irish history and legend. The high kings were seated here and it was the center of political and religious power before the arrival of Christianity. A *feis* (festival) at royal Tara was held at harvest or at the crowning of a king. Burial mounds here go back some 4,000 years, and there are earthworks dating from the Iron Age. All else of Tara's regal trappings must be left to your imagination as you view this low hillside. A presentation at the visitor center in St. Patrick's Church will give you a fuller understanding of its importance.

Five chariot roads led here from all parts of Ireland. The rath of the synods is an elaborate earthwork. The mound of the hostages, a Stone Age passage tomb that stands inside the royal enclosure, is an Iron Age hill fort and encloses the royal seat, a ring fort. On Cormac's House is the stone of destiny, used in the inauguration of the kings. Also here are the banquet hall, the enclosure of King Laoghaire, the sloping trenches and Grainne's enclosure. A statue of St. Patrick recalls his profound influence, but it was the coming of Christianity that led to the decline of Tara.

Return to the N3 and turn right. After 2 miles turn left, following signs to Skreen Church and Cross, go straight over two sets of intersections and follow an uneven road for 4.5 miles, then turn left toward Drogheda. After 1 mile turn left toward Slane on the N2. Follow the Battle of the Boyne marked route.

It does not take a great effort of the imagination to picture the field of battle in 1690, when the armies of William of Orange and James II met in a conflict that was significant for Ireland, Britain and Europe. A huge orange and green sign beside the deep waters of the Boyne marks the main site of the conflict, while helpful signs along the way show where the opposing armies camped, where battle was joined and where the river was crossed. The route passes along the Boyne Navigation Canal, once a link in Ireland's waterways system.

Take the N51 back to Drogheda.

river. Just to the east is the cottage of the poet Francis Ledwidge, who died during World War I.

Slane Castle on the banks of the Boyne river is the home of the Mount Charles family. Badly damaged by fire in 1991, the castle has been restored and tours are available in summer. The magnificent amphitheater in front of the house is used once a year as a stage for spectacular rock concerts.

Take the N51 for Navan, and after 1 mile turn right on the R163 for Kells.

In the sixth century, St. Colmcille founded a monastic settlement on this site. Kells, or Ceanannus Mór, became one of the great religious centers of Western Europe. This is where Ireland's most celebrated illuminated medieval manuscript, the famous *Book of Kells*, was written, now on view in the library at Trinity College, Dublin (see page 84). Facsimiles of the book are on display in the Kells Heritage Centre. St. Columba's Church at the top of Market Street was built on the original site. It is by far the most impressive building in the town. Four high crosses and a round tower are in the grounds.

Take the N3 (via Navan) for Dublin, and after 6 miles turn right signed for Tara.

The Hill of Tara commands majestic views over the fertile plains of Meath and beyond.

Dun Laoghaire

This is a place to promenade along the extensive harbor piers, past the villas on the seafront or through the parks. Savor the Victorian features of the place that was called Kingstown from the visit of George IV in 1821 until the establishment of the Irish Free State. When the granite piers were completed in 1859, the harbor was the biggest artificial haven in the world. Ships and ferries to England use the port and it is home to several yacht clubs, of which the Royal St. George and the Royal Irish are the oldest. The town also boasts Ireland's National Maritime Museum, housed in the Mariners' Church.

Built during the Napoleonic Wars in the early 19th century, the Martello Tower, which was home briefly in 1904 for James Joyce and Oliver St. John Gogarty, is now a museum displaying Joyce's personal letters, manuscripts, books, photographs, walking stick, waistcoat and other personal possessions. Lectures and poetry readings are held here, and there are marvelous sea views from the parapet. The Martello Tower and the nearby "Forty-foot" gentlemen's bathing place are vividly described in James Joyce's novel *Ulysses*.

An old stone jetty on the tranquil lakes of Glendalough

➕ C3

Tourist information ✉ Ferry Building, Dun Laoghaire
☎ 01 280 6600 🕐 Mon.–Sat. 10–6

James Joyce Tower and Museum ✉ Sandycove
☎ 01 280 9265 🕐 Mon.–Sat. 10–1 and 2–5, Sun. 2–6, Apr.–Oct. 🚆 DART Sandycove Station 💲 $$$

Glendalough

Glendalough, the glen of two loughs, is the loveliest and most historic of all its County Wicklow rivals. Two beautiful loughs lie deep in a valley of granite escarpments and rocky outcrops. On its green slopes are the gentle contours of native trees, on its ridges the jagged outline of pines. Add to this picturesque scene a soaring round tower and ruined stone churches in the valley, and you have a combination that makes Glendalough one of the most beautiful and historic places in Ireland. St. Kevin found solitude and spiritual peace in this place of exquisite natural beauty, and he lived a hermit's existence here for many years. Farther up the valley is St. Kevin's Bed, a precarious rocky ledge high on a cliff-face (only safely accessible by boat) where the saint used to sleep. When he died at an advanced age in 617, he left as his legacy a great school that had grown up around his teachings and had gained much respect throughout the Western world as an important institution of higher learning.

Throughout this mystical glen, ruins trace the history of his time here and the turbulent centuries since. The main group of ruins are just east of the Lower Lake. Among the most interesting are the Church of the Rock (*Tempall na Skellig*) and St. Kevin's Bed (a tiny hollowed-out hole) to the east of the oratory and about 30 feet above the lake. There are several stone churches, numerous crosses and a round tower. All in all, this is a place to linger, with an excellent choice of routes for keen walkers.

➕ C2

Glendalough Visitor Centre ✉ 7 miles east of Wicklow town ☎ 0404 45325; fax 404 45626 🕐 Daily 9:30–5:15, mid-Mar. to mid-Oct.; 9:30–4:15, rest of year (last admission 45 min. before closing) 🚌 St. Kevin's bus service from Dublin twice daily (check with tourist office for times of departure ☎ 01 281 8119; www.glendaloughbus.com) 💲 $

Howth

The pretty village of Howth sits at the northern end of Dublin Bay's curve, and Howth Castle crowns a steep hill with splendid views of the bay and village. While the castle is not open to the public, visitors are welcome to walk the pathways of its renowned 30-acre garden which is open all year. In May and June more than 2,000 varieties of rhododendron burst into bloom. The Transport Museum on the castle grounds holds a small collection of horse-drawn trams and buses, as well as other public and military forms of transportation. A growing suburb of Dublin, this fishing village still has a busy harbor.

✚ C3

Howth Castle Gardens and Transport Museum ☎ 01 848 0831 ⊕ Castle gardens: daily dawn–dusk;

museum: daily 10–5, Jun.–Aug.; Sat.–Sun. 2–5, rest of year ▯ 31, DART Howth Station ▯ Museum: $

Kilkenny

Kilkenny's narrow, winding streets and well-preserved structures make it a perfect example of a medieval town in Ireland today. Its Irish name is Cill Chainnigh (St. Canice's Church). A little monastery was established here by the saint in the sixth century on the grounds of the present St. Canice's Cathedral, whose round tower dates back to the original settlement. But it was the Normans and later the Anglo-Normans who built up the town as a trading center, which was protected by royalty until the mid-14th century.

It was in 1366 that the infamous Statutes of Kilkenny forbade any mingling of Anglo-Normans with the native Irish. By the time

The rocky promontory of Howth Head

The 150-foot Long Gallery in Kilkenny Castle – decorated with carved oak beams

Englishman Oliver Cromwell arrived in 1650, the city's population was demoralized, making it easy for him to seize the town, slaughter many residents and banish others to Connaght and confiscate their property.

Both Kilkenny Castle and the lovely St. Canice's Cathedral, built in the 13th century, were badly treated by Cromwell. Now beautifully restored, the cathedral is a repository for many fine medieval monuments, including 13th-century carvings and colorful stained-glass windows. In good weather you can climb its ninth-century tower for views over the town.

The impressive Kilkenny Castle (the seat of the Butler family) was also restored and continued to be used as a residence until 1935. In 1967 the Marquess of Ormonde gave it to the people of Kilkenny, who turned it over to the state two years later. Rich in artworks – there are miles of oil portraits – and elegant furnishings, it is open for tours conducted by guides well-versed in stories of the people who lived here. Ask about "Black Tom," then get set to hear some rather outrageous tales.

Taking a leisurely stroll around the streets of Kilkenny is a delight. Opposite the castle is Kilkenny Design Centre. Established in the 1960s, it is the spearhead of a crafts revival, showcasing carefully chosen pieces from more than 200 studios and workshops countrywide. Also be sure to visit the Rothe House on Parliament Street, a typical middle-class Tudor home, and the Tholsel, Kilkenny's city hall, which was erected in 1761 as a tollhouse and market.

Some 7 miles from Kilkenny is Dunmore Cave, chronicled as the site of a Viking massacre in 928. Once feared as a gate of hell, it is now well lit and fun to explore.
✚ B2

Tourist information ✉ Shee Alms House, Rose Inn, St. Mary's Lane ☎ 056 77 51500 🕐 Mon.–Sat. 9–6, Apr.–Nov. (occasional Sun. opening in summer); Mon.–Fri. 9–1 and 2–5, rest of year

St. Canice's Cathedral ✉ Irishtown ☎ 056 77 64971 🕐 Mon.–Sat.10–1, 2–5, Sun. 2–5, Easter–Oct. (until 4, rest of year) 🖐 $$ – joint ticket with Rothe House

Kilkenny Castle ✉ The Parade ☎ 056 77 21450 🕐 Daily 9:30–7, Jun.–Aug.; 10:30–5, Apr.–May; 10:30–12:45 and 2–5, rest of year 🖐 $$

Dunmore Cave ✉ Ballyfoyle, 7 miles from Kilkenny ☎ 056 77 67726 🕐 Daily 9:30–6:30, mid-Jun. to mid-Sep.; 10–5, mid-Mar. to mid-Jun. and mid-Sep to Oct.; Sat.–Sun. and holidays 10–4:30, rest of year
🖐 $

Kilkenny Design Centre ✉ Castle Yard ☎ 056 77 22118; www.kilkennydesign.com 🕐 Mon.–Sat. 9–6, Sun. 10–6, Apr.–Dec.; Mon.–Sat. 9–6, rest of year

Drive: Witches and Castles

Duration: 1–2 days

Norman castles, ecclesiastical ruins and tales of medieval witches haunt Kilkenny, the starting point for this 201-mile drive. Kildare's horse country appeals to followers of the sport of kings, and beautiful gardens near Portlaoise have universal appeal. Celtic kings and St. Patrick draw you onto Cashel.

From the tourist office in Kilkenny, take the R700 southeast for 11 miles to Thomastown.

This prosperous little market town on the banks of the River Nore is named after Thomas FitzAnthony Walsh, seneschal of Leinster, who built a castle and walled the town in the early 13th century. Among its interesting and ancient ruins are the remains of the 13th-century church where there are fragments of a high cross and some badly weathered effigies. Three miles away, the Kilfane church ruins have an impressive medieval stone effigy of a crusader in full armor. Grennan Castle, 1.5 miles to the southwest, is now in ruins. The most impressive remains of ancient buildings in the town are those of a large church dating to the 13th century.

Jerpoint Cistercian Abbey, 2 miles southwest of Thomastown on the N9, is one of Ireland's finest monastic ruins. Founded in the 12th century, it was dissolved and its lands given to the Ormonde family in 1540. The extensive remains are awe-inspiring, with the original Romanesque pillars, a fine chancel and the most decorative cloister arcade of any Irish church. The detailed secular and religious carved figures are an accurate portrayal of the armor and clothing of 15th- and 16th-century Ireland. A visitor center provides information on the abbey's long history. Jerpoint Abbey dates back to

Brimming with character and winding roads, the old town of New Ross sits along the River Barrow

1158, and the riverside ruins of the Benedictine and later Cistercian monastery contain many monuments and sculptures of saints and knights from medieval times. Here you'll find a 15th-century tower and cloister, and a small visitor center with picnic grounds.

Mount Juliet, signposted from the town center, was once one of Ireland's largest private estates, covering 1,411 acres of woodlands, pastures and landscaped lawns. Now a luxury hotel, the grounds provide an exceptionally beautiful drive off the main roads, and its public rooms are open to everyone.

Take the R700 southeast for 14 miles to Mountgarret Bridge, where it joins the N30 for the short drive to New Ross. There is much evidence of medieval origins in the narrow streets of New Ross, which was built on a steep hill overlooking the River Barrow. The town invites exploration on foot, as many of the streets are stepped and inaccessible to vehicles. The long bridge in the town center connects New Ross to County Kilkenny. The original bridge was built around 1200 and the town was soon walled. In 1643, it held off a siege by the Duke of Ormonde, but fell to Englishman

Oliver Cromwell just six years later. It was captured and then lost by insurgents in 1798, leaving the town in flames and many of its inhabitants slain.

The Tholsel (Town Hall) had to be rebuilt in 1806 when the original 18th-century structure fell victim to subsidence. It has a fine clock tower and holds the maces of kings Edward III and Charles II and ancient volumes of the minutes of the old town corporation. The 1798 memorial at the Tholsel depicts a "croppy boy," typical of the insurgents who assaulted the town.

Head north on the N30, turn left on the R700, then right after a short distance on the R705 for 23 miles to join the N9 at Leighlinbridge for the 7-mile drive into Carlow.

The village of Graiguenamanagh (the Granary of the Monks), between New Ross and Carlow, was once a place of great ecclesiastical importance. Occupying the site was the Abbey of Duiske, built between 1207 and 1240. It was suppressed in 1536, but determined monks stayed on for many years afterward before abandoning the extensive settlement. By 1774 it stood in ruins and the tower collapsed. A large part of the church was roofed in 1813 and Catholic services were resumed. In the 1970s, a group of dedicated locals undertook a major restoration, and today the completely restored abbey serves as the parish church.

The county town of Ireland's second smallest county, Carlow was an Anglo-Norman stronghold, strategically placed on the border of the English "Pale," a protected area around Dublin and its environs. The 640 insurgents who fell here during their 1798 attack on the town are remembered by a fine Celtic cross.

The west wall and the two flanking towers of 13th-century Carlow Castle can be seen near the bridge across the Barrow. This Norman castle was destroyed not by Cromwell, who captured it in 1650, but by one Dr. Middleton in 1814. In his zeal to convert it into an asylum, he tried to reduce the thickness of the walls with explosives, rendering it no more than a dangerous shell, most of which had to be demolished. The ruins of the castle, a stronghold of the earls of Thomond, are near the Barrow Bridge.

The Cathedral of the Assumption on Tullow Street is a fine Gothic-style building erected between 1828 and 1833. Of special interest are its 151-foot lantern tower and the marble monument of the 19th-century political writer Bishop Doyle by the renowned sculptor John Hogan.

Two miles east of Carlow on the L7, Browne's Hill Dolmen is thought to be Europe's largest, with a 100-ton capstone. Its exact purpose is a matter of speculation, but many believe the megalithic structure marks the burial place of an ancient local king.

Follow the R417 north to Athy. Turn northeast on the N78 for Kilcullen, then northwest on the R413 going under the M7 expressway, west to Kildare.
En route to Kildare, stop in Athy to view the strikingly modern Dominican church. Inside are George Campbell's outstanding Stations of the Cross. To the southeast of Athy, Castledermot's ecclesiastical ruins are a round tower, two high crosses and the remains of a Franciscan friary church.

In the heart of Ireland's horse-breeding and training country, the market town of Kildare sits on the edge of the vast Curragh plain,

and the National Stud, Ireland's most famous breeding ground, is nearby. Stroll around here and you'll understand why Irish horses are so prized around the world. You can visit the stalls and watch horses being groomed and exercised. The history of the horse from prehistoric times to the present day is represented in the Horse Museum. The Japanese garden, whose design symbolizes the lifespan of man, took four years to lay out (1906–10) and today is considered Europe's finest Oriental garden (see page 106).

East of town, horse racing has reigned supreme for centuries at the Curragh, where all the Irish Classics are run. The Curragh Camp, handed over to the Irish army in 1922, has been an important military station for a century. Here you can see the famous 1920 armored car "Slievenamon" in which Michael Collins was traveling when the fatal ambush of 1922 took place.

The Hill of Allen, legendary home of Irish folk hero Finn MacCool (see page 199) and the site of three royal residences in ancient Leinster, is northeast of town and is crowned by a 19th-century battlemented stone tower.

Take the N7 southeast through Monasterevin to reach Portlaoise.
Set at the intersection of the Dublin to Limerick and Dublin to Cork main roads, Portlaoise is also the site of Ireland's national prison. Four miles east of town, the Rock of Dunamase rises 200 feet above the plain, with the ruined 12th-century castle of Dermot MacMurrough, one-time king of Leinster.

Emo Court, 8 miles northeast of Portlaoise off the N7, is probably the premier attraction of County Laois. "Magnificent" is the only word for this neoclassical mansion designed in 1790 by the celebrated architect James Gandon, designer of the Custom House and several other Dublin landmark buildings. The grand house is open to the public by guided tour only. The formal gardens and extensive parkland are famous for their statuary, an avenue of giant sequoia trees and sweeping lawns dotted with neatly clipped yew trees, all providing a perfect foil for this fascinating mansion. If you enjoy walking, the superb lake and woodland areas are a real treat.

To the west of town, the many roads crossing the Slieve Bloom Mountains offer scenic drives.

Take the N8 for 9 miles south to Abbeyleix.

This attractive town has tree-lined streets, neat town houses and a fountain in the square. It is noted for the de Vesci Demesne, known as Abbeyleix House. The great house, which dates to 1773, is not open to the public, but the splendid grounds are. They include formal terrace gardens to the west of the house, a "wild garden" called the Paradise Garden, which is carpeted with bluebells in spring, and an American garden with magnolia trees. There is also a magnificent avenue of lime trees. The Heritage House in Abbeyleix is a fine example of Gothic architecture built in 1884 and designed to be a focus for visitors to this historic town. Interactive multimedia displays tell the story of Abbeyleix and the surrounding area.

Take the N8 southwest to the N75 turnoff to Thurles.

In ancient times, the O'Fogartys fortified this site on the River Suir, and although the Norman Strongbow's army was soundly defeated here in 1174, Anglo-Normans returned later to build a castle that would protect the crossing. Today it is a busy, well-laid-out marketing center for the surrounding agricultural area. It is also the cathedral town of the archdiocese of Cashel and Emly.

Take the R660 south for 13 miles to reach Cashel.

Cashel is a prosperous town best known for the Rock of Cashel (see page 129). Look above the first floor of the store opposite city hall to see the battlements and gargoyles of what was 15th-century Quirke's Castle, named after a family who lived there in the 19th century. At the southwest end of Main Street, the ornamental fountain is in memory of Dean Kinane and his efforts in bringing a much-needed extension of the railway to Cashel in 1904.

Take the R692 southeast to Fethard.

Fethard was an important Anglo-Norman settlement in medieval times. Remnants of the old town walls and their towers can still be seen. In the town center, there are keeps of

Fine monastic ruins at Jerpoint Abbey

three 15th-century castles, including that of Fethard Castle. Well-preserved remains of a priory contain several 16th- and 17th-century tombs. More than 1,000 exhibits depicting rural life in this part of Ireland are on display at the Folk, Farm and Transport Museum.

Take the R692 northeast to Mullinahone. Turn right for Callan, then turn north on the N76 for the 11-mile drive back to Kilkenny.

Jerpoint Abbey ✉ Thomastown, Co. Kilkenny
☎ 056 77 24623 ⏲ Daily 9:30–6, Jun. 1 to mid-Sep.; 10–5, Mar.–May and mid-Sep.–Oct.; 10–4 in Nov. 🖐 $$

The National Stud ✉ Tully, Kildare, Co. Kildare (off Dublin to Limerick road, N7) ☎ 045 522 963; www.irish-national-stud.ie ⏲ Daily 9:30–5, mid-Feb to mid-Nov. 🍴 Restaurant 🖐 $$$

Emo Court ✉ Emo, Co. Laois (6 miles northeast of Portlaois) ☎ 05786 26573 ⏲ Tue.–Sun. 12–6:30, mid-Jun. to mid-Sep.; gardens: daily dawn–dusk 🖐 $

The Heritage House ✉ Abbeyleix, Co. Laois
☎ 05787 31653; fax 05787 30059; www.heritagehousemuseum.com ⏲ Mon.–Fri. 9–5, Sat.–Sun. 1–5, May–Sep.; Mon.–Fri. 9–5, rest of year 🖐 $

Fethard Folk, Farm and Transport Museum ✉ Cashel Road, Fethard ☎ 052 31516 ⏲ Sun.11–4:30 🖐 $

Malahide

The speed at which Malahide is growing as a favored residential suburb of Dublin has not robbed it of its old-fashioned seaside atmosphere, and its popularity is enhanced by its many quality restaurants. There is a good beach to the east of the town, and an even better one farther along the coast at Portmarnock. There are two historic buildings on the way to Portmarnock – a martello tower, built in the early 1800s as a provision against Napoleonic invasion, and Robswall's Castle, a tower house to which a Victorian house has been added.

Malahide's most famous relic of history is its castle, one of the major showpieces of the Dublin area. Its core is medieval and, in spite of considerable changes from the intervening centuries, it still appears from the outside as a product of the Middle Ages. Malahide Castle is the stately residence that was occupied until 1973 by the descendants of Lord Talbot de Malahide, its founder in 1185. One of the many historic happenings within its walls occurred in 1690 when some 14 Talbot cousins sat down to breakfast together one morning before leaving to fight for King James II in the Battle of the Boyne, a battle in which all met their death.

Set in a 268-acre demesne whose formal gardens alone are worth a visit, the castle still retains traces of the original moat. Inside there is magnificent oak paneling and plasterwork, fine Irish period furniture and many paintings, including a rich collection of portraits of historical Irish figures on loan from the National Gallery in Dublin (see page 81). These are strikingly displayed in the great 17th-century dining hall. A separate building holds the Fry Model Railway Museum, the first of its kind in Ireland. On display are more than 300

Malahide Castle to the north of Dublin city houses much of Dublin's National Portrait Collection

handmade model trains, trams and railroad artifacts left by the late Cyril Fry, an enthusiastic railway engineer.

Farther north of Malahide is Newbridge House, another magnificent desmesne of 350 acres. Dating from 1737, this mansion has one of the finest Georgian interiors in the country. Its great red drawing room is just as it was when the Cobbe family was in residence here, giving you a perfect picture of how wealthy families entertained. To see how the house staff and the estate-workers kept the wheels turning, visit the kitchen and laundry, as well as the coach house, dairy, carpenter's shop and blacksmith's forge, all equipped with 19th-century implements. Within the grounds there's a 29-acre traditional farm, complete with farm animals that is always a hit with little ones.

✚ C3

Tourist information ✉ Dublin Tourism, Suffolk Street ☎ 01 605 7700 🕑 Mon.–Sat. 9–7, Sun. 10:30–3, Jun.–Sep.; Mon.–Sat. 9–5:30, Sun. 10:30–3, rest of year

The huge frontage of Russborough House displays heraldic lions

Malahide Castle and Fry Model Railway Museum
✉ Malahide ☎ Castle: 01 846 2184, www.malahidecastle.com; museum: 01 846 3779 🕑 Castle: Mon.–Sat. 10–5, Sun. 10–6, Apr.–Sep.; Mon.–Sat. 10–5, Sun. 11–5, rest of year. Museum: Mon.–Sat. 10–5, Sun 2–6, Apr.–Sep. 🍴 Restaurant 🚌 42 (from Beresford Place), DART Connolly Station to Malahide 💷 $$$ combined ticket

Newbridge House and Traditional Farm ✉ Donabate (12 miles north of Dublin on Belfast Road) ☎ 01 843 6534 🕑 Tue.–Sat. 10–1 and 2–5, Sun. 2–6, Apr.–Sep.; Sat.–Sun. 2–5, rest of year 🍴 Coffee shop 💷 House $$$, farm $

Russborough House

This, one of the most imposing of Ireland's Great Houses, was designed by architect Richard Castle for Joseph Leeson, later the Earl of Milltown. It was built from granite and in the Palladian style between 1741 and 1751. Its striking interior features fine stucco ceilings and sumptuous displays of silver, bronze and porcelain. The rhododendron garden is open in spring by arrangement only.

✚ C3

✉ Blessington, Co. Wicklow (about 2 miles south of Blessington) ☎ 045 865 239; fax 045 865 054 🕑 Daily 10–5:30, May–Sep.; Sun. 10–5:30 in Apr. and Oct; last admission 5 p.m. 🍴 Tearoom 💷 $$

A Long Tradition of Spectacular Gardens

Leinster is one of Ireland's most fertile regions. County Wicklow, in fact, bills itself as "The Garden of Ireland." Their annual Garden Festival from between May and August proves the point beautifully and colorfully (information from Wicklow Tourist Information, see opposite).

The gardens listed here are only a few of those you will want to visit. For *Gardens and Garden Centres*, an illustrated guide to Leinster gardens outside the Dublin area, contact Gail.Conaughton@failteireland.ie).

Fernhill Gardens

Overlooking Dublin Bay, Fernhill includes some 40 acres of parkland, woodland, rockery and water garden. Many of the trees date back over 200 years and were planted by Willliam Darley. A varying terrain provides a habitat for an unusually wide range of native plants and animals. The gardens are planted with rhododendrons, azaleas, camellias, magnolias and other acid-loving plants, as well as trees and shrubs from all corners of the earth. There is a rare example of an enclosed Victorian vegetable and flower garden. The Kitchen Garden is enclosed within clipped beech hedges divided into four quadrants with a now rarely seen potager-style layout. A long track, known as the Broadwalk, brings the visitor from the wide open areas around the house into a lovely light woodland full of beeches, oak and larches.

Japanese Gardens and St. Fiachra's Garden

On the grounds of the Irish National Stud (see page 102), the breathtakingly beautiful Japanese Gardens' underlying theme of the "Life of Man" depicts human progression from the cradle to the grave and beyond. Japanese lanterns, small brooks crossed by Japanese-style bridges and other Oriental touches make this garden (four years in the planning, 1906–10) unique in Ireland. It has won international accolades.

To celebrate the millennium, St. Fiachra's Garden was planted in 1999 around a natural setting of wetland, woodland, rocks, lakes and islands. The visitor center, with coffee shop, wine bar and craft shop is in the Japanese style, and there are picnic grounds.

Mount Usher Gardens

Mount Usher Gardens rank among the leading – and loveliest – horticultural centers in Ireland. Its 20 acres of flowers, trees, shrubs and lawns lie in the sheltered Vartry river valley and its plants come from many parts of the globe. Spindle trees from China, North American sweet gum and swamp cypress, the New Zealand ti tree, African broom and Burmese juniper are among those represented in a magnificent setting of superb landscaping. There's a spacious tea room at the entrance, as well as a shopping courtyard.

National Botanic Gardens

Since 1795 the National Botanic Gardens have fostered the native Irish affinity for all growing things. Their 50 acres (once home to poet Thomas Tickell) hold a variety of garden groupings, from decorative plantings to vegetable, herbal, scientific and medicinal plants and economic plants and exotic species from around the globe. There are fascinating tropical greenhouses and a small orchid room. Dedicated gardeners will delight in the wealth of botanical information, and even those who have never had dirt under their fingernails will find this a place of beauty and tranquility.

Powerscourt Gardens

Powerscourt Gardens were designed and laid out between 1745 and 1767. Perched on high ground with a view of Great Sugarloaf Mountain, magnificent Japanese and Italian gardens slope downward and are dotted with statuary and ornamental lakes. The 1,000-acre demesne, which straddles the River Dargle, holds rare shrubs, massive rhododendrons and a deer park. Powerscourt

The Italian and Japanese gardens at Powerscourt are renowned for their beauty

House, an impressive 18th-century mansion built on the site of an earlier castle, was gutted by fire in 1974, and a restored section now holds an audiovisual history presentation, shops and a restaurant.

St. Anne's Park Rose Garden

St. Anne's Park Rose Garden is one of the prettiest in Dublin, with climbers, floribunda, hybrid tea and old garden roses aplenty. In April and May, daffodils are in bloom. Much loved by Dubliners, this oasis of beauty is a horticultural bonus to city visitors.

Tullynally Castle Gardens

The 30-acre pleasure grounds and walled gardens on the estate of the massive Gothic revival Tullynally Castle date from the early 1800s. In addition to the two ornamental lakes and a grotto, there's a Chinese garden with pagoda and a Tibetan garden of streams and waterfalls. A note of fantasy is struck by fanciful sculptures by a local artist using roots and trees. An avenue of 200-year-old Irish yew trees lead to the walled gardens. Guided tours of the castle are available.

Fernhill Gardens ✉ Sandyford, Co. Dublin ☎ 01 295 4257; fax 01 2954257 🕐 Tue.–Sat. 11–5, Sun. 2–6, Mar.–Oct. 🚌 44 💶 $$

Japanese Gardens and St. Fiachra's Garden ✉ Tully,

Co. Kildare (Irish National Stud signposted from Kildare Town) ☎ 045 521 617; www.irish-national-stud.ie 🕐 Daily 9:30–6, mid-Feb. to mid-Nov. 💶 $$$

Mount Usher Gardens ✉ Ashford, Co. Wicklow ☎ 0404 40116; fax 0404 40205; www.mount-usher-gardens.com 🕐 Daily 10:30–6, mid-Mar. to Oct. 💶 $$$

National Botanic Gardens ✉ Glasnevin Hill Road, Glasnevin, Dublin ☎ 01 804 0300 🕐 Mon.–Sat. 9–6, Sun. 10–6, Mar.–Oct.; daily 9–4:30, rest of year 🚌 13, 19, 134 💶 Free; charge for parking

Powerscourt Gardens ✉ Enniskerry, Co. Wicklow ☎ 01 204 6000; fax 01 204 6900; www.powerscourt.ie 🕐 Daily 9:30–5.30; varies in winter months 💶 $$$

St. Anne's Park Rose Garden ✉ Mount Prospect Avenue, Clontarf, Dublin ☎ 01 833 1859 🕐 Daily 9–7, May–Sep., 10–dusk, rest of year 🚌 130 💶 Free

Tullynally Castle Gardens ✉ Castlepollard, Co. Westmeath ☎ 04496 61159; fax 04496 61856 🕐 Gardens: daily 12–6, Jul.–Aug.; Sat.–Sun. 12–6 May–Jun. 🍴 Tea room 💶 $$

For further information contact:
🛈 **East Coast and Midlands Tourism** ✉ Dublin Road, Mullingar, Co. Westmeath ☎ 044 934 8761; fax 044 40413; www.eastcoastmidlands.ie
🛈 **Wicklow Tourist Information** ✉ Rialto House, Fitzwilliam Square, Wicklow Town, Co. Wicklow ☎ 0404 69117; fax 0404 69118 🕐 Mon.–Sat. 9:30–5:30, Jul.–Aug.; Mon.–Fri. 9:30–5:15, rest of year

Wexford's church spire towers over this Viking town lying beside the River Slaney

Wexford

As the safest haven close to the southeastern point of Ireland, Wexford has always been a natural landing place for travelers from Wales, Cornwall in England, and France, and it was the first Irish settlement to fall to the invading Normans in 1169. But these were not the first invaders – the Vikings settled here in the ninth or 10th century and gave the town its name.

Wexford exudes an air of the past, its central streets still adhering to the medieval plan, and the quays, not so busy now as they once were, reflecting a long maritime heritage. Fragments of the medieval town walls survive. At the northern edge of town, near the train and bus station, the Westgate Tower is the only surviving gateway of five that once punctuated the old town walls, and it is fairly well preserved.

Nearby, Selskar Abbey stands on the site of an ancient pagan temple dedicated to Odin, and later a Viking church. King Henry II came here in 1172 to do penance for his murder of the devout Thomas à Becket.

Go by the wide intersection known as the Bull Ring at the north end of Wexford's Main Street and spend a few minutes reflecting on the bravery of the pikemen who are portrayed by the bronze statue there. Until Oliver Cromwell visited his wrath on the town in

1649, a great high cross stood here, and when Cromwell destroyed it, he slew some 300 people who knelt in prayer before it. While bull-baiting was once the main attraction here, there is now an open-air market every Friday and Saturday.

On Wexford's Crescent Quay, take a look at the Commodore John Barry (1745–1803) statue, and if you pass through Ballysampson, Tagoat (10 miles from Wexford), tip your hat to his birthplace. Homage is due to this seafaring Irishman, as he is credited with founding the U.S. Navy after being appointed by George Washington in 1797.

Take a drive down the scenic Hook peninsula through historic and quaint old villages. The ruins of the Knights Templar's foundation still stand at Templetown; Hook lighthouse, built more than seven centuries ago, is the oldest in Europe. Near Fethard-on-Sea, the Normans first landed in Ireland. At Ballyhack, catch the car-ferry over to Passage East on the County Waterford side for 10 minutes on the water to see these shores as they were seen by Viking and Norman invaders.

Just 3 miles west of Wexford, overlooking the River Slaney, the Irish National Heritage Park is a marvelous 35-acre park holding reconstructions of historic buildings from Ireland's past. These include a campsite, farmstead and portal dolmen from the Stone Age (7000–2000 BC) and a cist burial and stone circle from the Bronze Age (2000–500 BC). You can also view an ogham stone, ringfort and souterrain (an early Christian monastery), corn-drying kiln, horizontal water mill, Viking boathouse and an artificial island habitat known as a crannog, all from the Celtic and early Christian ages (500 BC to AD 1169). Also here are a Norman motte and bailey fortification and a round tower from the early Norman period (1169–1280). There's also a nature walk of real beauty, and an excellent craft and book shop.

In 1858, when Patrick Kennedy left Dunganstown (near New Ross, see drive page 101) for America, it was to escape the ravages of a famine. He left behind a thatched home set among stone farm buildings. A little more than a century later, his great-grandson, John Fitzgerald Kennedy, held the office of president of the United States and returned to visit his ancestral home.

The John F. Kennedy Park and Arboretum is the tribute paid to the president by the Irish government and United States citizens of Irish origin. It was officially opened by President Eamon de Valera in 1968 and covers 623 acres, of which more than 300 are set aside as the arboretum. Already there are 4,500 species of shrubs, and the number is expected to reach 6,000 in a few years.

In the Forest Garden, there are trees from all five continents, and lovely shaded walks throughout the park, with shelters and convenient resting spots. Follow the signposts to the top of Slieve Coillte and you'll be rewarded with a panorama of south Wexford and the splendid estuary of the Barrow, Nore and Suir rivers. Be sure to stop by the visitor center where you can see the unusal explanatory display fashioned in beaten copper.

Bird watchers should visit the reserve adjacent to Wexford Harbour, where more than 240 species of birds and more than a third of the world's Greenland white-fronted geese winter. There is an informative visitor center and observation tower.

⊞ C1

Tourist information ✉ Crescent Quay ☎ 05391 23111 🕐 Mon.–Sat. 9–6, Apr.–Nov.; Mon.–Fri. 9–5, rest of year

Irish National Heritage Park ✉ Ferrycarrig (3 miles outside town) ☎ 05391 20733; fax 05391 20911; www.inhp.com 🕐 Daily 9:30–6:30 🍴 Restaurant 🎫 $$$

John F. Kennedy Park and Arboretum ✉ New Ross, Co. Wexford ☎ 051 388 171; fax 051 388 172 🕐 Daily 10–8, May–Aug.; 10–6:30, Apr. and Sep.; 10–5 , rest of year 🎫 $

Wexford Wildfowl Reserve ✉ North Slob (3 miles east of Wexford town) ☎ 05391 23129 🕐 Daily 9–6, Easter–Oct.; 10–5, rest of year 🎫 Free

Munster

Dubbed "a most populous and plentiful country" by the poet Edmund Spenser in 1596, Munster's six counties are just as inviting and beguiling today.

Introduction and Map   **112**

Cork   **114**

Introduction and Map   **114**

Essential Information   **116**

Cork Sights   **117**

Walk: Cork's Mercantile Past   **120**

Feature: Cork's Cultural Scene   **122**

Drive: Island City, Magic Stone   **123**

Regional Sights   **126**

Drive: Ring of Kerry   **138**

Feature: Medieval Castle Banquets
        and Traditional *Céilí*   **144**

Feature: Kerry's Festivals   **147**

Mountain views between Kenmare and Glengarriff

Munster

Munster's six counties – Clare, Cork, Kerry, Limerick, Tipperary and Waterford – straddle the southern part of Ireland, which is a sort of mini Ireland. Outstanding examples of scenic, archeological, historical and cultural charms that make this country so special are liberally scattered across the face of Munster, a virtual grab-bag of sightseeing riches. Here you'll find the world-famous lakes of Killarney, Blarney's magical stone and Waterford's exquisite crystal. You'll also find the country's sunniest and driest climate in east Munster, the wettest in the west.

The dramatic coastline changes from wide, sandy beaches to steep, surf-fringed cliffs that soar above secluded coves and small fishing village harbors to deep-water commercial ports and craggy peninsulas. Mizen Head is Ireland's southernmost mainland point, crowned by a lighthouse whose summit perch overlooks striking cliffscapes. The bustling port cities of Cork, Limerick and Waterford encircle the coast, with reminders of their legends and history happily rubbing elbows with the sounds and sights of an astonishingly progressive present.

Inland mountain chains march across Munster, vibrant in spring with deep hues of rhododendrons, softened in the fall by more subtle shades of heather. To the east, the Comeragh and Knockmealdown ranges give way to the midland Galtees, Slieve Felims and Silvermines. Some of the earliest traces of the Stone Age inhabitants are found in Blackwater Valley. Ireland's highest peak, 3,400-foot-high Carrantouhill, is the star of Kerry's Macgillycuddy's Reeks, while the gentler slopes of the

Garinish Point harbor against the backdrop of Beara Peninsula

Slieve Mish range form the backbone of the Dingle Peninsula (Corca Dhuibhne), "the last parish before America." Ireland's famed "forty shades of green" create a glorious patchwork quilt of fertile stone-walled fields and Tipperary's Golden Vale plain. Sprinkled in this rural scene are small market towns. Amid all these scenic splendors, ancient ringforts, dolmens, cairns and other archeological relics bring to life a prehistoric landscape. Monasteries, massive castles and round towers trace Christian, Viking and Norman invasions over long centuries.

If cultural and artistic activities are high on your priority list, traditional Irish music is featured in many pubs. You may find your most memorable evenings happen when that same music spontaneously breaks out in the most unlikely rural settings. Munster's cities arrange year-round programs of opera, first-rate jazz and musical and theatrical productions. Its art galleries rank with the best in Europe. The Irish have an inborn flair for drama, and several local drama groups present surprisingly professional productions. Count yourself lucky if you run across a night of theater featuring an amateur troupe – when the last curtain falls, the cast often adjourns to the nearest pub along with members of the audience. It's great fun.

It's also great fun to show up for at least one day's racing at the three-day "meets" held at racetracks in Clonmel, Tramore, Mallow, Killarney and Limerick, where the atmosphere is not unlike that of old-time county fairs in the United States. For more energetic outdoor enthusiasts, excellent facilities for almost every sport, from golf to river (coarse fishing) and deep-sea fishing are never far away.

County Kerry's Dingle Peninsula and Ring of Kerry in County Waterford are important *Gaeltacht* (pronounced "Gwale-tuct") areas, where Irish is the thriving, everyday language.

In short, Munster is a shining example of modern Ireland building on and flourishing on the enduring foundation of its past.

Cork

Cork's charter dates to 1185, by which time the city already had a rich and colorful past. St. Finbar arrived in 650 to found a monastery on the small swampy island cradled by hills to the north and south and called it Corcaigh (Marshy Place). Since then, Cork has seen Vikings come storming in as plunderers in the ninth century, only to settle in as permanent residents, followed by Normans in the 12th century, who stayed on to build fortifications, great churches and abbeys. It was Englishman Oliver Cromwell who broke the pattern when he captured the city in 1649 and proceeded to impose a harsh repressive regime. Inevitably, resistance to such measures spawned a fierce sense of independence that even today underlies the Cork spirit.

Cork's status as a European Capital of Culture in 2005 resulted in a major facelift. These days, the cosmopolitan city is an important industrial and financial center, with a deep-water commercial harbor that comes right into the heart of the city. A busy ferryport

St. Patrick's Bridge elegantly spans the River Lee in the center of Cork

10 miles to the southeast at Ringaskiddy provides a convenient passenger service to France and Britain.

The People

The citizens of Cork are a lively, cultural bunch, among Ireland's most able traders and merchants, and much attuned to the arts. "Sure, it's only an accident of geography that Dublin is the capital of Ireland" is a sentiment readily expressed by Cork natives. That enormous civic pride is firmly rooted in the city's history and an implacable abhorrence of injustice.

The natives of Cork love nothing more than to show off their city, and they are quick to welcome strangers in their unique, lilting accent (delivered at breakneck speed), which may take a little getting used to. They have also retained in their everyday speech many words and phrases that have been long disused elsewhere. So if you overhear a woman described as mauzy, you'll know that, heavy of hips, she's really "a fine lump of a woman." Friendly they most certainly are, and perhaps because of their mercantile bent, that friendliness often expresses itself in practical terms.

Cork Cuisine

A leading Irish food critic based in Dublin recently wrote, "There are considerably more good restaurants per head of population in Cork than we can even dream of in the capital." In truth, you can name almost any ethnic cuisine, and you'll find it offered in at least one of those eateries. Menus run the gamut, from traditional boiled bacon and cabbage to gourmet Continental dishes. Unique to this city is *drisheen*, not unlike the black pudding you'll encounter throughout the country.

Cork is also home to the Beamish and Crawford brewery, now producing many varieties of beer as well as stout and tasty bitter. Cork Distillers Company (now Irish Distillers Ltd.) gave the world Cork Dry Gin, and at Midleton, east of the city, Jameson's whiskey is made and visitors are welcomed to the Jameson Experience visitor center.

Finding Your Way Around

Cork's compact city center sits on an island ringed by the two-prong Lee river, crossed by no less than 16 bridges – a bit confusing when you suddenly encounter another channel of the river you thought you had just left behind.

Vessels actually sailed up Patrick Street as late as 1760 (it was paved over in 1791), and in 1780 there was a canal down the center of the Grand Parade. The river cuts across the city from east to west and is bounded by hills on the north and south.

The major points of reference in the city center are St. Patrick's Street (just call it Patrick Street) and the Grand Parade. Other main arteries are Washington Street (which becomes Western Road as it runs past University College and heads out toward Killarney); South Mall, from which you turn onto Mary Street to reach Douglas Road en route to the airport; and MacCurtain Street, a busy one-way thoroughfare just across St. Patrick's Bridge that leads to both the main Cobh, Youghal and Waterford road and the Cork to Dublin highway. St. Patrick's Hill, at the foot of Patrick Street, is breathtakingly steep, its stepped sidewalk leading to a sweeping view of the city and harbor from the Montenotte section.

Essential Information

Tourist Information

● Cork Kerry Regional Tourism Authority
✉ Aras Fáilte (Tourist House), Grand Parade
☎ 021 425 5100; fax 021 425 5199;
www.info@corkkerrytourism.ie ⏲ Mon.–Fri. 9–6, Sat.–Sun. 9:30–4:30; Mon.–Fri. 9–5, Sat. 9:30–4:30, rest of year
● There is also a freephone information service in the arrivals terminal of Cork Airport.

Urban Transportation

Double-decker buses cover the city, with more than 14 routes running north to south. Hours are 7 a.m. to 11 p.m. Monday through Saturday, less frequently on Sunday. Most buses can be boarded on Patrick Street. A short walk from Patrick Street, the Parnell Place Bus Station (☎ 021 450 8188) offers frequent service to the airport and such nearby points as Blarney, Cobh, Kinsale and Crosshaven as well as major destinations around the country. They also conduct scenic tours from Cork to Blarney, Macroom and Killarney.

From late May until late September, an open-air double-decker bus will get you to such Cork highlights as the Cork City Gaol, City Library, St. Finbarr's Cathedral, Crawford Municipal Art Gallery, Triskel Arts Centre, English Market, Cork Opera House, Custom House and the Courthouse. Stay on the bus for the entire 70 minutes of the tour or opt to get off at an attraction and rejoin the tour on the next bus. You can buy a ticket, which is good for the day, at the tourist office or from the driver on the tour bus at one of its stops. Bus Eireann ☎ 021 450 8188.

Cork is well served by taxis, with major stands along St. Patrick's Street, the South Mall and many hotels. For taxi pickup elsewhere, call Cork Taxi Co-op ☎ 021 427 2222.

Cork Railway Station, Lower Glanmire Road (☎ 021 450 6766), about a five-minute walk from the city center, provides service to Cobh, Dublin, Mallow, Milstreet, Killarney and Tralee.

Airport Information

Located only 4 miles from the city center, Cork Airport (☎ 021 431 3131; www.corkairport.com) is reached via the Kinsale road and provides service to national and international destinations. There is a half-hourly Aircoach bus service from the main airport entrance to Cork city bus station The journey takes 30 minutes and the fare is €3.80. A taxi journey will take less time and costs around €15.

Climate: Average highs and lows

	Jan.	Feb.	Mar.	Apr.	May	Jun.	Jul.	Aug.	Sep.	Oct.	Nov.	Dec.
	8°C	8°C	9°C	12°C	14°C	16°C	16°C	18°C	16°C	13°C	10°C	8°C
	46°F	46°F	48°F	54°F	57°F	61°F	61°F	64°F	61°F	55°F	50°F	46°F
	4°C	4°C	4°C	5°C	8°C	10°C	12°C	12°C	11°C	8°C	5°C	4°C
	39°F	39°F	39°F	41°F	46°F	50°F	54°F	54°F	52°F	46°F	41°F	39°F

Blarney Castle, home to the famous Blarney stone

Cork Sights

Key to symbols

⊞ map coordinates refer to the Cork map on page 114; sights below are highlighted in yellow on the map ✉ address or location ☎ telephone number ◷ opening times 🍴 restaurant on site or nearby 🚍 nearest bus or railroad station 💷 admission charge: $$$ more than €6, $$ €4 to €6, $ less than €4 ℹ information

Ballymalloe Cookery School and Gardens

Food expert Darina Allen has brought international fame to the very best of Irish cuisine by fostering the proper use of seasonal local produce. The outstanding herb garden holds the largest collection of culinary and medicinal plants in Ireland, as well as fruit and vegetable gardens. Just for fun, wander through the Celtic maze. The restaurant practices what the school preaches in its lunch and dinner menus, and the adjoining shop stocks quality cookware.
⊞ C2 ✉ Shanagarry, East Cork, on N25 at Castlemartyr, between Youghal and Cork ☎ 021 464 6785 or 464 6422; www.cookingisfun.ie ◷ Gardens: daily 11–6, Apr.–Sep., guided tours by appointment; shop: daily Easter–Oct. 💷 Gardens: $$

Blarney Castle

There's a lovely sense of tranquility about the grounds and ruins of this historic castle – and a sense of magic about its stone that bestows the gift of eloquence on anyone who climbs its 120 steep steps to lean backward from the battlements and bestow a kiss on it.

The legend of its powers rose from Queen Elizabeth I's frustration in dealing with Irish chieftain Cormac MacCarthy, Lord of Blarney, and his smiling flattery that veiled wiliness with eloquence. Her declaration, "This is nothing but blarney – what he says, he never means!" added a new word to the English language and may have given rise to the legend of the "gift of eloquence" associated with the stone. But it was Father Prout who, in the 1830s, may have also bestowed magic on the stone when he wrote, "There is a stone there That whoever kisses Oh! He never misses To grow eloquent." However, by the time you've gone through all the exertions, you'll have earned a silver tongue! The Rock Close in the castle gardens is said to have been much favored by ancient Druids.

Take a short stroll from the castle and you'll find Blarney Woollen Mills, one of Ireland's oldest mills, turning out fine wools and cloths since 1741. These days, the large premises hold a vast collection of different

Irish crafts to see and buy, and there's a lovely traditional-style pub.

🚌 A2 ✉ Blarney (4 miles northwest of Cork city on N617, signposted from Cork city at Patrick Street Bridge) ☎ 021 438 5252; www.blarneycastle.ie ⏰ Mon.–Sat. 9–7, Sun. 9:30–5, Jun.–Aug.; Mon.–Sat. 9–6:30, Sun. 9:30–5, May, Sep.; Mon.–Sat. 9:30–dusk, Sun. 9:30–dusk, rest of year 🍴 Blair's Inn (see page 206) 🚍 Buses and coach tours from Parnell Street Bus Station, Cork 💲 $$$

Blarney Woollen Mills (retail shop) ✉ Blarney ☎ 021 451 6111 ⏰ Mon.–Sat. 9:30–6, Sun. 10–6

City Gaol and Radio Telefís Éireann Museum

This infamous building housed many a patriotic rebel in the late 1800s and early 1900s. Their grim prison existence is re-created vividly by appropriately dressed lifesize figures, the cells in which they lived and fascinating exhibits. On a happier note, in the former governor's house, the Radio Telefís Éireann Museum collection is well worth a visit. RTE operates Ireland's state-sponsored television and radio. Located in the original studio of 1927, exhibits cover the early days of radio. Allow two hours.

🚌 A2 ✉ Sunday's Well ☎ 021 430 5022; www.corkcountygaol.com ⏰ Daily 9:30–6, Mar.–Oct.; 10–5, rest of year 🚍 No bus service – short walk from city center 💲 Gaol: $; museum: $$$ (less expensive to buy a combined ticket)

Cobh Heritage Centre – The Queenstown Story

There is a strong tug of ancestry for many Americans descended from the thousands of Irish families who departed Queenstown, now named Cobh (Haven), as they fled the famine in search of a better life across the ocean in America. Sadly, many never reached those shores because of the awful conditions they endured in overcrowded and ill-equipped "coffin ships." The Queenstown Story in Cobh's Victorian railroad station tells their tale in heart-wrenching detail through a moving multimedia exhibition and startlingly lifelike figures of emigrant families.

While in Cobh, take time to visit the Gothic-revival St. Colman's Cathedral, with its 47-bell carillon, rose window above the main doorway, mosaic flooring and richly colored windows.

🚌 C2 ✉ Cobh Heritage Centre, Cobh, 15 miles east of Cork city, via Waterford Road (N25) to signposted turnoff for R632 ☎ 021 481 3591; fax 021 481 3595; www.cobhheritage.com ⏰ Daily 9:30–6 May–Oct.; 9:30–5, Jan.–Apr., Nov.–Dec. 22 (last admission 1 hour before closing) 🍴 Restaurant 🚍 Frequent rail service from Cork city 💲 $$$

English Market (City Market)

A leftover from colonial days, this cavernous market housed in a 1786 building carries on a Cork tradition that dates from the 1600s. Wall-to-wall foodstuff stalls peddle meats, vegetables, pastries and just about anything else that shows up on Cork tables. It's terrific for eavesdropping and a unique opportunity to mingle with Cork homemakers going about their daily lives.

🚌 B2 ✉ Entrances from Grand Parade, Patrick Street, Oliver Plunkett Street, and Princes Street ☎ 021 492 4258 ⏰ Mon.–Sat. 9–5 💲 Free

Fota Wildlife Park

More than 90 species of exotic animals, including giraffes, ostriches, zebras, oryx, kangaroos and lemurs, roam the park's 40 acres of open natural surroundings. More than just a zoo, the park is also heavily involved in conservation and rehabilitation of threatened species. The adjoining Fota Arboretum features trees and shrubs from China, Japan, Australia, the Himalayas and other countries around the world.

🚌 C2 ✉ Fota Island, Carrigtwohill, 10 miles east of Cork city on the Cobh Road ☎ 021 481 2678; www.fotawildlife.ie ⏰ Mon.–Sat. 10–6, Sun. 11–6 (last admission 5). Closed Christmas Day and Dec. 26 🍴 Coffee shop 🚍 Frequent rail and bus service from Cork city 💲 $$$

Old Midleton Distillery (Jameson Heritage Centre)

This marvelous old distillery traces the history of Irish whiskey since it was perfected by Irish monks in the 16th century, when they called it *uisce beatha*, "the water of life." There's an informative guided tour, ending with a complimentary glass of Jameson whiskey.

Cork

C2 ✉ Midleton, County Cork, 12 miles east of Cork ☎ 021 461 3594; fax 021 461 3642 🕐 Daily 10–6 (tours on demand), Mar.–Oct.; 3 tours daily 11:30, 1, 2:30 and 4, Nov.–Mar. 🍴 Restaurant 🚌 From Cork and Waterford 💶 $$$

St. Fin Barre's Cathedral

In a location that eventually proved to be Cork city's birthplace, this magnificent Church of Ireland, 1870 French Gothic cathedral is the descendant of the seventh-century monastery that grew into a seat of learning of international renown. Its ornate interior is a real draw with its unique mosaics and an impressive great west window.

A1 ✉ Bishop Street, three blocks past South Main Street Bridge ☎ 021 496 3387 🕐 Mon.–Sat. 9:30–5:30, Apr.–Oct.; 10–12:45 and 2–5, rest of year 💶 Free (donations welcome)

Shandon – St. Anne's Church and the Cork Butter Museum

St. Anne's is distinguished by its red-and-white "pepper pot" steeple, which houses its famous bells and its "four-faced liar" clock that never shows the same time on its four faces. Climb the winding belfry stairs and your reward is to follow numbers on the bell strings that send *The Bells of St. Mary's* ringing out over the city. Nearby is the interesting old Butter Exchange, which houses the Cork Butter Museum. Seemingly an unusual subject for a museum, but this place is well worth a visit.

A2

St. Anne's Church ✉ Church Street ☎ 021 450 5906 🕐 Daily 9–6, Apr.–Oct.; 10–4, rest of year 🍴 Isaac's (see page 207) 🚌 3 from city center 💶 $$

Cork Butter Museum ✉ O'Connell Square ☎ 021 430 0600; www.corkbutter.museum 🕐 Daily 10–1 and 2–5, Mar.–Oct. 🚌 3 from city center 💶 $$

University College Cork

The University College Cork campus is one of the jewels in Cork's crown in terms of its Gothic revival architecture, its gardens and wooded areas, stones with ancient Irish ogham inscriptions and the Crawford Observatory. Of special interest is the Honan Chapel that features Harry Clarke stained-glass windows. The Glucksman Gallery creates one of the most significant spaces for visual art in Ireland. Gallery shop and riverside restaurant.

A1 off map ✉ Western Road ☎ 021 490 3000; www.ucc.ie. Gallery: 021 490 1844; www.glucksman. org 🕐 Mon–Sat 9–5 (tours by appointment). Gallery: Tue.–Wed. Fri.–Sat. 10–5, Thu. 10–8, Sun. noon–5 🚌 5, 8 💶 Free 🛈 Guided tours

St. Patrick Street, Cork's main shopping thoroughfare

Walk: Cork's Mercantile Past

Refer to route marked on city map on page 114.

Free of urban pressure and appealingly compact, walking is without a doubt the best way to get around the city if you want to capture its true flavor and mingle with the people who give it life. Cork constantly challenges Dublin's supremacy, refusing to play second fiddle. Allow 90 minutes.

Begin at Bishop Lucey Park, across the Grand Parade from the tourist office.
Also known as City Park and named for a much-loved bishop of Cork, Bishop Lucey Park holds a section of the medieval city walls. The eight bronze swans adorning a sculptured fountain celebrate the 800th anniversary of Cork's 1185 charter.
Walk right to reach the junction of Grand Parade and South Mall, and turn left onto South Mall.
That impressive statue at the junction of the two streets commemorates Irish rebels in the 1798 and 1867 uprisings. Irishmen who perished in the two World Wars are honored by the War Memorial alongside the river, and the uncarved granite stone nearby is the Hiroshima Memorial. South Mall is a wide, tree-lined street that was once an open channel bringing ships right up to waterside cellars to unload merchandise.
Turn left on Winthrop Street.
The General Post Office on your left as you walk east on Winthrop Street was built on the site of the late 18th-century Theatre Royal, complete with busy coachyard facilities. Continue east and turn right on St. Patrick's Street (known simply as Patrick Street).
The statue in the center of the street at the foot of Patrick Bridge depicts Father Matthew, the "Apostle of Temperance" fondly remembered in these parts for his lifelong fight against Irish alcoholism in the 1800s.
Turn left across Patrick Street into Lavitts Quay, then left at the Opera House into Emmet Place.

Despite the opera house's resemblance to a lump of concrete, this 1960's addition to municipal culture regularly presents ballet, opera and drama productions (see page 122). By contrast, its next-door neighbor is an imposing building that houses the Crawford Art Galleryt. It was built in 1724, when ships could unload onto what is now the sidewalk, as the Custom House. Irish and international artists are represented in its fine collections, which include classical casts from the Vatican Galleries presented to Cork in 1818. The museum houses a collection of local landscape painting.
Turn left on Academy Street, then right on Patrick Street and look to your right for the three tiny streets described below.
The tiny lanes of French Church Street, Carey's Lane and Sts. Peter and Paul's Street became a safe haven for a colony of Huguenots who fled France in the 18th century to escape religious persecution and settled first in French Church Street. A few steps farther on, Carey's Lane was the site of a chapel in 1776, when Catholics were forbidden by law to have churches on main streets. The Huguenot graveyard is just behind the old wall on the right of the lane. Pause at the next small street on your right to feast your eyes on the elaborate stonework of the Church of Sts. Peter and Paul's, which blossomed from the original chapel in the lane and opened in 1868.
Follow Patrick Street to where it curves to the left into the Grand Parade and turn right to the junction of Cornmarket and Castle streets.
Once a lively and thriving open-air flea market, the Coal Quay (Cornmarket Street) was a vibrant part of the city's life for at least a century. It's lined with stalls presided over by shrewd, witty Irish countrywomen hawking odds and ends of every description. These days you're more likely to find second-hand clothing and furniture.
From Castle Street, turn left at North Main Street, then right on Washington Street and continue to Grattan Street, turn left, cross Clarke's Bridge, then right onto Wandesford Quay to Sharman Crawford Street and on to Bishop Street.

St. Fin Barre's Cathedral was designed by William Burges

Built in French Gothic style and designed by William Burges, the majestic limestone St. Fin Barre's Cathedral boasts three splendid spires and a magnificent interior with angels gazing down from a starry apse. It's a true "must see" (see page 119).

> **Turn right along French Quay and cross the bridge to South Main Street and continue walking east, then turn right on Tobin Street.**

At first glance, this narrow little street seems an unlikely setting for the arts, but the Triskel Arts Centre is alive with activity, from contemporary arts and crafts exhibitions to a variety of theatrical productions and some cutting-edge films.

> **Continue down Tobin Street to Grand Parade and cross over to the entrance of the English Market.**

Also known as the City Market (see page 118), the colorful English Market is the perfect place to end your walk, have a break, rest your feet and have a cup of tea or light meal in the balcony restaurant.

Cork's Cultural Scene

Cork city is packed with cultural activities, both traditional and contemporary. No matter what time of year you visit, you can count on attending a cultural event, and in most cases costs are moderate. The city was designated a City of Culture for 2005.

Cork's opera house presents plays and musical stage shows of the highest caliber, concerts by leading orchestras and musical stars, and ballet and other dance performances.

The Everyman Palace Theatre is housed in the venerable gilt-and-gingerbread Old Palace Theatre, a venue steeped in the city's theatrical history. It hosts high-quality performances of its resident company, as well as visiting troupes from around the country, Great Britain and America. There's coffee service at intermission, and audiences often mingle with actors who relax in the agreeable Theatre Bar.

Cork is the perfect place to enjoy traditional Irish music at its best, and the best of the best can be found in many of the city's numerous pubs. Ballads, jigs and reels liven the cozy atmosphere Wednesday through Saturday nights in An Bodhran, a century-and-a-half old pub frequented by university students as well as a nice mix of other age groups.

Bagpipes, bodhráns, fiddles and guitars hold forth just about every night of the week at the popular Lobby Bar featuring top traditional bands and soloists. Both pubs sometimes present contemporary music. Check local newspapers for other pubs featuring music, traditional and contemporary. Check also for weekend discos or clubs, which change times and places frequently.

Cork holds so many special events and festivals that it sometimes seems its citizens stand ready to throw a party at the drop of a hat. Choirs and dance teams from around the world descend on Cork in late July or early August for the Cork International Choral and International Folk Dance Festival, with most of the action set in the City Hall. In September the Cork Folk Festival keeps alive the deep-rooted music that is so much a part of Irish culture.

Considered by many to be the star of Cork's festivals, the Cork Guinness Jazz Festival in October attracts greats of the jazz world – the city rings with lively music pouring from pubs and theaters. It is ranked among the top three jazz festivals in the world. The equally famed Cork Film Festival in late September or early October gives independent film-makers a showcase for their work. It is one of Ireland's oldest and biggest film events. Established in 1956, the festival brings the best of international cinema to the Irish audience – and the visitors. It also gives Corkonians a chance to don their best bib and tucker for the many gala evenings that are so much a part of the festivities.

An Bodhran
✉ 42 Oliver Plunkett Street ☎ 021 427 4544
Cork's Opera House ✉ Emmet Place
☎ 021 427 4308; www.corkoperahouse.ie
The Everyman Palace Theatre
✉ 17 MacCurtain Street ☎ 021 450 1673;
www.everymanpalace.com
The Lobby Bar
✉ 1 Union Quay ☎ 021 431 1113

Drive: Island City, Magic Stone

Duration: 1–2 days

This 159-mile drive from the center of Cork heads to Blarney to kiss the famous stone and northwest through historic towns before turning east and south for the spectacular drive across the Vee.

Start at Tourist House, Grand Parade, in Cork. Cross Patrick Street Bridge and turn left for the signposted 6-mile drive northwest on the R617 to reach Blarney. The well-preserved ruins of Blarney Castle, built in 1446, draw visitors not just for their history, but also for the magical powers attributed to the famous stone embedded in its parapet wall. Kissing the stone involves lying on your back and hanging over an open space (see page 117). Close to the castle is the superb Scottish baronial mansion, Blarney Castle House, set amid lovely 18th-century gardens.

Leave Blarney on the R617. After a few miles, turn northwest on the R579 for Kanturk.

One mile south of town, unfinished Kanturk Castle was begun in 1609 by Irish chieftain MacDonagh MacCarthy, who planned the building as the largest mansion in Ireland, with a large quadrangle and four-story towers at each corner. Alarmed at its size and strength, the English Privy Council ordered work to cease, declaring that it was "much too large for a subject." The roofless, stout walls and towers have survived in remarkably good condition.

Drive southeast on the R576 to its junction with the N72, then turn east for 9 miles to reach Mallow.

Set on the River Blackwater, Mallow was a popular spa town during the 18th and early 19th centuries; its lively social life prompted the famous song "The Rakes of Mallow." The fine fortified 16th-century house replacing 12th-century Mallow Castle, which was burned in 1689 on the orders of King James II, now stands in fairly complete ruins in its own park by the river crossing. From the tourist office in Cork or Youghal, ask for the Blackwater drive map and chart that shows a wealth of historic relics.

About 9 miles north of Mallow via the N20, the little town of Buttevant saw the world's first steeplechase in 1752, run between its church steeple and the one in Doneraile. Buttevant was the model for "Mole" in Edmund Spenser's *The Faerie Queene*.

Early-evening sunshine lights up the clock tower in Youghal

The viewing points along this drive through a gap in the beautiful Knockmealdown Mountains provide spectacular panoramic views of some of the areas famous landscapes: Killballyboy Wood, Boernagore Wood, the Galtee Mountains, the Golden Vale of Tipperary, Bay Lough and the Comeragh mountain range.

Continue south on the R668 for 8 miles to Lismore.
This historic little town, site of an ancient monastic center, is beautifully located on the Blackwater river. Its most outstanding attractions are Lismore Castle, whose gardens are open to the public, the Protestant cathedral with grave slabs from the ninth and eleventh centuries, and the modern Romanesque-style Catholic cathedral. A program in the Heritage Centre depicts the town's history.

Take the N73 northeast for 21 miles to Mitchelstown.
Ten miles northeast of this tidy, attractive 19th-century town via the N8, the signposted Mitchelstown Caves are an underground wonderland of passages and high-ceiling limestone chambers, including the biggest chamber in the British Isles. The Old Caves were used as a refuge for a 16th-century Earl of Desmond, who had a price on his head. There are escorted tours through 2 miles of the fantastic netherworld.

Follow the N8 for 18 miles to Cahir.
Occupying a small islet in the River Suir, Cahir Castle was built in the 13th century by the de Berminghams and was held by the Anglo-Norman Butlers until 1599, when the Earl of Essex captured it after a three-day siege. Englishman Oliver Cromwell made a fierce show of force before the walls in 1650 and sent in surrender terms. Historians differ as to whether the garrison accepted the terms immediately or held out until they saw the heavy ordnance ranged against them. They did, however, surrender before another attack and the castle thus remained in sound condition. It has been restored and there is an excellent audiovisual show.

Head south on the R668 through Clogheen to begin the Vee mountain pass road en route to Lismore.

Take the N72 east for 4 miles to the bridge on the outskirts of Cappoquin and turn right on an unclassified road to a T-junction. Turn right on the road signposted Youghal that follows the Blackwater river south to the sea, then turn right on the N25 south for Youghal. Youghal (pronounced "yawl" meaning yew wood) is filled with mementos of its past. The picturesque harborside town was once the home of Sir Walter Raleigh, who brought the potato and tobacco to Ireland, and the setting for the 1954 movie *Moby Dick*. At the tourist office on the harbor, ask for their Tourist Trail booklet for information about the town's history and major sights, including the impressive 1776 clock tower, which now holds a museum featuring Walter Raleigh memorabilia, remnants of the old town walls, and Myrtle Grove, the home of Sir Walter Raleigh. Harbor cruises are sometimes available, and deep-sea fishing charters can be booked at the tourist office.

Eight miles east of Youghal, via a signposted turnoff from the N25, is the pretty little seaside village of Ardmore (see page 126). It has a fine group of ecclesiastical remains, including one of the most perfectly preserved round towers in Ireland. There are also bracing cliff walks along the sea's edge.

Follow the N25 west for 28 miles to return to Cork.

Tourist information ✉ Heritage Centre, Market House, Market Square, Youghal ☎ 024 20171 🕔 Mon.–Fri. 9–5:30, Sat.–Sun. 9:30–5, Apr.–Oct.

The Mitchelstown Caves are a massive pre-glacial underworld

Munster

Regional sights

Key to symbols

Ardmore

One of the most perfectly preserved round towers in Ireland rises some 98 feet above the attractive little seaside village of Ardmore. St. Declan came from Wales to found a monastic settlement here in the fifth century, and the tower is just one of several remarkably intact remains still on view. Look for the incredibly tiny St. Declan's Oratory – legend says that the grave in one corner is that of St. Declan himself. Traces of architectural styles of the 10th to 14th centuries are visible in the ruins of the cathedral, and of special interest are a set of panels on its west gable, which holds

Mizen Head Signal Station guides vessels along the rocky coastline

sculptured biblical scenes such as the Adoration of the Magi, the Weighing of Souls and the Judgment of Solomon. This pretty village invites a leisurely stroll along the sandy beach.

✚ C1

Tourist information ✉ Seafronts parking lot, Ardmore ☎ 024 94444 ⏰ Seasonal opening

Bantry and the Beara Peninsula

Named for an ancient Celtic chieftan, the little town of Bantry sits at the head of 21-mile-long Bantry Bay, surrounded by hills. Twice (in 1689 and 1796) the French attempted naval invasions of Ireland from this inlet, only to be defeated by great storms and faulty communications. Between Bantry and Glengarriff, look for an "Artist's Studio" roadside sign in Ballylickey, which marks the studio of Raymond Klee, a fine, Welsh-born, award-winning artist whose remarkable paintings of the Irish landscape are popular with visitors.

Bantry House sits on the southern outskirts of town in a magnificent demesne, where landscaped lawns and gardens look out over the bay. The 1750 Georgian mansion is the ancestral home of the Earls of Bantry, and holds an impressive collection of European antiques, paintings, sculptures, tapestries and many other precious items.

Within the grounds you'll find the French Armada Exhibition Centre, where you can view the remarkably preserved remains of the frigate *Surveillante*, which came to a watery end when it was scuttled after the 1796 expedition led by Wolfe Tone and the United Irishmen came to a disastrous end, and lay buried on the sea-bed for 200 years. Extracts from Wolfe Tone's journal bring an immediacy to those long-ago events. You can visit the house and exhibition center jointly or individually.

The 30-mile Beara Peninsula is a narrow, mountainous finger of land stretching out to sea between Bantry Bay and the Kenmare River. Its northwest corner falls within County Kerry, marked by the Cork–Kerry border that runs along the Caha mountain range. Glengarriff sits at its head, and a drive

The classical pavilion in the Italianate gardens on Garinish Island, off Glengarriff

through the wild, sparsely populated landscape of the peninsula is a pleasant three- or four-hour diversion when you're traveling from Glengarriff to Kenmare or Killarney.

About a mile offshore from Glengarriff, in a sheltered inlet of Bantry Bay, is the lovely little Garinish Island, whose elaborately landscaped Italianate garden has brilliantly hued plants and flowers collected from around the world, interspersed with classical pavilions and meandering pathways. A ferry ride from Gengarriff takes you over to these splendid gardens, thriving in the warming effects of the Gulf Stream. Playwright George Bernard Shaw loved the place, and parts of *St. Joan* were written here.

Gougane Barra's densely wooded mountains have over the centuries been a natural refuge for those desperately seeking religious freedom. St. Finbar chose an island in the lake at its center as the setting for his sixth-century monastery. During the time of the Penal Laws, when they were forbidden to celebrate Mass, Irish worshippers held services in this secluded setting. The woods are laced with lovely walkways, making this a delightful stop.

Mizen Head is Ireland's most southerly mainland, and its signal station sits high above the wild Atlantic water. A breathtaking 172-foot suspension bridge soars 150 feet above crashing waves at the cliff base below. Views of the coasts are simply magnificent. The visitor center is located in the keeper's house and engine room, with audiovisuals, archives, maps and a bird and sea look out.

🕂 A1

Tourist information ✉ The Courthouse, The Square, Bantry ☎ 027 50229 🕔 Daily 9:15–6, Jun.–Aug.; Mon.–Sat. 9:15–5, Apr.–May, Sep.–Oct.

Bantry House and 1796 Bantry French Armada Exhibition Centre ✉ Bantry (on the east side of the town) ☎ House: 027 50047 🕔 House: daily 10–6, Mar.–Nov.; Armada Centre: daily 10–6, Mar.–Nov. 🍴 O'Connor's Seafood Restaurant in Bantry (see page 206) 🎟 House, gardens and Armada Centre: $$$; Armada Exhibition Centre and gardens: $$; www.bantryhouse.ie

Garinish Island ✉ Glengarriff ☎ 027 63040 🕔 Mon.–Sat. 10–6:30, Sun. 11–5, Apr.–Sep.; Mon.–Sat. 10–4:30, Sun. 1–5 in Mar. and Oct. 🚤 Boat to island: $$$; Island: $$

Mizen Head Signal Station Visitor Centre ✉ Mizen Head, 6 miles west of Goleen ☎ 028 35115; fax 028 35422 🕔 Daily 10–6, Jun.–Sep.; 10:30–5, mid-Mar. to May and in Oct.; 11–4, rest of year 🎟 $$

Gougane Barra National Forest Park ✉ 15 miles northeast of Bantry off R584, signposted on the Macroom to Glengarriff road 🎟 Free; $$ parking fee Jul.–Aug. and weekends Apr.–Oct.

Cahir Castle sits inside the protection of a forbidding stone curtain wall

Cahir

Cahir, a rocky islet in the River Suir, has been the natural site of fortifications as far back as the third century. It was one of Brian Ború's homes during his reign as high king of Ireland. The present magnificent castle was built by the 13th century Normans and held by the Anglo-Norman Butlers until Queen Elizabeth I's favorite, the Earl of Essex, captured it in 1599. Articles ending the Cromwellian wars were signed here in 1652, and title was held by Butler descendants until 1961. The state took over in 1964 and restored the castle to near-original condition and refurnished residential apartments with authentic reproductions that bring alive its centuries-old history. Guided tours of the castle are available on request. Don't miss the excellent audiovisual show, "Partly Hidden and Partly Revealed."

The town of Cahir is something of a time warp and some of its shops and houses appear little changed for decades. Unusual for towns in the Irish Republic, there is a war memorial in the main square dedicated to the local men who joined Irish regiments and fell in World War I.

The other curiosity is the quaint Swiss Cottage that stands in pretty woodland gardens by the riverside just outside the town. Its thatched, corkscrew timbered building with "eyebrow windows" looks like something out of *Hansel and Gretel* rather than the Swiss Alps. Designed in 1810 by British architect John Nash for the Butler family, it was rescued from dereliction in 1985–89 by enthusiastic conservationists and extensively restored. The original hand-painted French wallpapers and fabrics have been faithfully copied, and it is now elegantly furnished with many period pieces.

✚ C2

Tourist information ✉ Castle parking lot, Cahir
☎ 052 41453 ⏰ Daily 10–5, Apr.–Oct (times can vary)
Cahir Castle ✉ Castle Street, Cahir (on the east side of the town) ☎ 052 41011 ⏰ Daily 9–7, mid-Jun. to mid-Sep.; 9:30–5:30, rest of year 🍴 Crock of Gold Tea Room, across the road 💷 $

Swiss Cottage ✉ Ardfinnan Road ☎ 052 41144
🕐 Daily 10–6, mid-Apr. to mid-Oct.; Tue.–Sun. 10–1
and 2–4:30, mid-Oct. to mid-Nov.; Tue.–Sun. 10–1 and
2–6, mid-Mar. to mid-Apr. 💲 $

Carrick-on-Suir

The town of Carrick is noteworthy for its
beautiful Tudor mansion – rare amid Ireland's
hundreds of fortresses and abbeys. Despite its
name, Ormond Castle is completely
unfortified. The original 15th-century castle
fell into ruins centuries ago. Not so the
adjoining Elizabethan manor house, built by
the 10th Earl of Ormond ("Black Tom") to
entice Queen Elizabeth I to visit. The grand
edifice never did succeed in that effort, but it
did survive the centuries to stand as Ireland's
best example of that period. Two of the 15th-
century towers are consolidated into the
manor house, and the fine decorative
plasterwork is among the best in the country.

There is probably no truth in the legend
that Ormond Castle was the birthplace of
Anne Boleyn, mother of Queen Elizabeth I.
Today the town is much prouder of a more
recent hero, Sean Kelly, the racing cyclist who
was ranked world champion for five
consecutive years. Carrick rejoiced when
Kelly won the 1988 Tour de France. A square
in the town is named after him.
✚ C2

Ormonde Castle ✉ Castle Park (off Castle Street),
Carrick-on-Suir ☎ 051 640787 🕐 Daily 10–6 (last
admission 5 p.m.), mid-Jun. to Sep. 💲 Free
ℹ Access by guided tour only

Cashel

Undoubtedly Ireland's most majestic
historical landmark, the lofty Rock of Cashel
soars 300 feet above the town of Cashel and
its surrounding plains. After you view the
audiovisual "Strongholds of the Faith,"
wander among the ancient stones and ruins,
climb to the top of the cathedral tower to
wonder at Tipperary's Golden Vale plains,
and gaze at the stone Cross of Cashel with a
base that may have been a pre-Christian
sacrificial altar. Ancient Celts worshipped
here, and Irish kings built their palace on the
sacred site. It was here that St. Patrick came
in the year 450 to preach to Aengus, king of
Munster, using the shamrock as a symbol of
the Trinity. Aengus saw the light, and he and
his family accepted baptism.

Murtough O'Brien presented the Cashel
of the Kings to the church in 1101, and in
1127 Cormac MacCarthaigh built the little
chapel that bears his name. It's a miniature
gem of Romanesque style. In the years that
followed, the fortunes of the sacred place
vacillated with the fluctuations of royalty and
church power. In 1748 the archbishop of the
day left it abandoned and unroofed because –
so the Irish say – his coach and four horses
could not make it up the steep incline to its
great west door.

No visit to the Rock of Cashel is complete
without a look at the Brú Ború Heritage
Centre next door. The Brú Ború traditional
musicians and dancers perform most days
during the summer, and facilities include a
subterranean exhibition and an information
center, craft center and folk theater.

Although the town tends to be
overshadowed by the Rock, as one of
Ireland's designated Heritage Towns it is well
worth a visit in its own right. A good place to

The sense of history is intense at the Rock of Cashel

start is the town hall's Folk Village, an attractive reconstruction of local village lifestyles. Wandering from one thatched village shop to another is a step back in time. In the informal setting, shops are interspersed with other facets of daily life, including a forge and the Penal Chapel. Cashel's ecclesiastical prominence predates the arrival of St. Patrick, as changing exhibitions at the Heritage Centre portray. On permanent display is a large-scale model of the town in the 1640s, and the "Royal Heirlooms and Relics of the House of McCarthy Múr" exhibit provides a little glimpse into the lifestyles of ancient Gaelic royalty.

From June to September, the quaint old Cashel heritage tram departs the center to tour the historic sites in the town. Adjoining the Georgian St. John the Baptist Cathedral and nearby 14th-century town walls, the GPA Bolton Library holds fascinating manuscript collections, some of which date to the 12th century. The complete works of Machiavelli are here, as is the Nuremberg Chronicle of 1493, works by Dante and a host of other larger-than-life figures, including part of Chaucer's *Book of Fame*, printed by Caxton.
➕ C2

Tourist information ✉ Town Hall, Main Street ☎ 062 61333 🕐 Daily 9:30–5:30, Mar.–Oct.; Mon.–Fri. 9:30–5, rest of year

The Rock of Cashel ✉ Cashel ☎ 062 61437 🕐 Daily 9–7, mid-Jun. to mid-Sep.; 9–5:30, mid-Mar. to mid-Jun. and mid-Sep. to mid-Oct.; 9–4:30, rest of year 💰 $$

Brú Ború Heritage Centre ✉ Cashel ☎ 062 61122 🕐 Daily 9–11:30, mid-Jun. to mid-Sep.; Mon.–Fri. 9–1 and 2–5, rest of year 🍴 Restaurant 💰 Center: free; show: $$$ ℹ Ask about banquet and show evenings available in summer months

Cashel Folk Village ✉ Dominic Street (near the Rock of Cashel) ☎ 062 62525 🕐 Daily 9:30–7:30, May–Oct.; 10–6, Mar.–Apr. 💰 $

Cashel Heritage Centre and Tram Tour ✉ Town Hall ☎ 062 62511 🕐 Daily 9:30–5:30, mid-Mar. to Nov. 30; Mon.–Fri. 9:30–5:30, rest of year 💰 Free

Colorful buildings line the streets of Dingle town

St. John the Baptist Cathedral and GPA Bolton Library
✉ John Street ☎ 062 61944; fax 062 62511
🕐 Mon.–Fri. 10–4.30 🎫 $

Dingle Peninsula (Corca Dhuibhne) and the Blasket Islands (Na Blascaodai)

The Dingle Peninsula is the most westerly point of land in Europe, its offshore Blasket Islands the "last parish before America." Its beginnings are shrouded in the mists of prehistory, which left its marks scattered over the face of the Slieve Mish mountains, along its coves and rocky cliffs and in the legends that persist to this day. You may feel the very essence of Celtic magic has been distilled into the air of the Dingle Peninsula. Or perhaps it is only the soft, lyrical accents of the Gaelic, used here, that make it seem so.

West of town, Ventry (Ceann Trá) Harbour was, according to legend, the scene of a fierce and bloody battle between "King of the World" Daire Doon and King of Ireland Finn MacCool (see page 199). Still farther west, Dunbeg Fort perches on a high promontory, one side surrounded by earthen trenches, and its 22-foot-thick wall riddled with an elaborate *souterrain* (inner passage).

From the high cliffs of Slea Head (Ceann Sléibhe) you get the most sweeping view of sheltered coves below and the Blasket Islands. The last of their tiny population was moved to the mainland in 1953, when the fishing industry failed to provide a living wage and the government gave land grants for small farm holdings on the peninsula. Visitors from Springfield, Massachusetts may feel a special bond to the people of the Blaskets, since many islanders emigrated to that city.

Boats go out from Dunquin (Dún Chaoin) Harbour on an intermittent basis during summer months. There are very good potteries on the peninsula: Louis Mulcahy operates a pottery studio and workshop at Clogher Beach, Ballyferriter (Baile an Fheirtéaraigh) where he trains local potters in the production of many unusual items.

Ballyferriter is also the focal point for a summer-school program that brings students to study Gaelic and live with local families who use the language in their everyday lives. Stop at the old schoolhouse in the center of the town, now the Oidhreacht Chorca

Dhuibhne (Corca Dhuibhne Regional Museum). Dingle's long history is illustrated by more than 200 photographs, artifacts and text, and you'll leave with more than a nodding acquaintance with the region's beehive huts, standing stones, mysterious graves, ring forts and other relics.

One of the peninsula's most astonishing remains is Gallarus Oratory between Dunquin (Dún Chaoin) and Ballyferriter. It's a marvelous specimen of early Christian architecture. Built in an inverted-boat shape, it has remained completely watertight for more than a thousand years, its stones perfectly fitted without benefit of any kind of mortar. Look also for the Alphabet Stone in the churchyard of the ancient ruined Kilmalkedar church. The pillar is carved with both the Roman alphabet and ogham strokes.

In a low, sprawling building that seems to nestle into its waterside setting in Dunquin, the Blasket Centre presents the story of the Blasket Islanders in innovative displays and productions that bring to vivid life the harshness of their daily lives and the richness of their literary works. Every image inside is enhanced by the clear view of the islands through a seaward-looking wall of glass.

Dingle (its ancient Irish name is An Daingean, The Fortress) is a busy market town that sits at the head of the Dingle Peninsula. Both town and peninsula have become a mecca for some of Ireland's most talented crafts people, and you may want to pick up at least one Irish treasure here. There's good crafts browsing at The Wood in Ceardlann Na Coille, a cluster of small cottages housing crafts workshops. Here you will find expert silversmith Brian de Staic, who fashions unique necklaces with your name inscribed in strokes of the ancient ogham language.

In 1983, Fungi the dolphin moved in to Dingle Bay (Bá na Daingin), promptly becoming the beloved pet of locals and visitors alike. He's fun to watch as he cavorts through the water, following the small boats that bring visitors out for a closer look (trips daily year round) and perhaps a swim with the playful dolphin.

To reach the northern shores of the peninsula, take the Connor Pass road from

Dingle town to Castlegregory. The views from the pass and up along the coastal road stretching from Castlegregory into Tralee are just spectacular.

➕ A2

Tourist information ✉ Strand Street, Dingle ☎ 066 915 1188 🕐 Mon.–Sat. 9–7, Sun. 10–5, Jun.–Sep.; Mon.–Sat. 9–5, rest of year ℹ You can make reservations on one of the many boats that visit Fungi daily during summer months

Louis Mulcahy ✉ Ballyferriter ☎ 066 915 6229 🕐 Daily 9–7, Jun.–Aug.; 10–5:30, rest of year

The Blasket Centre ✉ Dunquin ☎ 066 915 6444 🕐 Daily 10–6, Easter–Nov. 30 🍴 Café 💲 $$

Corca Dhuibhne Regional Museum ✉ Ballyferriter ☎ 066 915 6333 🕐 Daily 10–6, Apr.–Oct.; by appointment rest of year 🍴 Coffee shop 💲 $

The Wood ✉ Ceardlann Na Coille, less than a mile west of Dingle on the coast road

Returning to pasture along the clifftop road near Dingle

Doolin

Such is the international reputation of this tiny village as a focal point for traditional Irish music, that musicians from around the world flock here to play in O'Connor's Pub. The appreciative audiences are as diverse as the musicians.

Don't be put off by Doolin's ungainly sprawl as it is an excellent base for exploring the Burren. There is a good choice of cafés and restaurants, and it's advisable to book hotels ahead during summer months. It is the closest mainland point to the Aran Islands (Oiléan Árann), and boats leave the pier daily for the 30-minute voyage to Inishmore (Inis Móir) and Inisheer (Inis Óirr) islands. There are also boat trips to view the Cliffs of Moher (see page 135).

In 2006 Doolin Cave opened to the public. It contains the longest stalactite in the northern hemisphere (the largest in the world that you can actually visit), which measures 20 feet and hangs from the roof of a cathedral-like cavern. The one-hour tour (maximum 20 people) starts with 120 steps down to the mouth of the cave, then, kitted out with hard hat and flashlight, you begin the exciting underground experience.

✚ B3

Tourist information ✉ The Cliffs of Moher, Liscannor ☎ 065 708 1171 🕐 Daily 10–5, mid-Mar. to May 30; 10–6, Jun.–Sep.

O'Connor's Pub ✉ Doolin ☎ 065 707 4168

Doolin Cave ✉ Doolin (pick up at Bruach na hAille restaurant) ☎ 065 707 5761; www.doolincave.ie

Trees force their way up through the limestone of the Burren

Ennis and County Clare

Ennis is a bustling market town with many historical buildings and tiny, winding streets. Of special note is the 13th-century Franciscan friary on Abbey Street. For detailed exploration of the town, stop by the tourist office for *Ennis – A Walking Trail,* an excellent guide for an hour-and-a-half tour. County Clare's incredible history is captured in displays at the County Clare Museum, located in a former convent.

The Craggaunowen (pronounced "Crag-an-owen") Project brings a sense of reality to everyday Irish life during the Bronze Age and early Christian era. The small castle has an interesting display of medieval art objects. In the lake a short walk away is a fascinating re-creation of a crannog (a Bronze Age lake dwelling). There's a cooking site of the Iron Age, and the earthen ring fort on the grounds holds a reconstructed farm home of some 15 centuries ago. Of special interest is the glass shelter that has been built to house the tiny leather curragh built by Tim Severin for his daring voyage across the Atlantic to retrace St. Brendan's legendary route of AD 700.

There's an eerie moonscape look to much of the 100-square-mile limestone area of the Burren. Its sense of remoteness belies its rich plant life at first glance. Make your first stop the Burren Display Centre to view exhibits to explain what you'll see. Nearby in Carran, the Burren Perfumery has an organic herb garden and demonstrations of essential oil extraction. Walking all or part of the 26-mile signposted Burren Way is the best way to discover the relics of ancient civilizations, and the astonishing flora thriving in such an unlikely setting. Nearby, a local farmer discovered Aillwee Cave about 50 years ago. Its awesome stalactites, stalagmites, waterfall and relics of brown bears who eons ago hollowed out snug pits have made it one of the most popular visitor attractions in the Shannon region. This region has many ancient buildings, often carefully restored to achieve full tourist potential. Besides well-known Bunratty (see page 144), there are tower houses like Knappogue Castle, which was built in 1479 and whose restoration has been faithful to that 15th-century character.

If you've been looking for a mate, Lisdoonvarna, 7 miles north of Ennistymon good weather. Clifftop walks are tempting, but call for caution, as there is a real danger that the ground may give way.

The Visitor Experience at the Cliffs of Moher, incorporating the Atlantic Edge interpretative center, is in a cavernous underground building, reached via a downward spiraling ramp. This gives access to the fascinating interactive exhibits and displays about the ocean, geology and plantlife of the area. There are stories from folklore and real life, a film of an aerial tour of Clare and a computer-generated cliff-ledge experience.

✠ B3

Tourist information ✉ Arthur's Row, Ennis ☎ 065 682 8366 🕐 Daily 9:30–5:30, Jun.–Oct.; Mon.–Sat. 9:30–5:30 in May and Oct.–Jan.; Mon.–Fri. 9:30–5:30, rest of year

Aillwee Cave ✉ Ballyvaughan, Ennistymon (28 miles from Ennis) ☎ 065 707 7036 🕐 Daily 10–6:30, Jul.–Aug.; 9:30–5:30, Jan.–Jun. and Sep.–Nov.; by appointment, rest of year 🍴 Café 💺 $$$

County Clare Museum ✉ Arthur's Row, Ennis ☎ 065 682 3382 🕐 Mon.–Sat. 9:30–5:30, Sun. 2–5, Jun.–Sep.; Tue.–Sat. 9:30–5:30, rest of year 💺 Free

Craggaunowen Project ✉ Quin, Co. Clare, 10 miles from Ennis, signposted from Quin, north on R469 ☎ 061 360 788 🕐 Daily 10–6 (last admission at 4), mid-Apr. to mid-Oct. 🍴 Tearoom 💺 $$$

Burren Display Centre ✉ Kilfenora, 8 miles northwest from Ennis on the Lahinch Road ☎ 065 708 8030; www.theburrencentre.ie 🕐 Daily 9:30–6, Jul.–Aug.; 10–5, Mar.–Jun. and Sep.–Oct. 🍴 Tea shop; Vaughan's Pub in Kilfenora 💺 $$

Burren Perfumery ✉ Carran ☎ 065 708 9102 🕐 Daily 9–7, Jun.–Sep.; 9–5, rest of year 💺 Free

Clare Heritage and Genealogical Centre ✉ Church Street, Corofin, 6 miles northwest from Ennis on the Lahinch Road ☎ 065 683 7955; fax 065 683 7540 🕐 Geneological Centre: Mon.–Fri. 9–1, 2–5; museum: daily 10–6, May–Oct.

Knappogue Castle ✉ Quin (9 miles from Ennis, south on R469) ☎ 061 368 103 🕐 Daily 9:30–5:15 (last admission at 4:15), May–Oct. 💺 $$$

Visitor Experience at the Cliffs of Moher ✉ Cliffs of Moher ☎ 065 708 6141; www.cliffsofmoher.ie 🕐 Daily 8:30–8:30 May–Sep.; 9–6, Mar.–Apr. and in Oct.; 9–5:30, Jan.–Feb.; 9:30–5, Nov.–Dec. Capacity-controlled entry by timed ticket 🍴 Restaurant and café 🚌 From Ennis bus station 💺 $$

on road N67, is the place to be in September. That's when Europe's largest matchmaking festival imbues this little North Clare town with song, dance, storytelling, serious matchmaking and all-round gaiety. The tourist office in Ennis can fill you in on exact dates. Lisdoonvarna is also famous for its Victorian Spa Complex and Health Centre, where you can drink or bathe in the therapeutic mineral waters which have been dispensed here since the 18th century.

If you have any County Clare ancestors, it is quite likely you can trace them among the thousands of family records at the Clare Heritage and Genealogical Centre (write for a Genealogical Research Form). Even if you aren't engaged in tracing your roots, you will find the "Ireland West 1800–60" exhibition fascinating as it takes you through famine and emigration years.

The 5-mile stretch of the Cliffs of Moher that rise to as high as 754 feet can only be described as breathtaking. They are best viewed from O'Brien's Tower, built on the highest cliff to afford a good vantage point for early 19th-century tourists. Mountains as far apart as Kerry and Connemara and the Aran Islands (*Oileáin Árann*) are clearly visible in

Killarney

The friendly, ebullient residents of Killarney more than offset what is a popular perception of the town as more commercial than any other town in Ireland. "Commercial," in Killarney's case, simply translates into an abundance of good accommodations, eateries and entertainment.

Killarney's wealth of natural beauty can be a bit overwhelming. Not to worry – the jarveys (drivers of open horse-drawn vehicles), boatmen and bus-tour people have it all worked out. Their routes will take you to the high points, and although it is perfectly possible to wander around on your own, do go along for at least one of the organized tours, whether by car, boat or coach. It's great fun. The guides know and love the scenery and embellish every spot with the folklore that will make the experience even more memorable. If you're ready for a break from driving, Bus Eireann runs several good day trips to nearby locations, such as the Ring of Kerry and the Dingle Peninsula (page 131).

For a lasting memento of your visit, stop in the Frank Lewis Gallery, which specializes in landscapes of the area, portraits and sculptures by local artists.

A broad valley holds the three main lakes, with Lough Leane (the Lower Lake) closest to Killarney and separated from the Middle Lake by Muckross peninsula. It was on one of its 30 islands that dedicated monks faithfully recorded Irish history from the 11th to the 13th century in the *Annals of Innisfallen*. The Middle Lake covers 600 acres, holds four islands, and is connected to the small, narrow Upper Lake and its eight islands by a broad river called the Long Range. The lakes and streams are connected to the Atlantic by the River Laune. Their waters catch the shimmering reflections of birch, mountain ash and arbutus, while hovering over all are the peaks of some of Ireland's finest mountains: Macgillycuddy's Reeks, with Carrantuohill, the country's highest mountain; the Tomies; the Mangerton range; and Torc. As a Killarney jarvey was once thought to have said, "Sure, 'tis a grand sight, one of God's blessings."

Killarney's boatmen are legendary for their skillful navigation of the lakes and their store of wondrous tales. Boats depart in summer from the Ross Castle pier for two-and-a-half-hour tours, which include the Gap of Dunloe, Ross Castle, Muckross House, Gardens and Traditional Farms, and Torc Waterfall. Check at the tourist office for times and reservations. These sights are on the Ring of Kerry Drive (see pages 138–140).

Set on 11,500 acres of parkland and surrounded by marvelously landscaped gardens, the Victorian mansion Muckross House was built in 1843, bought by Americans in 1911, and presented as a gift to the Irish people in 1932. The first two floors are furnished in the manner of the great houses of Ireland, while its upper floors hold fascinating exhibits of maps, prints and other documents, as well as a small wildlife and bird collection. A folk museum and crafts shop bring to vivid life the Kerry country lifestyle of a time long past. The surrounding gardens feature azaleas and rhododendrons.

A strong feeling of having stepped back in time is inevitable at the Muckross Traditional Farms, where Irish farm life of years gone by continues in living exhibits – crops are sown and harvested, homemakers go about their daily chores, and carpenter, blacksmith and wheelwright carry on their trades. Adults and

Narrow shopping street in the small, neat town of Killarney

children will delight in the authentic barnyard with its animal occupants.

The tower house and two rounded towers that join remnants of a curtain wall are all that remain of Ross Castle, a late 15th-century O'Donoghue Ross stronghold on the shores of the Lower Lake, about 2 miles from town. Your imagination will help resurrect it to its life as an Irish chieftain's home. Late 16th- and early 17th-furnishings are on display, and the view from the top is superb.

Near Cahirsiveen, Valencia Island is joined to the mainland by a causeway. Silhouetted against the horizon, 10 miles offshore, the sharply pointed Skellig Islands are home to thousands of puffins, gannets and other seabirds. It was not always a sanctuary for birds. For it was on Skellig Michael (An Sceilg Mhicil), a massive rocky hulk that rises steeply 700 feet above the sea, that a colony of sixth-century monks did the seemingly impossible when they built a retreat of stone beehive huts. For six centuries it was an impenetrable monastic refuge, abandoned in the 12th century.

Today the Skellig Islands are a 45-minute boat ride from the mainland in good weather, and you reach the ruins after a climb of no fewer than 640 steps. Your climb is rewarded with magnificent views and a sense of

wonder at the stone beehive huts, that have survived all these centuries without mortar, two oratories and a church.

Begin or end your visit to the Skelligs with a stop in the Skellig Heritage Centre on Valencia Island. The stone building, framed by grassy mounds, seems to grow right out of the landscape. Here you can view programs and displays on the area's history. Pick up an excellent guide book from the crafts shop, and ask for ferry service information.
✚ A2

Tourist information ✉ Beech Road ☎ 064 31633; fax 064 34506 🕐 Daily 9:15–5:15, Jul.–Sep.; Mon.–Sat. 9:15–5:15, rest of year

Muckross House ✉ Kenmare Road (N71) ☎ 064 31440; fax 064 33926; www.muckross-house.ie 🕐 Daily 9–5:30 (until 6 Jul.–Aug.). Farms: daily 10–6, Jun.–Sep.; 1–6, May; Sat.–Sun. 1–6, Mar.–Apr., Oct. 🍽 Restaurant in craft center 🚌 From Killarney 💵 House and farm: $$$

Ross Castle ✉ Ross Road, off Muckross Road (N71) ☎ 064 35851 🕐 Daily 9–6:30, Jun.–Aug.; 9–5:30 mid-Mar. to May, Sep. to mid-Oct.; Tue.–Sun. mid-Oct. to mid-Nov. 💵 $$

The Skellig Experience ✉ Skellig Heritage Centre, Valencia Island, 7 miles off the Ring of Kerry on R765 ☎ 066 947 6306; www.skelligexperience.com 🕐 Daily 10–6 (until 7, Jun.–Aug.), Apr.–Dec. 🍽 Café 💵 $$

Old farm machinery and peat mound at Glenbeigh bog village

Drive: Ring of Kerry

Duration: 1–2 days

The 112-mile Ring of Kerry takes top billing on this tour as you travel from one scenic wonder to the next. The route skirts the edges of the Iveragh Peninsula to Kenmare, then circles back over the mountains via Moll's Gap and Ladies' View to Killarney. Mountains, lakes, sandy beaches and offshore islands form a superb panorama, and Killarney town has its own fair share of lakes and legends.

Starting at the tourist office on Beech Road in Killarney, take the N72 northwest for 13 miles to Killorglin.
Perched on hills above the River Laune, Killorglin is an ideal starting point for this drive. In mid-August, this quiet town is abuzz with the three-day Puck Fair dating from 1613 (see page 147). Pubs stay open around the clock, and every sort of street entertainment goes on non-stop. This is also a traditional gathering place for the country's traveling people, who come to engage in some hard-driving horse trading.

Turn southwest on the N70 to Glenbeigh.
On the main street of this village, look for the bog village adjoining the Red Fox Inn. Bogs have always played an important role in Ireland, and this re-creation is an authentic depiction of the lives of the peatbog communities.

Follow the N70 southwest to Cahersiveen.
The drive along the southern banks of Dingle Bay (Bá na Daingin) from Glenbeigh to this small town at the foot of the Bentee Mountain is one of island-dotted coastal scenery and fields studded with prehistoric stone ring-fort ruins, with clear views of the Dingle Peninsula (Corca Dhuibhne) across the water. At Cahersiveen, Valencia Island comes into view (see page 137). There is a ferry service, and it is accessible by car via a causeway at Portmagee. The island is noted for its superb scenery of cliffs, mountains, seascapes and vivid subtropical flowers.

Drive 10 miles south on the N70 to Waterville (An Coireán).
Set on a strip of land that separates Ballinskelligs Bay (Bá na Scealg) from the island-sprinkled Lough Currane (Loch Luíoch), this popular resort and fishing center is also known for its superb golf

course. Mountains rise from the lake's shores, and on Church Island there are ruins of a 12th-century church that was dedicated to a sixth-century holy man, St. Fionan.

Continue south, then east on the N70 for 22 miles toward Sneem.

Just beyond Coomakista Pass on the N70, and one mile before Caherdaniel (Cathair Dónall), is Derrynane House. Set in the wooded National Historic Park, this was the birthplace of Daniel O'Connell in 1775. The house is maintained as a museum containing memorabilia on Ireland's beloved "Liberator." Most of O'Connell's political life was spent here; Cahersiveen's Heritage Centre includes displays on his life.

On the drive east on the N70 from Waterville to Sneem, just east of Caherdaniel, is Castlecove where, about a mile and a half north of the road, you will see Staigue Fort, one of the country's best-preserved Iron-Age stone forts. The circular stone walls, 13 feet wide and 18 feet high, have held over the centuries without the benefit of mortar. Along their interior are several flights of stairs in near perfect condition.

Derrynane National Historic Park covers 320 acres and incorporates semitropical plants and coastal trees and shrubs, as well as fine coastal scenery. There is a well-marked

nature trail, and swimming is accessible to visitors. The pretty town of Sneem, situated where the Ardsheelaun estuary joins the Kenmare River, is popular for brown trout and salmon fishing, and its fine sandy beaches provide safe swimming. George Bernard Shaw wrote part of *St. Joan* here. Sneem is also the last resting place of Father Michael Walsh, who was a parish priest in the area for 38 years in the 1800s and was immortalized as "Father O'Flynn" in a well-known Irish ballad. Two miles to the south in Parknasilla, the elegant Great Southern Hotel is famed for its rock gardens and colorful sub-tropical blooms.

Continue east on the N70 for 17 miles to Kenmare.

The drive from Sneem along the banks of the Kenmare River has lovely views of the Caha and Slieve Miskish mountains on the opposite shore. Kenmare faces the broad Kenmare River estuary, with impressive mountains at its back.

Known as Ceann Mara (Head of the Sea) by the ancients, today it is a lively heritage town, noted for its sea fishing, safe swimming, walks and climbs, homespun woolen industry and lace. Kenmare is one of Ireland's planned estate towns, dating from 1670. The Heritage Centre details its history, as well as

Moll's Gap in Killarney

covering such intriguing exhibits as the Nun of Kenmare, the Landlords of Kenmare, the Effects of the Famine, and Kenmare Lace Exhibition. A Heritage Trail map focusing on historical sites within walking distance from the center is provided at no charge.

Turn north on the N71 to reach Moll's Gap.

The drive north to Moll's Gap is one of rugged mountains and stone-strewn valleys. The viewing point at this gap affords sweeping views of Macgillycuddy's Reeks and of Ireland's highest mountain, 3,414-foot Carrantuohill. The restaurant and craft shop make this a good refreshment stop.

Follow the N71 northeast for 3 miles to Ladies' View.

This excellent mountainside viewing point allows far-reaching views over the broad valley of the Killarney lakes. Queen Victoria and her ladies-in-waiting were so enthralled by this view that it was promptly named in their honor.

Some 9 miles north on the return to Killarney are the well-preserved ruins of Muckross Abbey. The abbey dates from 1448 and was built on the site of an earlier religious establishment. Elizabethan-style Muckross House is surrounded by landscaped gardens that slope down to the lake (see page 136).

The first two floors are furnished in the manner of the great houses of Ireland, while its upper floors hold exhibits of maps and prints, as well as a small wildlife and bird collection. The basement houses a folk museum, weavers' workshop, an audiovisual display about nature and an exhibition about Killarney's copper mines and oak woods. The Muckross Craft Centre comprises craft workshops, a restaurant and gift shop. Muckross Traditional Farms is a working museum that farms the land with the methods used in the 1930s (see page 136).

About 1 mile before Muckross House, a signpost on the N71 directs you to a scenic footpath up a mountain slope to the 60-foot Torc Waterfall. Continue to the top of the falls for magnificent views, if you've brought a picnic, this is the ideal spot. Alternatively, there is a good tea-shop at Muckross House.

Continue for 11 miles northeast on the N71 to Killarney.

Cahersiveen Heritage Centre ✉ Bridge Street ☎ 066 947 2724 🕐 Mon.–Fri. 10–5, Sun. 12:30–5, Apr.–Oct.; phone to confirm winter hours 🎫 $$

Derrynane House ✉ Caherdaniel ☎ 066 947 5113 🕐 Mon.–Sat. 9–6, Sun. 11–7, May–Oct.; Tue.–Sat. 1–5, Apr. and Oct.; Sat. –Sun. 1–5, rest of year 🎫 $$

Kenmare Heritage Centre ✉ The Square ☎ 064 41233 🕐 Daily 9–7, Jul.–Aug.; 9–5 Apr.–Jun., Sep.–Oct.; Mon.–Sat. 9–5, rest of year 🎫 Free

Kinsale

As picturesque a fishing and boating town as you're likely to encounter in the whole of Ireland, Kinsale (18 miles south of Cork city via N71) is a gateway to a meandering coastline drive through west Cork. From its beginnings in 1333, it has witnessed – and participated in – the ebb and flow of Irish history, which is traced through exhibits and photos housed in Kinsale's Regional Museum in the Old Courthouse, built in 1600.

Today Kinsale is a popular yachting center, and home to several top-rated gourmet restaurants. Its narrow, winding streets make for great strolls through the town. The Earl of Desmond built Desmond Castle in the 1500s as a custom house, but over its long history it has served as a prison, wine storage depot and a workhouse during the famine years. These days it holds an International Museum of Wine, illustrating Ireland's contribution to the wine trade.

South of town at Castlepark, you can visit the remains of James Fort, which dates back to 1602. The Old Head of Kinsale is a narrow promontory with a ruined 12th-century castle atop a high cliff. It overlooks the spot where in 1915 the *Lusitania* was sent to a watery grave by a German submarine, with the loss of 1,198 souls.

In Summer Cove on the eastern side of the estuary stands the still intact Charles Fort. Built in 1683 and in constant use until 1922, the fort was designed in the classic star-shaped style. It sits high on a clifftop, with spectacular views of Kinsale Harbour.

Timoleague Abbey, 10 miles southwest of Kinsale, is one of Ireland's best preserved Franciscan friaries, built in the middle of the 13th century. Nearby, the Castle Gardens have been maintained by the same family for the past 150 years.

➕ B1

Tourist information ✉ Pier Road ☎ 021 477 2234 ⏰ Daily 9:15–1 and 2:15–5:30

Kinsale Regional Museum ✉ Market Square ☎ 021 477 2044 ⏰ Wed.–Sat. 10:30–4:30, Sun. 2–5; reduced hours in winter 💶 $$

Fishing boats resting in the still waters of Kinsale Harbour

Fine walking countryside around Lough Gur

Desmond Castle ✉ Cork Street ☎ 021 477 4855
🕐 Daily 10–6, Easter–Oct. 31 🍴 The Vintage ☎ 021
477 2502 ✉ Main Street) 🎟 $
Charles Fort ✉ Summer Cove ☎ 021 477 2263
🕐 Daily 10–6, mid-Mar. through Oct. 31; Sat.–Sun.
10–5, rest of year (last admission 1 hour before
closing). Closed Dec. 25 🍴 Man Friday (see page 208)
🎟 $ ℹ️ Wear suitable shoes for the uneven terrain.
Parking nearby

Limerick

Limerick, Ireland's third largest city, gets its
name from the Irish Luimneach (Bare Spot).
Centuries ago, that's just what was here – a
barren, hilly bit of land on an island, and
because the island sat at the lowest ford of
the Shannon, it is believed early Celts built
an earthen fort at its highest point. Then
came the Danes in 831 to build a base from
which to launch their plundering. More than
a century later, Brian Ború sent them packing
and installed the O'Briens as rulers. St. Mary's
Cathedral, built in the oldest part of the city,
has a fine view from its bell tower and holds
some intriguing antiquities.

Next came the Normans, building their
stout city walls and castles. Portions of their
walls remain to this day, as does King John's
Castle, whose impressive fortification on the
banks of the Shannon has guarded Limerick

since the early 1200s. The imaginative
admissions building sits atop excavated
remains of ancient city walls and homes of
pre-Norman residents. The massive gate
house, corner towers, curtain walls and
battlements reflect the authority of royalty,
while in the courtyard medieval war
machines usually seen only in period movies
beguile the imagination. Don't rush through
this one – it is a definite "don't miss."

The marvelously restored 15th-century
Bunratty Castle was built for the O'Briens,
earls of Thomond, and its restoration
includes furnishings that look as though
they've been here since the days of those first
residents. Enter across a drawbridge into the
vaulted Great Hall, the center of castle life
where elaborate feasts are served up nightly
just as they were in days of yore (see page
144). Some of the reconstructions in the Folk
Park include a blacksmith shop, post office,
draper, tea room and a tiny pub.

During the 18th century, Limerick took
on its present-day form, with stylish
townhouses going up along broad avenues
extending far beyond the old boundaries of
Irish Town and English Town.

With 800 years of turbulent history
behind it, Limerick has in transformed itself
from a town with a slightly grubby image to
one of progressive modernity built around its
cherished monuments from the past. There is
a variety of sightseeing attractions, with a
plentiful supply of all the facilities expected
of a city of this size.

Modern places of interest include
the worthwhile Hunt Museum, one of the
finest art museums in the country outside the
National Gallery in Dublin (see page 81). It
contains works by Picasso, Renoir and
Leonardo de Vinci. Along with medieval
statues in stone, bronze and wood, there are
Egyptian, Greek and Roman artifacts, as well
as Neolithic flints and other Irish relics.

If flying is your passion, you'll know that
the first commercial direct flight between the
United States and Europe was flown by Pan
Am's luxury flying boat *Yankee Clipper*, which
landed at Foynes on the broad estuary of the
Shannon. Now restored and preserved, the
Foynes Flying Boat Museum translates

nostalgia for that era into exhibits, an audiovisual show and the radio and weather room with original navigation equipment.

At Lough Gur, in addition to the lake dwelling that dates between AD 500 and 1000, there's a wedge tomb from 2500 BC, one of Ireland's largest stone circles and replicas of weapons, tools and pottery found in this area. The remains of animals no longer seen in Ireland (giant Irish deer and bear) have been unearthed in nearby caves.

✚ B2

Tourist information ✉ Arthurs Quay ☎ 061 317 522
🕐 Mon.–Sat. 9–6, Sun 9–1, 2–5:30, Jul.–Aug.;
Mon.–Sat. 9:30–5:30, rest of year

St. Mary's Cathedral ✉ Bridge Street ☎ 061 310 293
🕐 Daily 9:30–5 💷 Donation: $

King John's Castle ✉ Nicholas Street ☎ 061 360 788
🕐 Daily 9:30–5:30, Apr.–Oct.; 10:30–4:30, rest of year
💷 $$$

Bunratty Castle and Folk Park ✉ Shannon Airport
Road (N18) ☎ 061 360 788 🕐 Daily 9–6 or 6:30,
Jun.–Sep.; 9:30–5:30, rest of year 🍴 Tearoom in folk
park 🚌 Limerick and Shannon Airport bus 💷 $$$

Lough Gur Stone Age Centre ✉ Lough Gur, 16 miles
from Limerick ☎ 061 385 186 🕐 Daily 10–6 (last
admission at 5:30), May.–Sep. 💷 Access to lake: free;
centre: $$ 🛈 Regular walking tours conducted to
archeological features

Hunt Museum ✉ The Custom House, Rutland Street
☎ 061 312 833 🕐 Mon.–Sat. 10–5, Sun. 2–5
🍴 Restaurant 💷 $$$

Foynes Flying Boat Musuem ✉ Foynes, 23 miles
west of Limerick via N69 ☎ 069 65416;
www.flyingboatmuseum.ie 🕐 Daily 10–6, Apr.–Nov.
🍴 Café 💷 $$$

Lismore

Among the several scenic drives around the Cappoquin and Lismore area, undoubtedly the most spectacular is the one that takes you through a gap in the Knockmealdown Mountains, known as the Vee. From the outskirts of Lismore, it climbs through larch and rhododendron, and heather-covered mountainsides, to the V-shaped pass. The sweeping views from numerous stopping points overlook Tipperary's Golden Vale, before descending to the little town of Clogheen in County Tipperary. High on one mountain slope stands a most curious grave,

The austere facade of Bunratty Castle, Limerick

that of Samuel Grubb, one-time owner of Castle Grace, who decreed he should be buried upright overlooking his lands. There's a small pathway leading up to the stone cairn that is his final resting place.

✚ C2

Tourist information ✉ Lismore ☎ 058 54975
🕐 Seasonal

Listowel

There is a decidedly literary bent to this north Kerry town, 17 miles northeast of Tralee. It has nurtured several of Ireland's leading writers, including John B. Keane and Bryan McMahon. The tradition lives on during Writer's Week in late June or early July, when lectures and workshops are designed to encourage new writers. Theater thrives with performances by Irish and international troupes in St. John's Arts and Heritage Centre on the square. If you're visiting in September, pay a visit to the Listowel Races.

✚ A2

Tourist information ✉ St. John's Church,
The Square ☎ 068 22590 🕐 Mon.–Sat. 10–6,
Jun.–Sep.

St. John's Arts and Heritage Centre ✉ The Square,
Listowel ☎ 068 22566 🕐 Mon.–Sat. 10–1, 2–6 (times
may vary)

Enjoy an evening of feasting and merriment at Knappogue Castle

Medieval Castle Banquets and Traditional *Céilí*

The medieval banquets at Bunratty and Knappogue castles and the traditional *céilí* at Bunratty Folk Park are each a unique experience and appeal to all age groups. No matter which you choose, you'll not be disappointed – at least one should go on your "don't miss" list. You stand a good chance of being disappointed though if you fail to make reservations through a travel agent or the banquet reservations manager, Shannon Castle Banquet, before you leave home. If you arrive without a reservation, any tourist office in Ireland will try to make one for you (with as much advance notice as you can give them). There is free parking, and tourist offices in Ennis or Limerick can furnish information about bus transportation.

Any "lord and lady of the castle" spirit you might anticipate for the medieval banquet at Bunratty Castle quickly dissolves into one of great fun and hilarity. Even the stuffiest of type joins in as story follows story and song follows song. The internationally famed Bunratty Singers serve up enchanting melodies, and the golden notes of an Irish harp melt the stoniest heart.

Somewhat harder to reach than Bunratty (it's 19 miles from Limerick, 9 miles from Ennis, signposted from Quin, south on R469 and there's no public transportation), Knappogue Castle's banquet is slightly more sedate, but far from stuffy. The group is smaller and more intimate, and the colorful entertainment focuses on the women of Ireland, both mythical and real – queens, saints and sinners from a Celtic past.

In the great barn in the Bunratty Folk Park, the traditional Irish céilí are strictly not for upper-crust nobility! The traditional music of pipes, fiddle, bodhran and accordion is what the people of Ireland have made their own and handed down through the centuries. This is the most informal of the three feasts, where audience and performers join together in song and dance, and the menu here features wholesome dishes such as Irish stew, soda bread and fresh homegrown garden produce.

Shannon Castle Banquets ✉ Town Centre, Shannon ☎ 061 360 788 ⌚ Twice nightly 5:30 and 8:45; Knappogue Castle's banquet: 6:30, Apr.–Oct.; Bunratty Folk Park; banquets 5:30 and 8:45 year-round

Thurles

A large market town on the River Suir, Thurles (pronounced "Thur-less") has two castles and a splendid Italianate cathedral, based on the one at Pisa in Italy. The town's Semple Stadium is a major venue for all Gaelic games, and it was in the Hayes Hotel that the Gaelic Athletics Association was founded in 1884 to codify and encourage Irish sports.

On the west bank of the River Suir 4 miles south of Thurles, Holy Cross Abbey was founded in 1168 and was ever after a revered place of pilgrimage. Among its treasures was a particle of the True Cross preserved in a golden shrine dating from 1110, now in the Ursuline Convent in Blackrock, Cork. Restored in 1971, the abbey still contains many religiously significant ruins, and Sunday pilgrimages continue to take place from May through September.

➕ C2

Tourist information ✉ Excel Building, Mitchell Street, Tipperary town ☎ 062 80520 🕐 Mon.–Sat. 10–6

Tralee

The county town of Kerry, and the northeast gateway to the Dingle Peninsula (Corca Dhuibhne), Tralee grew around the 13th-century Desmond Castle, of which a tiny portion can be seen where Denny Street meets the broad Mall. The history and heritage of the area is revealed in three separate presentations at the multimedia exhibition called Kerry the Kingdom and housed in the Ashe Hall. "Kerry in Colour" spotlights the county's landscape and historic monuments; the Kerry County Museum follows the area's evolution over some 7,000 years, with exhibits of the Stone, Bronze, Iron, Celtic and early Christian ages, while "The Story of Kerry" charts the history of modern Ireland; and "Geraldine Tralee" is a time car ride that takes you through the streets of the town in the Middle Ages, when Kerry, Cork and Limerick were under the control of the powerful Desmond Fitzgeralds (Geraldines). Touring the narrow, winding streets of the town, you'll see the Gothic-style Holy Cross Church designed by Pugin, with splendid stained glass by Michael Healy.

Flower-clad pub entrance in Tralee

St. John's includes a statue of a notable Kerry saint – Brendan the Navigator.

Two miles out of town brings you along an old ship canal to a 65-foot-high windmill at Blennerville. Built in 1800, it worked continually until 1850, and was restored to full working order in the 1990s. The exhibition center tells the story of 19th-century emigration from Blennerville port. Train buffs will not want to miss the scenic, narrated 2-mile ride from Tralee to Blennerville on the beautifully restored narrow-gauge steam train. Trains leave Tralee on the hour, Blennerville on the half-hour.

For entertainment, don't miss the superb Siamsa Tire (pronounced "Sheem-sa Tee-ra" – it means merrymaking), Ireland's National Folk Theatre troupe, who regularly perform in Tralee. This is Irish theater with a difference – a depiction of rural life in the past through music, song, dance and mime. Performances are in the Irish language, but don't let that put you off – the meaning of every stage action is made clear. Another popular event is the summer Rose of Tralee Festival, when young women with Irish roots come from around the world and compete to become the "Rose" (see page 19 and 147).

Twenty-one miles northwest of Tralee, Ballybunion is home to some of Kerry's most

The National Folk Theatre, Tralee

glorious beaches, overlooked by soaring cliffs, crowned by 14 Celtic promontory forts. For panoramic views, walk at least a portion of the cliff walk that climbs to the summit of Knockanore. Ballybunion is home to a seaside golf course that challenged President Clinton during his 1998 visit. The Ballybunion Busking (street entertainment) Festival is held in August.

✚ A2

Tourist information ✉ Ashe Memorial Hall, Denny Street ☎ 066 712 1288 🕐 Mon.–Sat. 9–7, Sun. 9–6, Jul.–Aug.; Mon.–Sat. 9–6, May–Jun., Sep.; Mon.–Sat. 9:15–5, rest of year

The Holy Cross Church, Tralee

Kerry the Kingdom ✉ Ashe Memorial Hall, Denny Street ☎ 066 712 7777 🕐 Daily 9:30–5:30, Jun.–Aug.; Tue.–Sat. 9:30–5, Apr.–May and Sep.–Dec.; Tue.–Fri. 10–4:30, rest of year 🍽 Café 💲 $$$ ℹ Tralee tourist office on site

Blennerville Windmill and Steam Train ✉ Windmill: on R559, 3 miles west of Tralee; steam train: Ballyard, Tralee ☎ 066 712 1064 🕐 Windmill: daily 10–6, Apr.–Jun., Sep.–Oct.; 9–6, Jul.–Aug.; steam train: daily 11–5:, May–Sep. 🍽 Coffee shop 💲 $$

Siamsa Tíre ✉ National Folk Theatre, Town Park ☎ 066 712 3055 🕐 Box office: daily 9–6, call for performances 💲 $$$

Tramore

Tramore's 3-mile sand beach and 50-acre amusement park are ideal for families. Kids will love the beach and Splashworld, an enclosed swimming complex. The Tramore Golf Club is nearby and welcomes visitors to its 18-hole course. That giant of a statue looking down from Great Newtown Head is known locally as "Metal Man," and although the statue was erected to protect mariners, legend has it that any unmarried female who hops three times on one foot around its base will then hop down the aisle within the next 12 months.

✚ C2

A modern take on a traditional theme – dancing at the Rose of Tralee International Festival

Kerry's Festivals

For five days and nights in August, international beauties with Irish ancestry gather in Tralee to decide who best fits the time-honored description "...lovely and fair as the rose of the summer." The Rose of Tralee International Festival, however, is a far cry from other such competitions. This festival is one of light-hearted fun and frolic that entails parades, pipe bands, street entertainment and the crowning of the "Rose." It's five days and nights of merriment and a grand time to be in County Kerry.

If you'd like to be part of the fun, there are several package deals that cover transportation and accommodations available from local tourist offices. Be sure to make arrangements well in advance, whether you plan to stay in Tralee or in Killarney, 20 miles to the south.

Lighthearted also best describes Killarney's Roaring Twenties Festival during St. Patrick's weekend in March. The streets teem with high-spirited high-society types, gangsters, bootleggers and other assorted Roaring Twenties characters for four days of revelry. Barbershop quartet competitions, an Al Capone party and the gala Gatsby Ball are just a few of the highlights.

In mid-August, the hillside market town of Killorglin lets its hair down in three days of what many Irish call sheer madness disguised under the name of the Puck Fair. This bacchanalian event has been held every year since 1613, originally to celebrate the beginning of the harvest. Things get off to a rowdy start when a tremendous male (or puck) goat is hauled up to a high platform in the square and crowned as "King of the Fair." What follows is a free-for-all carnival and country fair, with most pubs staying open around the clock. There are all sorts of street entertainment, and over on the green, you can witness some pretty serious horse and cattle trading.

Just how all this began is a matter of dispute: some say a goat bleated to alert a shepherd boy of approaching enemy forces and he then alerted the town. This is traditionally a gathering place for the country's traveling people, who come to drive hard bargains in the horse-swapping business, catch up with tinker gossip and indulge in non-stop revelry.

Rose of Tralee Festival Office ☎ 066 712 1322; fax 066 712 2654; www.roseoftralee.ie ✉ Ashe Memorial Hall, Denny Street, Tralee

Crystal comes in all shapes and sizes at the Waterford Visitor Centre

Waterford

Waterford, Ireland's fourth-largest city with a population of 50,000, reflects virtually every phase of Irish history. Its fine harbor, which is the main seaport of the southeast, is as alive with freighters along the broad River Suir as it was in the days when Viking long-ships plied its waters.

Prehistoric dolmens, promontory forts and passage graves speak of the earliest settlers. Legends of valor and incredibly beautiful Iron Age metalwork mirror the two sides of the flamboyant, battle-loving and artistic Celtic clan of the Deise.

The most extensive remains of Viking walls in the country and massive Reginald's Tower (which has stood intact for a thousand years) remind us of those fierce sea-raiders who came in 853 for a safe sea-haven from which to launch their plundering forays. They stayed here and become settlers and traders for more than 300 years.

Dozens of towers are legacies of the Normans, who claimed the city in 1170. Reginald's Tower has stood sentinel at the end of the quay for 1,000 years. Originally, the River Suir lapped at its 12-foot-thick walls, and entry was only from inside the city walls. As the strongest fortification on the river, it has resisted attacks from a variety of forces, including those of Oliver Cromwell.

Now a fascinating museum, its treasures include King John's mace and sword, many of the city's 30 royal charters and an interesting display on "Timbertoes," a wooden bridge designed by Boston architect Lemuel Cox in 1797. Some of the rebels involved in the 1798 uprising were hanged from its beams.

It is the modern Waterford Crystal Factory that is the city's most persistent claim to fame. Tours of production areas of the factory are one of Ireland's most popular attractions and give an informative insight into the skills required to blow, cut and polish the glassware, from a small wine glass to sparkling chandeliers. The Waterford Crystal Gallery has the world's largest display of Waterford Crystal. Visitors are also invited to view a 17-minute audiovisual presentation, which details glassmaking from its ancient beginnings to the present.

In the 1980s, Waterford underwent extensive excavations that unearthed fascinating details of the lives of its ancient inhabitants. Special attention is given to the period 1000 AD to 1500 AD. Waterford Museum of Treasures – the massive riverside renovated stone granary that holds an overflowing cornucopia of Waterford's historic treasures – is also where you'll find the tourist information office. A glass elevator transports you to the third floor and an important collection of artifacts showcasing Waterford's rich Viking, Anglo-Norman and medieval history. Highlights include a gold kite-shaped brooch of around 1150, a curved Viking flute made from a swan or goose bone from the same era and the ornately illustrated 14th-century Great Charter Roll. The second floor covers the 18th century and has an audiovisual show about the 19th century.

In the heart of Waterford city on Barronstrand Street, Holy Trinity Cathedral turns a plain, unadorned face to passersby. But a surprise awaits those who step inside to view extravagant decorations and Waterford crystal chandeliers. The magnificent 1770s Christ Church Cathedral sits on the site of an 11th-century cathedral. Its Renaissance style was designed by John Roberts, a noted Waterford architect. Each Monday and Friday evening at 8 during July and August, there's a 45-minute audiovisual presentation of the city from its beginnings to the present.

As for the people of Waterford – an amiable blend of all those who came over the centuries as settlers, conquerors, and artisans – they are especially warm in their welcome to visitors. One-hour walking tours conducted by knowledgable and entertaining storytellers are scheduled daily at 11:45 and 1:45 from the Granary and depart from the Granville Hotel on the quay at noon and 2. The Green Plaque Trail is a self-guided walking tour outlined in a helpful booklet and map available at the tourist office.

✚ C2 (regional map on page 112)

Tourist information ✚ B2 ✉ The Granary, The Quay ☎ 051 875 788; fax 051877 388 ◷ Daily 10–6, Easter–Oct.; Wed.–Sun. 10–5:30, rest of year 🍴 Restaurant 🎟 $$

Reginald's Tower ✚ C1 ✉ The Mall, Waterford ☎ 051 304 220 ◷ Daily 9:30–6:30, Jun.–Sep.; 10–5, rest of year 🎟 $

Waterford Museum of Treasures ✚ B2 ✉ The Granary, Merchant's Quay ☎ 051 304 500; www.waterfordtreasures.com ◷ Mon.–Fri. 9:30–6, Sat. 11–6, Apr.–Sep.; Mon.–Fri. 10–5, Sat. 11–5, rest of year 🎟 $$$

Christ Church Cathedral ✚ C1 ✉ Cathedral Square ☎ 051 858 958 ◷ Mon.–Sat. 10–5, Sun. 11–5, Easter–Oct. 31 🎟 Presentation: $

Waterford Crystal Visitor Centre ✚ Off the map ✉ Kilbarry, Cork Road ☎ 051 332 500; fax 051 332 716; www.waterfordvisitorcentre.com ◷ Daily 8:30–6, Mar.–Oct.; 9–5, rest of year; tours: daily 9–4, Mar.–Nov.; Mon.–Fri. 9–3, rest of year 🍴 Restaurant 🎟 Tour $$$

© Govt of Ireland

Ulster and Northern Ireland

Ulster's landscape lends credence to the heroic myths and legends that have been spawned within its borders.

Introduction and Map   **152**

Belfast **155**

Introduction and Map   **155**

Essential Information   **159**

Belfast Sights   **160**

Walk: Between Old and New   **167**

Drive: Strangford Lough   **169**

Regional Sights   **172**

Feature: American Connection   **176**

Feature: In St. Patrick's Footsteps   **182**

Drive: Fermanagh Lakeland   **186**

Feature: The Inishowen Peninsula   **198**

Feature: Finn MacCool   **199**

The astonishing hexagonal rock formations of the Giants' Causeway

Ulster and Northern Ireland

▶ **Since 1921, the ancient province of Ulster has consisted of the six counties of Northern Ireland – Antrim, Armagh, Down, Fermanagh, Londonderry and Tyrone – and the three Republic of Ireland border counties of Cavan, Donegal and Monaghan.**

Border Counties

At the very top of Ireland, County Donegal is awash with scenic beauty, its jagged coastline bordered by wide strands backed by steep cliffs, inland mountains cut by deep valleys and a countryside filled with antiquities and legends. In the rhythmic patterns of Donegal speech can be heard the distinctive cadence of Ulster, and the Irish language thrives in Gaeltacht (Gaelic speaking) areas. From Donegal cottages come some of the world's most beautiful hand-woven tweeds, prized the world over.

The great Irish poet Patrick Kavanagh was born in County Monaghan, and wrote of his home county, "O stoney grey soil of Monaghan, You burgled my bank of youth." Although early on he managed to "escape" to make Dublin his home for 30 years, his poetry is sprinkled with references to and influences of the nearly flat, faintly rolling land that seems to nurture creative talent, from literature to exquisite hand-made lace. In the end, he was brought back home to Inishkeen and laid to rest in his native county.

Cuilcagh Mountain, at the Northern Ireland border just south of Enniskillen, rises to 2,188 feet, the highest point in County Cavan's gently undulating landscape of water-splashed rolling hills. The Shannon, Ireland's longest river, rises on its southern slopes, and the Erne flows northward from Lough Gowna through the center of the county into the Upper Erne river, spreading its waters into myriad lakes along the way. Fishing and water sports draw modern-day residents and visitors alike to the more than 365 lakes in the county.

Northern Ireland

Like the Republic to the south, Northern Ireland is a veritable cornucopia of travel treasures and experiences. Its green fields, cliff-studded and cove-indented coastline, forest-clad mountains and above all its hospitable inhabitants invite a visit to this unique part of Ireland. Highlights not to be missed include the gentle shoreline of County Down with its romantic Mountains of Mourne that sweep down to the sea; its firm claim on a good part of St. Patrick's sojourn; quiet little villages on the Ards Peninsula that look across to Scotland (clearly visible in many places); a countryside dotted with Norman castles; Strangford Lough, the largest sea lough in the British isles; County Fermanagh's Lough Erne and its 300 square miles of exquisite scenery; the fabulous Marble Arch Caves; Devenish Island; Armagh's two cathedrals – one Protestant, one Catholic, both named for St. Patrick; the Sperrin Mountains of County Tyrone; a unique folk park that depicts the rural lives of Irish immigrants on both sides of the Atlantic, and Londonderry's massive old city walls.

The Erne forms a stunning string of loughs and waterways from County Cavan to Donegal Bay

The Ulster Way provides excellent walking along 435 miles of interconnected and well-marked footpaths through all six counties.

Northern Ireland spreads before the visitor a wealth of other scenic splendors throughout all six counties. Because the province is small (about the size of Connecticut), in the space of one week it is possible to comfortably visit most of the major attractions. Beyond all those, there are elements found only here that will add a special dimension to your Irish experience.

Myths

It was in this part of Ireland that the champion Cuchulainn singlehandedly guarded the border against the onslaught of Connaught's Queen Maeve when she set out to capture the Brown Bull of Cooley. This was home territory for Finn MacCool (see page 199) and his faithful Fianna warriors. And the beautiful Deirdre o' the Sorrows played out her life's tragedy within the borders of Ulster.

The People

The accents of the North fall on the ear with the soft burr of Scotland, mingled with the clipped speech of native English and the lilting Irish brogue of the Republic. It's an enchanting mix, and don't be at all surprised if you find yourself ending sentences with the distinctive lift that characterizes so much of what you hear.

Along with their speech, these descendants of Britain's plantation-era families have put into the mix strong elements of their cultures. Squash and cricket are sports you'll rarely find in the Republic, but they flourish above the border; the strains of traditional Irish music are interspersed with music of a distinctly British or Scottish flavor. Belfast's magnificent Opera House is as likely to play an English drawing-room comedy as an Irish classic by O'Casey or Synge.

Although one-third of Northern Ireland's population is concentrated in Belfast, because of their largely rural heritage Ulster people tend to be outdoor people who make the most of the plentiful natural resources lavished on them by nature.

With the British Isles' largest lake (Lough Neagh), 50 miles of tranquil cruising waters on Lough Erne and rivers teeming with fish, water sports rank high in leisure activities, from fishing, both fresh water and coastal to deep-water sea angling, to boating and water skiing. Golf, hiking and cycling follow closely behind.

Politics

There is no question that long-standing tensions exist around, among other things, such Unionist activities as the famous Orange parades of July 12 (to celebrate their beloved King Billy's victory at the 1690 Battle of the Boyne) and the Catholic St. Patrick's Day parade on March 17 (equally celebrated in many parts of America), and, on August 15, the Ancient Order of Hibernian parade to celebrate the Feast of the Assumption. Now the awful strife that has infected Northern Ireland since that fateful day in 1969 is much muted and the political parties from both sides have begun to talk and work together for a peaceful solution.

Since the ending of the hostilities, the economy of Northern Ireland has begun to thrive again, with new industries starting up and a lot of city regeneration in evidence. There's a vibrant atmosphere and an air of confidence and optimism about the place.

One thing is certain: both traditions welcome visitors warmly and are equally proud of the natural beauty and historical monuments of their homeland. Perhaps because of their turbulent recent history, Northern Ireland natives are also especially anxious that visitors return home with positive memories.

Belfast

In ancient times, Belfast was a castle built at a ford of the River Lagan and prehistoric earthworks can still be seen on neaerby hilltops. Its name in Irish is Beal Feirste, Mouth of the Sandy Ford. A small village developed around the castle, and in the 17th century Protestant settlers from Scotland and parts of England moved in, and native villagers were moved out by order of English rulers, thus establishing the character of the city that grew at a steady pace until the end of the 1700s, thanks in large part to a thriving linen industry.

In 1791 Wolfe Tone founded the United Irish Society in Belfast to bring together Protestants and Catholics who chafed under the repressive Penal Laws. In 1798 their efforts led to an uprising, one which was quickly squelched by English forces.

The shipyard that was to become one of the largest in the world and contribute so much to the city's growth was opened in 1791. By the time the Industrial Revolution was in full bloom during the 19th century, both ship-building (the *Titanic* was built here) and the linen trade welcomed newer, more modern operating methods. Both prospered, and Belfast's population grew rapidly.

© Crown copyright

Built in Portland stone, the Victorian Belfast City Hall dominates Donegall Square

The city today is a bustling, energetic center of industry. Belfast's unique character has developed through the combination of economic and political struggle, hard work and a special brand if Irish humor. For the visitor it is easy to get around and has many points of interest. The most prominent landmark must be credited to Queen Victoria, whose statue adorns Donegall Square and whose era of architectural style is in evidence around the city. Belfast's ambience today, however, is far from Victorian. Both the city center and the riverfront are taking on a new face, incorporating pedestrian areas dotted with benches and street entertainers. The big millennium building project

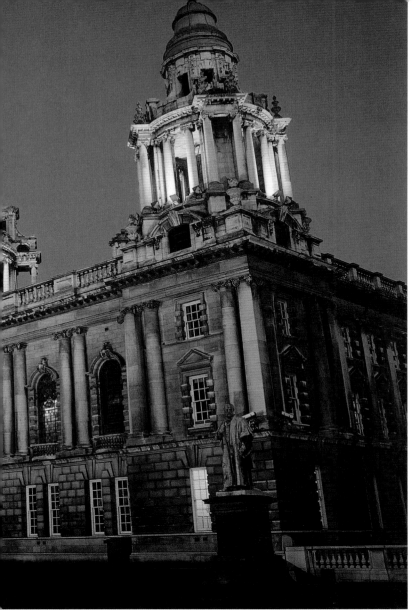

"Odyssey" has had a huge impact (see page 164). Belfast is a leading tourist destination within Europe with more than 400 places to eat and drink. The city center is a first-rate shopping mecca, with many of Britain's leading stores, as well as shops selling native crafts.

Belfast city center is fairly compact and most of the important sights are within easy walking distance. To explore the city on foot, take it neighborhood by neighborhood and use local buses to get you from one to another. The Shankill Road area (Protestant, loyalist) is northwest of the center; the Falls Road area (Catholic, nationalist) is to the west; Malone and Ballynafeigh areas are to the south; and the Sydenham, Bloomfield, Belmont and Ballymacarrett areas are to the east.

The City Hall marks Donegall Square as the hub of Belfast city center. From the square, Donegall Place leads north to the important shopping area along Royal Avenue, while to the south, Bedford Street leads into Dublin Road and the Queens University area.

With the easing of political tensions, a vibrant cultural scene has emerged in this relatively young city. It caters to all tastes, from classical music and theater to the latest in popular music led by Van Morrison, who began his career with a Belfast rhythm-and-blues group.

Venues are as varied as the choice of performances. The Waterfront Hall and Conference Centre on the Lagan river presents a variety of entertainment, as does the Grand Opera House on Great Victoria Street (see page 163). Ulster Orchestra and Northern Ireland Symphony Orchestra concerts are regularly scheduled in Ulster Hall (closed until end 2008 for renovation) on Bedford Street, while the international superstar concerts are likely to be in Kings Hall Exhibition and Conference Centre.

Traditional, folk, jazz, blues and rock music are found in such pubs as the Duke of York (off Lower Donegall Street), the Front Page (Donegall Street) and Kelly's Cellars (Bank Street just off Royal Avenue). One of the best is the Rotterdam Bar on Pilot Street, in the docks area, which features original rock bands. If you want to sample the famous Irish humor, head for the Empire Bar on Botanic Avenue on a Tuesday evening.

Irish and international plays are staged in the Lyric Theatre on Ridgeway Street, and visual and performing arts are featured at the Old Museum Arts Centre on College Square North.

Tracing Your Roots

If tracking down your Northern Ireland ancestors is your top priority, collect as much information about your forebears as possible before leaving home. It is also a good idea to contact Northern Ireland genealogical organizations well in advance of your arrival in the province. They will reply to every letter, but you are requested to enclose three international reply coupons with your query to help with the cost of mailing to you.

The Public Record Office is the main source for genealogical research in Ulster. While they do not conduct individual genealogical research, members of the public are welcome to search the records themselves.

The General Register Office has records of births and deaths from 1864 and marriage registrations since 1922. For a small fee, the Registrar General will arrange searches of any births, marriages or deaths in Northern Ireland prior to 1922.

You can, of course, employ a professional to do your research. For a list of members and the services they offer, write to:
Association of Ulster Genealogists and Record Agents (AUGRA) Glen Cottage, Glenmachan Road, Belfast BT4 2NP.

Public Records Office
✉ 66 Balmoral Avenue, Belfast BT9 6NY
☎ 028 9025 5905; fax 028 9025 5999;
www.proni.gov.uk
🕐 Mon.–Fri. 9:15–4:45, Thu. until 8:45

The General Register Office
✉ Oxford House, 49–55 Chichester Street, Belfast BT1 4HL
☎ 028 9025 2000
🕐 Mon.–Fri. 9:30–4; opens at 10 first Tue. of month

The rich interior of the Crown Liqour Saloon in Belfast

Essential Information

Tourist Information

Belfast Welcome Centre ✉ 47 Donegall Place ☎ 028 9024 6609; fax 028 9031 2424; www.gotobelfast.com 🕐 Mon.–Sat. 9–7, Sun. 11–6, Jun.–Sep.; Mon.–Sat. 9–5:30, rest of year

Urban Transportation

In Belfast, Metro operates a network to all parts of the city, with departures from Donegall Square East, West and North, Upper Queen Street, Wellington Place, Chichester Street and Castle Street. Information on which buses go where is posted at Donegall Square West, and routes are listed on the Belfast city map available from the tourist office.

For details of bus services (both Metro and Ulsterbus), contact Translink Call Centre ☎ 028 9066 6630; www.translink.co.uk 🕐 Daily 7a.m.–8p.m. Translink can also provide information on Northern Ireland Railways.

There are many guided coach tours of Belfast and its environs available, an excellent way to gain an overview of the city. City Sightseeing runs tours departing every half-hour 10–4:30 in summer, every hour 10–4 in winter; ☎ 028 9062 6888. Mini-coach tours, guided by historians, tour the city's landmarks. Tickets available from Belfast Welcome Centre.

Taxi stands are at main rail stations, ports and airports. Black cabs are metered and service stands are at Central Station, both bus stations and City Hall. When using a taxi without a meter, be sure to agree on a price before you get in.

Airport Information

Belfast International Airport is 19 miles northwest of the city center in Crumlin. The Belfast City Airport is 2 miles to the northeast. Most flights from the U.S. and Canada set down at George Best Belfast International Airport, and there are frequent Airbus services to and from the city. Passengers arriving at George Best Belfast City Airport can take the Airlink bus into the city. ☎ Belfast International Airport: 028 9448 4848; Belfast City Airport: 028 9093 9093 🚌 Airbus fare £6 one-way, £9 round trip; taxi fare from Belfast City Airport starts at £6; Airlink bus £2.20 for round-trip.

Climate: Average highs and lows

Jan.	Feb.	Mar.	Apr.	May	Jun.	Jul.	Aug.	Sep.	Oct.	Nov.	Dec.
8°C	9°C	11°C	13°C	16°C	18°C	19°C	19°C	17°C	14°C	11°C	8°C
46°F	48°F	52°F	55°F	61°F	64°F	66°F	66°F	63°F	57°F	52°F	46°F
3°C	3°C	4°C	6°C	8°C	10°C	13°C	13°C	11°C	8°C	6°C	4°C
37°F	37°F	39°F	43°F	46°F	50°F	55°F	55°F	52°F	46°F	43°F	39°F

The 1865 Albert Memorial Clock Tower, named after Queen Victoria's husband

Belfast Sights

Key to symbols

⊞ map coordinates refer to the Belfast map on page
155; sights below are highlighted in yellow on the map
✉ address or location ☎ telephone number
🕐 opening times 🍴 restaurant on site or nearby
🚌 nearest bus or tram route
🎫 admission charge: $$$ = more than £6,
$$ = £3 to £6, $ = under £3
ℹ information

Albert Memorial

The Albert Memorial Clock Tower designed
by W. J. Barre, looks loftily towards the River
Lagan on High Street and pays tribute to
Prince Albert, Queen Victoria's beloved
consort. It is affectionately known as Belfast's
"leaning tower" because it is slightly less than
straight (more than a yard off true vertical).
Unfortunately, you'll have to admire the lean
from the outside as the tower is not open
to the public.
⊞ B2

The elegant Palm House in the Botanic Gardens – a 19th-century technical marvel of iron and glass

Belfast Castle

From its perch on Cave Hill, 400 feet above sea level, Belfast Castle was built in the late 1800s as a family residence and was a gift to the city in 1934 from the Earl of Shaftesbury. Used primarily for private functions, its Scottish baronial architecture features a six-story square tower, but the Victorian arcade cellar holds shops, a bar and cellar restaurant open to the public daily. The refurbished Visitor Centre has information on Cave Hill as well as the castle itself. There are also pleasant walkways in the castle's 200-acre estate, and an adventure playground.

✚ A3 ✉ Antrim Road (2.5 miles from the city center, signposted from Antrim Road) ☎ 028 9077 6925; www.belfastcastle.co.uk ☻ Mon.–Sat. 9 a.m.–10 p.m., Sun. 9–5:30 🍴 Cellar Restaurant 💷 Free

Belfast Zoo

The Belfast Zoo, with its dramatic mountain site and marvelous views of the city, is a delight. Its gorilla and chimp houses have won animal welfare awards, and some species roam free. Don't miss the penguin and sea lion enclosures with underwater viewing. Of note, too, are the spectacled bears – this is the only zoo in the United Kingdom that keeps them.

✚ A3 ✉ Antrim Road (4 miles north of city on slopes of Cave Hill) ☎ 028 9077 6277; www.belfastzoo.co.uk ☻ Daily 10–5, Apr.–Sep.; 10–2:30, rest of year 🍴 Restaurants 💷 $$$

Belvoir Park Forest

Comprehensive information on Ireland's feathered population is readily available at the Royal Society for the Protection of Birds Visitor Centre in the pleasant woodland of Belvoir Park Forest. This is a must for dedicated bird watchers.

✚ B1 ☎ 028 9049 1264 ☻ Dawn–dusk 💷 Free

Botanic Gardens

Established in 1827, these outstanding gardens are noted for the Victorian-style 1839 Palm House glass house and its rare plants, including banana, aloe, rubber, bamboo and

Victorian facade of the Crown Liquor Saloon, decorated with splendid mosaic tiles

bird of paradise flower. In the 1889 Tropical Ravine, or Fernery, a profusion of tropical plants in a sunken glen can be viewed from the observation balcony. The outdoor gardens, first planted in 1927, feature colorful rose beds.

✚ A1 ✉ Stranmillis Road (signposted from M1/M2, Balmoral exit) ☎ 028 9031 4762 ◉ Gardens: Daily until dusk. Palm House and Tropical Ravine: Mon.–Fri. 10–12, 1–5; Sat.–Sun. 1–5, Apr.–Sep.; Mon.–Fri. 10–12, 1–4, Sat.–Sun. 1–5, rest of year ◉ Metro 7 to College Park, 8 to Queens University ◉ Free

Cave Hill Country Park

Neolithic men carved the five caves that give this popular public park on the slopes of a 1,200-foot basalt cliff its name, and the caves have provided shelter for generations that followed. From the top there are spectacular panoramic views of Belfast and the valley. Rebellion was on the minds of Wolfe Tone, Henry Joy McCracken and other United Irishmen when they met here for two days in 1795 to plot the 1798 uprising. There are more walks in the park (remember which color arrow you need to follow for your specific route) and for children there's an adventure playground.

✚ A3 ✉ 3 miles north of city, off Antrim Road.

Numerous access points; parking at Castle or Zoo ☎ 028 9077 6925 ◉ Daily dawn–dusk; center: Mon.–Sat. 9 a.m.–10 p.m., Sun. 9–5:30 ◉ Free

City Hall

This massive two-story Portland stone building crowned with a copper dome and set around a central courtyard in Donegall Square was 10 years in construction (begun in 1888). Inside is all elegance with Greek and Italian marble; the dome rises above the central staircase at the heart of the exuberant interior of rich mosaic, stained glass, marble and wood paneling. The interior is undergoing major renovation and will reopen for tours in 2009. In the meantime the grounds will remain open and outdoor events will continue.

✚ B2 ✉ Donegall Square South ☎ 028 9027 0456 ◉ No tours until renovation complete ◉ Free

Colin Glen Forest Park

It is well worth a stop at the visitor center in this 200-acre park at the foot of Black Mountain to view the audiovisual presentation and other displays before setting out on one of the several nature trails.

✚ A1 ✉ Stewartstown Road (5 miles west of the city) ☎ 028 9061 4115 ◉ Park: daily dawn–dusk; center: Mon.–Fri. 9–5, Sat. 11–3 ◉ Free

Crown Liquor Saloon

Bend an elbow at least once or go by for lunch at the Crown Liquor Saloon, which dates from 1849. It's a marvelous old Victorian pub, the Corinthian pillars flanking the entrance give way to the ultimate in casual elegance with an interior of carved woodwork, marble counters and painted ceramic tiles. Some chrome-and-mirror addicts got their hands on it a few years back and nearly modernized the character out of it, but the National Trust conservation organisation came to the rescue and it is now back to its original state. The saloon is still lit by gas lamps and to call for service you'll need to use the antique system of bell pulls. ✚ A1 ✉ 46 Great Victoria Street ☎ 028 9027 9901; www.crownbar.com 🕐 Mon.–Sat. 11:30 a.m.–midnight, Sun. 12:30–11 🍴 Restaurant

Dixon Park

Named for Sir Thomas and Lady Dixon, the beautiful rose gardens in this park have won international acclaim and are widely acknowledged to be among the world's finest. From July to September, the City of Belfast International Rose Trials are held here. In addition to more than 20,000 rose bushes, there's an interesting Japanese garden and wooded areas and shrubberies on several levels plus a play area for the youngsters. ✚ A1 ✉ Upper Malone Road ☎ Center: 028 9060 3359 🕐 Daily dawn–dusk 🍴 Restaurant 🎫 Free

First Presbyterian Church

Situated in the pedestrianized main shopping center, this 1783 church is notable for its elliptical interior with enclosed pews, each entered by a door and designed by John Wesley. Free lunchtime concerts are occasionally offered. ✚ B2 ✉ Rosemary Street

Giant's Ring

This impressive Bronze Age antiquity is within easy reach of Belfast. The huge circular structure is more than 600 feet in diameter, and the enigmatic Druid's Altar dolmen inhabits its center. Its original purpose is a matter of speculation. Prehistoric rings were commonly thought to be the home of fairies,

Ornamentation on the wall of the magnificent Grand Opera House

and consequently treated with respect, but in the 18th century they were found to make terrific race courses. The earthen bank surrounding the ring, 20 feet wide and 12 feet high, is a natural grandstand. ✚ B1 ✉ Near Edenderry village, a mile south of Shaw's Bridge, off B23 🎫 Free

Grand Opera House

Following the inclusion of a £10 million extension, the Grand Opera House remains Northern Ireland's premier venue for cultural performance. The stunning late-Victorian masterpiece includes 24 gilt elephant heads separating boxes sporting canopies, Buddhas scattered about the draperies, and lots of gold and maroon. ✚ A2 ✉ 2–4 Great Victoria Street ☎ 028 9024 1919; www.goh.co.uk 🕐 Tours by appointment 🎫 $$$

Harbour Commissioner's Office

Built in 1854, this is probably the grandest building in Belfast. Exquisite mosaic floors inlaid with marble and beautiful stained-glass windows reflect Belfast's Victorian prosperity. In the upstairs, barrel-roofed Barnet Room, maritime paintings adorn the walls and stained glass depicts the arms of colonial

partners such as Canada and Australia.
🔲 B3 ✉ Corporation Square ☎ 028 9055 4422
🕐 Tours by appointment 🚌 $$

Lagan Boat Company

Climb aboard the M.V. *Joyce Too* for a trip
along the River Lagan or a Titanic Special
that takes in the Harland & Wolff shipyards
with commentary about the fated luxury
liner. Passengers can embark or disembark
outside the Odyssey Centre. Check for sailing
times as weather can affect the trips.
🔲 C3 ✉ Departures from Donegall Quay ☎ 028 9033
0844/07718 910423 (mobile) 🕐 Lagan tours: Tue.–Thu.
12:30, 2, 3:30 Apr.–Sep., Tue.–Thu. 12:30, Mar. 2, Oct.;
no tours Nov.–Feb. Titanic tours: Fri.–Mon. 12:30, 2,
3:30 Apr.–Sep., Fri.–Mon. 12:30, 2 Mar., Oct.; Sat.–Sun.
12:30, Nov. 2–Dec.; no tours Jan.–Feb. 🚌 $$$

Lagan Valley Regional Park and Minnowburn Beeches

A walk over the 9 miles of paths along the
banks of the River Lagan from Belfast to
Lisburn takes you past old locks and lock
houses from the late 1700s, when horses
towed coal barges. If you are here in the fall,
the blazing colors of the Minnowburn
Beeches woodlands are not to be missed. You
can enjoy pleasant walks from the Beeches to
Edenderry village and the Giant's Ring.
🔲 B1 ✉ Towpath begins near Belfast Boat Club in
Stranmillis and runs upstream from Moore's Bridge,
Hillsborough Road in Lisburn. Minnowburn Beeches
are 3.5 miles south of Belfast at Shaw's Bridge on
Milton Road ☎ 028 9049 1922 🚌 Free

Linen Hall Library

Established in 1788 to "improve the mind
and excite a spirit of general enquiry," this is
the oldest library in the city. It began life as a
charitable project and is still supported by
public subscription. Among its notable
collections are books on heraldry, books by
Robert Burns, documents of local history and
an impressive array of press coverage during
the "Troubles" that began in 1969. Thomas
Russell, librarian here in 1803, was executed
for his revolutionary activities.
🔲 A2 ✉ 17 Donegall Square North ☎ 028 9032 1707
🕐 Mon.–Fri. 9:30–5:30, Sat. 9:30–1. Tours must be
arranged in advance 🍴 Café 🚌 Free

Odyssey

Belfast's big millennium project is a complex
covering 23 acres of the riverfront. It includes
a science center (called W5) with over 100
interactive exhibits, an IMAX theater, a 14-
screen multiplex cinema and huge arena, and
the Pavilion has restaurants, bars and shops.
🔲 C3 ✉ 2 Queen's Quay ☎ 028 9045 1055;
www.theodyssey.co.uk 🕐 Science center: Mon.–Sat.
10–6, Sun. noon–6. Phone for times of other attractions
🚌 $$–$$$

Queen's University and Visitor Centre

Queen's University is the hub for a cluster of
art galleries, restaurants, accommodations
and shops. The campus is a charming
mixture of little mid-Victorian row houses
(largely occupied by arts and law faculties),
complete with front gardens, and the very
formal Tudor-revival-style main building
designed by Charles Lanyon in 1849. There's
a strong emphasis on science studies, and the
full-time student body numbers about
14,000, with another 10,000 part-time
students. The visitor center features
exhibitions and memorabilia associated
with the university.
🔲 A1 ✉ University Road ☎ 028 9097 5252
🕐 Visitor centre: Mon.–Fri. 10–4 (also Sat. 10–4,
May–Sep.). Campus tours weekdays 🚌 Free

Sinclair Seamen's Church

Charles Lanyon, who designed so many
Belfast buildings, was the architect for this
unique 1857 church, whose interior is very
much like a maritime museum. Sailors must
feel right at home as they listen to sermons
delivered from a pulpit built like a ship's
prow. The nautical theme is carried over
to the organ, which has both port and
starboard lighting.
🔲 B3 ✉ Corporation Square ☎ 028 9071 5997
🕐 Wed. 2–5; Sun. services at 11 and 6

St. Anne's Cathedral

Belfast Cathedral (St. Anne's) was built
between 1899 and 1904 and has a fine
mosaic showing St. Patrick landing in Ireland
at Saul in AD 432, which you will find over
the entrance to the Chapel of the Holy Spirit.

Stormont stands proudly overlooking its sweeping drive on the outskirts of Belfast

✚ B3 ✉ Donegall Street ☎ 028 9032 8332; www.
belfastcathedral.org 🕐 Mon.–Sat. 10–4, Sun. outside
services. Services Mon.–Sat. 1, Sun. 10, 11, 3:30

St. Malachy's Church

Its striking turrets overlooking the Upper
Markets area, St. Malachy's Roman Catholic
Church opened in 1844 and boasts a fine
fan-vaulted ceiling.
✚ B1 ✉ Alfred Street ☎ 028 9032 1713 🕐 Daily
8:30–5:45

Stormont

A mile-long avenue leads up to the massive,
gleaming white building that has been, since
it opened in 1932, the seat of Northern
Ireland self-governing parliaments that come
and go as negotiations for self-rule wax and
wane with the political climate. This is where
the Good Friday Agreement of 1997 was
hammered out, and it was also the seat of the
resultant executive committee of the
Northern Ireland Assembly.

The statue standing squarely in the
middle of the avenue is of Sir Edward
Carson, who was largely responsible for
maintaining Northern Ireland's position as a
part of the United Kingdom when he led the
opposition of Irish home rule in 1912. The
building itself is not open to the public, but
the beautifully maintained grounds are open
to all daily until 7:30p.m.
✚ C2 ✉ Upper Newtownards Road 🚌 Bus 20A, 23

Ulster Folk and Transport Museum

The Ulster Folk and Transport Museum is set
on 176 acres of the beautiful parkland estate
of Cultra Manor. The open-air museum is
composed of a fascinating collection of
buildings and rural and urban shops, all
furnished in 1900s style. Many were moved
stone by stone from original locations and
rebuilt here.

The result is a microcosm of Ulster life
from the 18th to the 19th century. Traditional
Irish cottages, watermills, farms, a 1792
church, a pub, a flax-scutching mill, schools,
printer's workshops and even a small town, in
addition to many other buildings make this
enchanting place well worth a visit.
Costumed interpreters and a schedule of

Exhibits at the popular Ulster Folk and Transport Museum

craft demonstrations and other activities bring the place to life.

The Transport Museum has exhibitions of many modes of transport and includes the largest locomotive (*Old Maeve*) built in Ireland, trams, buses, cars, horse-drawn carts and all sorts of motorized machines. Always popular is the "Titanic" exhibition on the "unsinkable" liner, which was built in Belfast's shipyards and foundered after hitting an iceberg on her maiden voyage. Take in the "Flight Experience", an interactive exhibition.

In addition to the permanent exhibitions and buildings, the museum has lots of special events during the year such as horse-ploughing, music days and Halloween fun.
✚ C3
✉ Bangor Road, Cultra Manor, Holywood, Co. Down (7 miles east of Belfast on A2, the road to Bangor) ☎ 028 9042 8428 🕐 Mon.–Fri. 10–5, Sat. 10–6, Sun. 11–6, Mar.–Jun.; Mon.–Sat. 10–6, Sun. 11–6, Jul.–Sep.; Mon.–Fri. 10–4, Sat. 10–5, Sun. 11–5, rest of year (last admission one hour before closing) 🍴 Tearoom
💳 Combined ticket: $$$

Ulster Museum

In the lovely surroundings of the Botanic Gardens, the Ulster Museum has given remarkable insight into the life and history of the province. A £12 million project is underway to revitalize this important cultural institution. The museum has comprehensive collections of Irish art, history, natural sciences and archeology is the Early Ireland Gallery, which concentrates on the flora and fauna of 10,000 BC to 1500 BC.

Also of interest are the superb collections of fine and applied arts ranging from works by Turner and Gainsborough to pieces by contemporary Irish artists.
✚ A1
✉ Stranmillis Road, next to Botanic Gardens ☎ 028 9042 8428; www.ufm.org.uk 🕐 Closed for major renovation until Spring 2009. Contact the tourist information office for opening details or call the contact number 🍴 Café 🚌 69, 70 💳 Free

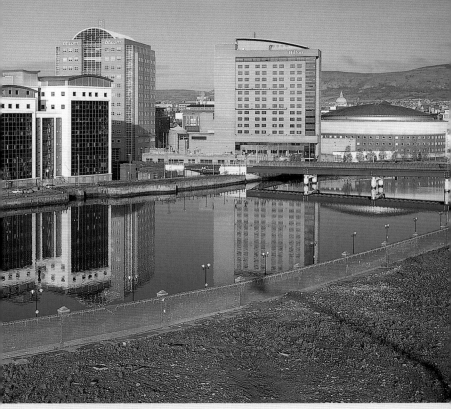

Bright new buildings now edge Belfast city waterfront

Walk: **Between Old and New**

Refer to route marked on city map on page 155.

This walk combines some of Belfast's major attractions and a portion of the exciting and ongoing rejuvenation of the city's waterfront, which is helping to make Belfast a popular European tourist destination. As you walk, notice the contrast between Belfast's distinctive Georgian, Victorian and Edwardian buildings and the newer structures along the river. Begin your tour at St. Anne's Cathedral. Allow about one-and-a-half hours.

Located on Lower Donegall Street, the imposing Hiberno-Romanesque St. Anne's is sometimes called Belfast Cathedral. Take a look at the striking mosaic inside depicting the arrival of St. Patrick on his return to Northern Ireland (see page 182).

From the cathedral, turn left and walk down Donegall Street to Waring Street, then left to reach Albert Square.
Poor old Prince Albert lists slightly to one side, due to the fine silty soil on which he stands, left by a glacier at the end of the last Ice Age (some of Belfast's substantial Victorian buildings have also fallen victim).

From the Albert Memorial, turn right to reach Donegall Quay.
The Lagan Weir, beautifully spotlighted at night, is located close to the spot where Belfast began and maintains the river level close to the high-tide mark. The small conical building at the west end of the weir

housed the former Lagan Lookout. Just near here you can take a boat tour of the shipyard's where the *Titanic* was built (see page 164).

Leaving the Lagan Boat Company jetties buy the *Big Fish* sculpture, cross the bridge and follow the signposted Riverside Walk.

Notice the huge block of art nouveau flats, quite a departure from Belfast's traditional architectural style.

At the beginning of a curve in the river, look across to the opposite bank for a view of the Waterfront Hall, the most strikingly modern resident of Belfast's riverfront. There's a bit of irony that its location is Lanyon Place, named for Sir Charles Lanyon, the architect largely responsible for the city center's Victorian buildings. A wonder of glass and metal, the badly needed concert and conference center seats 2,500 and is sometimes the venue for Belfast-born rock star Van Morrison. Made of bronze, the auditorium exterior will eventually turn green over time and reflect the dome of the City Hall.

Next-door neighbors to the Waterfront Hall, the massive Hilton hotel and huge British Telecom Call Centre offices are tall, red-brick structures that could be called Belfast's skyscrapers.

Cross the river at Albert Bridge and walk along East Bridge Street to the

intersection with Oxford Street.

One peek inside St. George's Market and it's a sure bet you'll linger to explore this covered marketplace that has been a Belfast tradition for generations. It has been renovated and revitalized. There's everything from fresh produce and fish to discount and used clothing to second-hand videos and odds-and-ends.

Exit the market and turn left on May Street and continue forwards to Donegall Square.

Built of white Portland stone in 1906, the Edwardian City Hall facade is 300 feet long, with a copper dome rising 173 feet. Equally impressive interior features are the marble grand staircase and main entrance. The city council meets here, and in its custody is the Charter of Belfast granted by King James I in 1613 (see page 162).

Cross to Donegall Square North.

If you're interested in Irish politics or any phase of Northern Ireland culture, you'll want to allow time to browse through the collections at Linen Hall Library, one of the oldest subscription libraries in the United Kingdom (see page 164).

End your tour here, or walk north to Donegall Place for shopping, or head south on Bedford Street and Dublin Road to reach the Queen's University area.

The Waterfront Hall is set in the city's commercial area, close to the river

The 19th-century Mount Stewart House surrounded by splendid gardens

Drive: **Strangford Lough**

Duration: 1 day

This is an 87-mile drive around Belfast city encompassing its strong industrial ship-building tradition. The city is rich in Victorian and Edwardian architecture, from the magnificent City Hall to the atmospheric 1849 Crown Liquor Saloon.

Take the A2, which leads east out of the city center, and follow the signposts for Bangor. After 7 miles turn left for the excellent and not-to-be-missed Ulster Folk and Transport Museum.

The Ulster Folk and Transport Museum, in the grounds of Cultra Manor, tells the story of the province's past through buildings that have been saved and meticulously reconstructed at this site. You can wander through a thatched cottage, a rectory and a terraced house, and watch demonstrations of traditional crafts. A church, schoolhouse, water-powered mills and other buildings give a vivid picture of the past. The transport section spans the history of transport, from creels used by a donkey carrying turf,

through the grand ocean-going liners built in Belfast, to ultra-modern aircraft from the Belfast firm Short Brothers and Harland. This is undoubtedly one of the best museums in Ireland (see page 165).

Turn left and follow the A2 for 4 miles. Turn right following the signpost for Newtownards, 3 miles farther.

This thriving town lies among some of the richest arable land in Ulster. St. Finnian founded Movilla Abbey in AD 540, and the Dominican priory was established by the Normans in the 13th century. The hollow, octagonal, 17th-century market cross also served as the town watch and jail. The impressive town hall was built around 1770 by the Londonderry family who also built Scrabo Tower overlooking the town.

Take the A20, following signs for Portaferry to Greyabbey.

The village derives its name from the 12th-century Cistercian abbey. North of the village is Mount Stewart, a magnificent garden where many exotic plants flourish in formal terraces and parterres or in natural settings. Lady Londonderry, the renowned hostess and leader of London society, created this unique garden after World War I. Each garden is given a name such as Tir n'an Og (the Land of Eternal Youth), the Mairi

Garden, Peace Garden, the Dodo Terrace and the Italian Garden. The lake is particularly beautiful. The house, the early home of Lord Castlereagh, contains the 22 chairs used at the Congress of Vienna and a masterpiece by the painter Stubbs ranks among its treasures. Designed as a banquet house, the Temple of the Winds is an exquisite piece of 18th-century landscape architecture.

Follow the A20 for 4 miles to Kircubbin. Take a left turn on to the B173 for 3 miles, then turn left for Portavogie.
Up to 40 boats fill the attractive harbor of Portavogie when the fleet is in. Shellfish are plentiful and hotels also serve a good variety of fresh fish. Seals regularly follow the boats into the harbor to scavenge for food before the load is auctioned on the harborside.

Take the A2 south for 2 miles. At Cloghy turn left and follow signposts to Kearney. After 1 mile, turn left for Kearney and follow signposts at two left turns for Kearney, about 3 miles.
Kearney is a tiny village in the care of the National Trust conservation organization. Once a fishing village, it now offers fine walks along its rocky shoreline.

At Temple Cowey and St. Cowey's Wells on a remote and peaceful shore are a penance stone and holy well at a site founded in the seventh century and later used for worship in penal times. Mass is still celebrated here from time to time.

Turn left and left again to follow the road around the tip of the peninsula by Barr Hall and Quintin Bay to Portaferry.
One of Ulster's most beautiful villages, Portaferry's attractive waterfront of colorful cottages, pubs and shops is framed by green meadows and wooded slopes. No fewer than five defensive tower houses guard the narrow neck of the lough. The Marine Biology Station, part of Queen's University in Belfast, is opposite the ferry jetty. Nearby is the Northern Ireland Aquarium, Exploris, beside a pleasant park, which explains the unique nature of the marine life of Strangford Lough. More than 2,000 species of marine animals thrive in the waters of Strangford, including large colonies of corals and sponges in the fast-flowing tides of the Narrows, with sea anemones and brittle stars in the quieter waters. The lough is home to large fish, including tope and skate. A regular, five-minute car-ferry service to Strangford gives stunning views of the lough.

Take the car ferry to Strangford. Boats leave at half-hour intervals.

Scrabo Hill, topped by a 135-foot tower in memory of the 3rd Marquess of Londonderry

Strangford is a small village with two bays, pretty houses and a castle. Close by is Castle Ward, set in a fine parkland with excellent views over the lough. This fascinating 18th-century mansion is an architectural hodgepodge – part pseudo-Gothic and part Classical. Restored estate buildings show the busy organization that once supported a country house including formal gardens, a Victorian laundry and theater in the stableyard, and a sawmill. One mile south on the A2 to Ardglass, a stop-over to Cloghy Rocks is a great place for viewing seals when the tide is right. Farther south is Kilclief Castle and Killard Point at the narrowest point of the neck to the lough. This lovely grassland area with low cliffs and a small beach is rich in wild flowers.

Take the A25 to Downpatrick.
Down Cathedral stands on the hill above the town, while English Street, Irish Street and Scotch Street jostle together below (see page 183). Quoile Pondage is an area of meandering freshwater wetland between wooded shores, with fine walks. Southwest is the popular Downpatrick race course.

Follow the A22 to Killyleagh.
A fairy-tale castle with towers and battlements overlooks this quiet loughside village. The Hamilton family has lived here for 300 years, and although the original castle was built by the Normans, its present appearance owes more to the 19th century. Sir Hans Sloane, the physician and naturalist whose collection formed the nucleus of the British Museum in London, was born in Killyleagh in 1660 and educated in the castle.

It is said that the famous Emigrant's Lament: "I'm sitting on the stile, Mary," written by Lady Dufferin, a guest at the castle during the Famine, was inspired by the stile at Killowen Old Churchyard.

Follow the A22 for 5 miles to Balloo crossroads. Turn right at the sign for Killinchy, and continue for 4 miles, then carry straight on to Comber. After 2.5 miles, turn right, following the sign for Nendrum Monastic Site.
A place of great tranquility, Nendrum monastic site was established on one of the many islands along Strangford's calm middle waters; it is now reached by a causeway. The site is one of the most complete examples of an early monastery, and the ruins, in three concentric rings, include the stump of a round tower, monks' cells and a church.

Return across the causeway, and after 3 miles turn right for 3 miles to join the A22 to Comber, then back to Belfast.

Mount Stewart Gardens ✉ Portaferry Road (A20 from Newtownards towards Greyabbey) ☎ 028 4278 8387; www.nationaltrust.org.uk 🕐 Gardens: Daily 10–8, May–Sep.; 10–6 in Apr. and Oct.; 10–4, rest of year 🖉 $$

Exploris Aquarium ✉ The Ropewalk, Castle Street, Portaferry ☎ 028 4272 8062; www.exploris.org.uk 🕐 Mon.–Fri. 10–6, Sat. 11–6, Sun. noon–6, Apr.–Sep.; closes at 5, rest of year 🍴 Café 🖉 $$$

Castle Ward ✉ 1.5 miles west of Strangford Village on A25 ☎ 028 4488 1204 🕐 House: Daily 1–6, Jul.–Aug.; Sat.–Sun. 1–6, Apr.–Jun. and in Sep. Grounds: Daily 10–8, May–Sep.; 10–4, rest of year 🍴 Tearoom 🖉 $$

The handsome observatory at Armagh is the oldest meteorological station in the British Isles

Regional Sights

Key to symbols

🗺 map coordinates refer to the region map on page
152; sights below are highlighted in yellow on the map
✉ address or location ☎ telephone number
🕐 opening times 🍴 restaurant on site or nearby
💷 admission charge: $$$ = more than £6, $$ = £3 to £6,
$ = under £3 ℹ️ information

Ards Peninsula

Some 23 miles of unspoiled countryside, the
Ards Peninsula lies between Strangford
Lough and the Irish Sea and runs from
Bangor to Ballyquintin Point. Only about
5 miles wide, this long finger of land is
dotted with picture-postcard villages,
windmills and ancient ring forts. A bird
sanctuary and wildlife reserve emphasize the
peninsula's natural beauty. Of the two roads
running down the peninsula, the lough road
(A20) is more scenic than the coast road
(A2). Drive out to the little 19th-century
village of Kearney for a taste of history. The
car ferry that crosses from Portaferry to
Strangford gives you a look straight out to
sea, but look quickly because the entire
crossing takes only four minutes.
🗺 C2 ✉ 10 miles east of Belfast

Armagh

Your exploration of County Armagh's
sightseeing treasures will be more meaningful
if you make St. Patrick's Trian and Land of
Lilliput your first stop. Dramatic
presentations of the Armagh Story and Least
of the Faithful provide an insightful
background for other attractions, and the
Land of Lilliput's gigantic reclining Gulliver
surrounded by Lilliputians will delight the
entire family.

Myths and legends of Queen Macha and
the Red Branch Knights surround Armagh,
but historical fact outshines them all. At first
glance, Navan Fort, a grassy 250-yard
enclosure around a large mound, gives few
clues to the fabulous kingdom that inhabited
this site. You have to use your imagination to
unfold the stories of Queen Macha's palace:
Deirdre of the Sorrows, who first met her
lover Naisi here; Cuchulain, who polished his
martial arts skills here; and the Red Branch
knights. A 120-foot wide by 40-foot high
Celtic temple once crowned its top. Navan
was the capital of the kings of Ulster from
600 BC to AD 332, and the burial in 1014 of
the high king of Ireland, Brian Ború, is
commemorated in the Church of Ireland
Cathedral of St. Patrick. Standing on the site
of a church founded in AD 445 by St. Patrick

himself, this cathedral has been altered and added to over the centuries, whereas the Roman Catholic St. Patrick's Cathedral, built between 1838 and 1873, is a light Gothic-style building with a lavish interior.

The town's excellent county museum houses outstanding collections reflecting Northern Ireland life from prehistoric times to the present in an Ionic schoolhouse that dates from 1833. In addition to an extensive library, there are maps, photographs, and paintings by Armagh-born James Sleator and George Russell.

Armagh is without doubt Northern Ireland's most interesting cathedral town (St. Patrick called it "my sweet hill"), with imposing Catholic and Protestant edifices facing each other from their respective hilltops. Red hats of every cardinal archbishop of Armagh and medallions for each of Ireland's saints can be seen in the Catholic cathedral.

The city also has many beautiful buildings and some delightful old streets – Abbey Lane, lined with quaint shops, the Cathedral Close and Castle Street, which follows the contours of an ancient ring fortress. The tree-lined Mall, once a racecourse, is now one of Ireland's finest parks and is surrounded by Armagh's best Georgian buildings including the imposing Court House, the splendid Public Library and the Royal Irish Fusiliers Museum, where a large model of the Battle of Barossa in 1811 is only one of the exhibits that tell the story of the Royal Irish Fusiliers regiment from 1793 to 1968.

In the Palace Stables Heritage Centre, costumed guides successfully re-create and bring to life the activities in the archbishop's palace in 1786. At the entrance to the house is Ireland's longest friary, now in ruins – the 13th-century 153-foot-long Franciscan friary that was founded by Archbishop O'Scanail.

A 10-minute walk from town, off the Friary Road, will bring you to the grounds of Armagh Observatory, which although not open to the public does take groups around on request. On the grounds is the Armagh Planetarium, reopened in 2006 following a major renovation. The

The elegant entrance to St. Patrick's Roman Catholic Cathedral

planetarium features Ireland's first full-dome 3D Digital Theatre.

Southeast of Armagh is Gosford Forest Park, where rare breeds of cattle and deer roam in open paddocks and there are marked nature trails and an arboretum.
➕ B2

Tourist information ✉ 40 English Street ☎ 028 3752 1800 🕐 Mon.–Sat. 9–5, Sun. 2–5 (12–5, Jun.–Aug.)

St. Patrick's Trian and Land of Lilliput ✉ 40 English Street ☎ 028 3752 1801 🕐 Mon.–Sat. 10–5, Sun. 2–5 🍴 Restaurant 🎟 $$

Armagh County Museum ✉ The Mall East ☎ 028 3752 3070 🕐 Mon.–Fri. 10–5, Sat. 10–1 and 2–5 🎟 Free

Royal Irish Fusiliers Museum ✉ Sovereign's House, The Mall East ☎ 028 3752 2911 🕐 Mon.–Fri. 10–12:30 and 1:30–4 🎟 Free

Palace Stables Heritage Centre ✉ Friary Road ☎ 028 3752 9629 🕐 Sat. 10–5, Sun. 12–5, Apr., May, Sep.; Mon.–Sat. 10–5, Sun. 12–5, Jun.–Aug. 🍴 Restaurant 🎟 $$

Armagh Friary ✉ At entrance to Palace Stables Heritage Centre 🎟 Free

Armagh Planetarium ✉ College Hill ☎ 028 3752 3689 🕐 Tue.–Fri. 1–5 (show 3p.m.); Sat. 11:30–5 (shows 12, 1, 2, 3, 4) 🎟 $$$

Gosford Forest Park ✉ Markethill, off A28 ☎ 028 3755 1277 🕐 Daily 10–dusk 🍴 Restaurant 🎟 $$

Ballycastle and the Glens of Antrim

Under the Fair Head promontory, the beautiful seaside town of Ballycastle has a wide strand to the east and the lovely Glens of Antrim stretching away inland. At the heart of the town is The Diamond (Market Square), packed with the stalls, entertainments and horse dealing of the famous Ould Lammas Fair at the end of August each year. For about a hundred years St. Patrick's Day has been celebrated with a horse show, and in June there is a festival of Irish music, dancing and games. Just outside the town are the ruins of Bonamargy Friary, founded by Rory MacQuillan around 1500 and burial place of the MacDonnell chiefs, including the notorious Sorley Boy. Amazingly, the eastern range of cloister, gatehouse and church have remained virtually intact, lacking only the roof. Beyond Fair Head is the scenic Murlough Bay, which is now in the care of the National Trust conservation organization.

Ballycastle's museum illustrates the folk and social history of the Glens of Antrim. At the harbor is a memorial to Gugliemo Marconi, who carried out the first practical test on radio signals between White Lodge, on the clifftop at Ballycastle, and Rathlin Island in 1898. You can travel by boat to Rathlin and savor the life of the 30 or more farming families who live here. The island is a mecca for divers and birdwatchers.

From the shore you can follow the B15 coastal route west to Ballintoy, then, turning right, following the signpost to Carrick-a-Rede.

The mainland clifftops are connected to the small rocky island of Carrick-a-Rede by a swinging rope bridge that is strung across a deep 60-foot-wide chasm. The water here is too treacherous to cross in any other way. If you dare, cross over the wooden planks and grip the rope handrails, but be warned, this is definitely not for the fainthearted. The bridge is put up each year by salmon fishermen who use Carrick-a-Rede, "the Rock in the Road," as a good place to net the fish in their path to the Bush and Bann rivers. The rope bridge is approached from Larry Bane, a limestone head that was once quarried. Some of the quarry workings remain at Larry Bane, the quarry access to the magnificent seascape that provides guaranteed birdwatching. You can sit in your car and spot kittiwakes, cormorants, guillemots, fulmars and razorbills, though you might need binoculars to see the puffins on Sheep Island farther out to sea.

The nine green Glens of Antrim run through mountainous terrain between Cushendun and Larne before reaching the sea. All nine have individual names and virtually all have stories to tell: Glentaisie (Taisie's glen, named for a daughter of the king of Rathlin), Glenshesk (sedgy glen), Glendun (brown glen), Glencorp (glen of the dead), Glenaan (blue glen), Glenballyeamon (Eamonn's townland glen), Glenariff (ploughman's glen), Glencloy (glen of hedges) and Glenarm (glen of the army). "The Capital of the Glens," Cushendall sits on a pleasant, sandy bay below Glenballyemon, Glenaan and Glencorp and in the curve of the Dall River. The rugged peak of Lurigethan broods over the village, while the softer Tieveragh Hill is supposed to be the capital of the fairies. Cushendall owes much to an East Indian nabob, Francis Turnley, who built the Curfew Tower in the center as a "place for the confinement of idlers and rioters."

Water of Life

Spelling apart, Irish whiskey is distinctively different from its Scottish sister. In Scotland, the malted barley is dried over an open peat fire, imparting its characteristic smoky flavor. Irish whiskey is distilled three times and dried in smoke-free kilns producing a clear, clean taste; most spirits are distilled twice. The art of distillation was introduced to Ireland by Christian missionaries around AD 600. The elixir was originally named Uisce Beatha (pronounced "Ish'ke Ba-ha", meaning water of life).

Intrepid visitors cross the Carrick-a-Rede rope bridge, 80 feet above the sea

Larne is the terminus for the shortest sea-crossing between Ireland and Britain. It also marks the start of the scenic Antrim Coast Road, constructed in the 1830s to link the remote Glens of Antrim to the rest of Ulster. To the north is Carnfunnock Park, which has a maze in the shape of Northern Ireland.

Ballycastle ✚ C3
Tourist information ✉ 7 Mary Street ☎ 028 2076 2024; fax 028 2076 2515 🕐 Fri. 9:30–7, Sat. 10–6, Sun. 2–6, Jul.–Aug.; Mon.–Fri. 9–5:30, rest of year

Ballycastle Museum ✉ 59 Castle Street ☎ 028 2076 2942 🕐 Mon.–Sat. noon–6, Jul.–Aug. (or by arrangement) 💷 Free
Bonamargy Friary ✉ A2 (half a mile east of Ballycastle) 💷 Free
Larne tourist information ✉ Narrow Gauge Road, Larne ☎ 028 2826 0088 🕐 Mon.–Fri. 9–5, Sat. 10–4
Carrick-a-Rede rope bridge ✉ Larrybane, County Antrim (5 miles northwest of Ballycastle off A2) ☎ 028 2076 9839; www.nationaltrust.org.uk 🕐 Daily 10–7, Jul. and Aug.; 10–6, Mar.–Jun. and Sep.–Oct. 💷 $

American Connection

America's military links to northern Ireland date back as early as 1778, when John Paul Jones scored America's first naval victory when he sailed the USS *Ranger* up Belfast Lough and captured the HMS *Drake* within sight of the 12th-century Carrickfergus Castle (see page 177). During those turbulent times, America's Declaration of Independence was printed by John Dunlap from Strabane, County Londonderry (who went on to found the *Philadelphia Gazette*, America's first daily newspaper). At least five of those who signed the Declaration of Independence were from Northern Ireland.

Among American presidents, Andrew Jackson's parents came from Carrickfergus; Andrew Johnson's grandfather was from Larne; Chester A. Arthur's father was born near Ballymena; Grover Cleveland's grandfather was a County Antrim merchant; William McKinley's great-great-grandfather emigrated from Conagher, near Ballymoney; and Theodore Roosevelt's maternal ancestors hailed from Larne. It is certainly an impressive list.

Plenty of other American heroes had Northern Ireland roots, including Davy Crockett, Sam Houston, Mark Twain and Neil Armstrong. The founder of the American Presbyterian Church, Francis Makemie, sailed from Northern Ireland for America in 1682, and John Hughes, first Roman Catholic archbishop of New York, emigrated in 1817.

In June 1942 American troops arrived in Northern Ireland to begin intensive training in preparation for World War II battles.

All those connections take on even more meaning at the Ulster American Folk Park at Camphill just north of Omagh, County Tyrone (see page 194). The re-created cottages and working conditions of 250,000 18th-century emigrants give a real insight into their reasons for crossing the Atlantic, and the replicas of their log cabin settlements in America kindle a new appreciation of their contribution to U.S. history. Ask at tourist information centers for the Heritage Trail brochure that lists restored ancestral homes of U.S. presidents.

American hero with Irish roots: Neil Armstrong, the first man on the moon

The lough beside Carrickfergus Castle provides a harbor for small boats

Carrickfergus

The main landmark of this small seaside town is its massive Norman castle, an impressive sight from land and sea. Dating from the late 12th and early 13th centuries, the almost perfectly preserved fortress was actually garrisoned until 1928. In 1778, Commander John Paul Jones of the fledgling American Navy stood offshore just below Carrickfergus Castle in the *Ranger* and captured the much larger British *Drake*. In 1611, a defensive stone wall was built around Carrickfergus (the only place in the North where English was spoken at the time), and more than half of the wall is still intact.

Begin your exploration of the town at the Carrickfergus Museum and Civic Centre to learn about the town's history. Starting in AD 581, maritime, military and historical stories unfold before you during the monorail ride. There is also an excellent exhibition of gas equipment and other machinery as well as an audiovisual presentation at Flame – The Gasworks Museum of Ireland. Built in 1855 to light street lamps, these are the only Victorian coal-fired gasworks in Ireland and were in service until 1964.

The ancestral home of American President Andrew Jackson was just beyond the north end of Carrickfergus' seafront promenade at Boneybefore, a site now marked by a plaque. Just a few yards away, the Andrew Jackson Centre, in a replica of a simple thatched cottage of the 1700s, gives insight into the life of his forebears before they left for America in 1765, as well as his career and that of other U.S. presidents with Ulster connections. In the grounds of the Jackson Centre, the U.S. Rangers Centre features an exhibition on the First Battalion U.S. Rangers (the U.S. Army's most decorated unit) and their strong connections with Carrickfergus in 1942. It contains photographs and other memorabilia.

✚ C2

Tourist information ✉ 11 Antrim Street ☎ 028 9335 8049 🕐 Mon.–Sat. 10–6, Sun. 1–6, Apr.–Sep.; Mon.–Sat. 10–5, Sun. 1–5, rest of year

Carrickfergus Castle ✉ Marine Highway ☎ 028 9335 1273 🕐 Mon.–Sat. 10–6, Sun. 2–6, Jun.–Sep.; Mon.–Sat. 10–4, Sun. 2–4, rest of year 🍽 Café ♿ $$

Flame – The Gasworks Museum of Ireland ✉ Irish Quarter West ☎ 028 9336 9575 🕐 Daily 10–5, Jul.–Aug.; 2–5, Apr.–Jun. and in Sep. ♿ $

Carrickfergus Museum and Civic Centre ✉ The Heritage Centre, 11 Antrim Street ☎ 028 9335 8049 🕐 Mon.–Sat. 10–6, Sun. 1–6, Apr.–Sep.; Mon.–Sat. 10–5, Sun. 1–5, rest of year ♿ Free

Andrew Jackson Centre and U.S. Rangers Centre ✉ 2 Boneybefore ☎ 028 9335 8049 🕐 Mon.–Fri. 10–1 and 2–6, Sat.–Sun. 2–6, Jun.–Sep.; Mon.–Fri. 10–1 and 2–4, Sat.–Sun. 2–4, rest of year ♿ Free

Breathtaking Atlantic views from Mussenden Temple, Downhill

The Causeway Coastline

The most distinguishing feature of the north Antrim coast is the Causeway Coast and a string of such small towns as Ballycastle, Portstewart, Larne and Portrush. Inland from Larne, Ballymena, the county town of Antrim, boasts as one of its sons Timothy Eaton, who founded Eaton's Stores in Canada.

The fantastic Giant's Causeway is much more impressive when you walk its basalt columns (there are 37,000!) than any photograph can possibly convey. How they came to be packed so tightly together that they form a sort of bridge from the shoreline out into the sea, submerge, and then surface on the Hebrides island of Staffa is a matter of conjecture. Scientists will tell you that they're the result of a massive volcanic eruption 60 million years ago, when molten lava cooled and formed into geometric shapes. But Irish legend will tell you that it was the giant, Finn MacCool (see page 199), who built the causeway between Ulster and Scotland and it was his Scottish counterpart, Finn Gall, who destroyed all but the bit you see today.

Be that as it may, you will not want to miss this mass of symmetrical basalt columns jutting out into the sea from the foot of a steep cliff. The visitor center houses a 25-minute audiovisual show telling the story of

the formation of the Causeway, together with fascinating pictoral exhibits, a tourist information office and book shop and tearooms. A minibus service from the visitor center to the foot of the cliff is a decided bonus if you don't want to walk.

Generations of imaginative guides have embroidered stories and created names for the remarkable formations – the Giant's Organ, the Giant's Harp, the Wishing Chair and Lord Antrim's Parlour. One story absolutely based on fact is of the *Girona*, a fleeing Spanish Armada galleon, wrecked in a storm one night in October 1588. A diving team retrieved a treasure hoard from the wreck in 1967, and it's now on display in the Ulster Museum in Belfast (see page 166). The wreck still lies under cliffs in Port na Spaniagh, one of a magnificent array of bays and headlands on the causeway.

Portrush, west of the Giant's Causeway, is a typical seaside resort that flourished with the rise of the railways. It has three good bays, with broad stretches of sand, ranges of dunes, rock pools, white cliffs and a busy harbor. Nearby, there could hardly be a more dramatic sight than the craggy headland crowned by the great lump of ruined 13th-century Dunluce Castle sitting on – almost overhanging – the very edge of the cliff. Back in 1639 a storm actually picked up and dumped the kitchens, the cooks and all the pots into the sea below. Silhouetted against the skyline, it was in its day the largest castle in the north.

Here also is the Dunluce Centre. It features the Finn McCool Playground, a themed and interactive game environment, and the Treasure Fortress, Motion Simulator and Turbo Tours that supply unexpected thrills. Panoramic views from the tower are spectacular and there's a shopping arcade, all of which makes for a good family day out. Portrush's indoor water center, Waterworld, is the perfect place to take a break from the rigors of travel and enjoy the fun pools. There are giant water flumes, water cannon, swings, a rope bridge and even a pirate ship.

The neat village of Bushmills close by is the home of the world's oldest legal distillery. Licensed since 1608, it's still turning out the "wine of the country" after all these centuries. There's a marvelous exhibition of its history, and a whiskey tasting nicely rounds off the one-hour guided tour through the distilling process. The water from St. Columb's Rill, or stream, is said to give the whiskey its special quality. The Bush River is rich in trout and salmon, and its fast-flowing waters not only supported the mills that gave the town its name, but they also generated electricity for the world's first hydroelectric tramway, which carried passengers to the Giant's Causeway between 1893 and 1949.

Panoramic views of the coast are nothing short of breathtaking at Downhill, which is perched on the very edge of a cliff overlooking the Atlantic. Mussenden Temple, a beautiful 18th-century rotunda modeled on Tivoli's Temple of Vesta is only part of this ruined estate that once belonged to the 4th Earl of Bristol, Frederick Hervey. The Earl was an eccentric collector and traveler who gave his name to the Bristol hotels throughout Europe. A glen walk leads from the Bishop's Gate to the Mussenden Temple. ✚ C3

Tourist information ✉ 76 Church Street, Ballymena ☎ 028 2563 8494 🕐 Mon.–Fri. 9–5:30, Sat. 10–4, Jul.–Aug.; Mon.–Fri. 9–5, Sat. 10–4, rest of year

Whiskey barrels waiting for delivery in the warehouse at Old Bushmills Distillery

Giant's Causeway Visitor Centre ✉ 44 Causeway Road, County Antrim (2 miles north of Bushmills on B146) ☎ 028 2073 1855 🕐 Daily 10–7, Jul.–Aug.; 10–5, Jun., Sep. and Oct.; 10–5, Mar.–May; 10–3, rest of year 🍴 Tearoom open Mar.–Nov. 🎟 Causeway: free; audiovisual: $; guided walk $; parking $$

Dunluce Castle ✉ On the A2, 3 miles east of Portrush ☎ 028 2073 1938 🕐 Mon.–Sat. 10–6, Sun. noon–6, Jun.–Aug.; Mon.–Sat. 10–6, Sun. 2–6, Apr.–May and in Sep.; Tue.–Sat. 10–4, Sun. 2–4, rest of year 🎟 $

Dunluce Centre ✉ 10 Sandhill Drive, Portrush ☎ 028 7082 4444; www.dunlucecentre.co.uk 🕐 Daily 10:30–6:30, Jul.–Aug.; Sat.–Sun. noon–5, rest of year 🍴 Café 🎟 $$$

Waterworld ✉ Portrush, end of Portrush harbor ☎ 028 708 2001 🕐 Mon.–Sat. 10–8, Sun. noon–8, Jul.–Aug.; Mon.–Sat. 10–6, Sun. noon–6, Jun.; Sat. 10–7, Sun. noon–7, Sep.; Sat.–Sun. noon–6, Easter–May 🍴 Café 🎟 $$$

Old Bushmills Distillery ✉ 2 Distillery Road, Bushmills ☎ 028 2073 3218; www.bushmills.com 🕐 Mon.–Sat. 9:30–5, Sun. noon–5 (last tour at 4), Apr.–Oct.; reduced tours Nov.–Feb. 🍴 Coffee shop 🎟 $$

Mussenden Temple ✉ Mussenden Road, Castlerock, County Londonderry ☎ 028 2073 1582 🕐 Daily 11–5, Jul.–Aug.; Sat.–Sun. 11–5, May–Jun. and in Sep.; grounds all year dawn to dusk; telephone for temple openings 🎟 Temple: $

Donegal

At the head of Donegal Bay, on the estuary of the River Eske, Donegal is a pleasant town with the splendid central Diamond (square) – a triangular marketplace flanked with buildings and streets radiating from each side. In the center stands a 2-foot-tall obelisk.

Historically, it was the seat of the O'Donnells and Donegal Abbey, now in ruins, which was a Franciscan friary founded by Red Hugh O'Donnell and his mother, Nuala O'Connor. *The Annals of the Four Masters* was written here in the 17th century, charting the history of Ireland up until 1616. This important chronicle is now in the National Library in Dublin. Red Hugh also built the west tower of Donegal Castle (1505) on the banks of the Eske beside the Diamond when he rebuilt an earlier castle on the site. He made this the chief O'Donnell stronghold. The rest was added by Sir Basil Brooke in 1607 and features a mammoth Jacobean fireplace, and windows and gables in the house he built around the old tower. The remains have been beautifully restored.

The Donegal Railway Heritage Centre comprises a museum and information center that recalls a now redundant scenic line known as "The Wee Donegal." The center has given a new purpose to the original Old Station House where it is housed.

Donegal is an attractive and strategic place for exploring the northwest, and is known worldwide for its shopping. Its main store, Magee's, is one of the best-known places to buy tweed, a quality fabric still produced in the town. Other crafts are showcased at the Donegal Craft Village, just outside Donegal on the Ballyshannon road, where workshops include a glass-blower, hand-weaver, jeweler, sculptor and stone carver.

On a much larger scale is the Belleek Pottery, east of Ballyshannon. Their intricate "basket weaving" has to be seen to be believed. There's a small museum (some pieces on display are more than 100 years old), and the visitor center conducts guided tours to let you see craftspeople creating, glazing and decorating the world-famous porcelain. The shop features tableware, vases, clocks, ornaments and a host of other

products – this is the place to buy a future heirloom to carry home! On the road to Ballyshannon is Murvagh Beach, a beautiful 1-mile stretch of beach backed by sand dunes and the Murvagh Forest.

The drive to Glencolumbkille (Gleann Cholm Cille) travels west of Donegal through lonely mountain country with occasional glimpses of the sea. It is a journey that goes back as far as 5,000 years through a culture that has changed little since the days of Bonnie Prince Charlie. Try to get to the picturesque little harbor town of Killybegs (west of Donegal on the R263) in the late afternoon, and go down to the pier to watch the fishing fleet come in – it's a memorable experience, hundreds of seagulls swarm and screech overhead and half the town gathers together to greet the fishermen.

Lying below Beefan Mountain, Glencolumbkille Folk Village displays the story of Irish peasant life

Modest in size, Glencolumbkille Folk Village is one of Ireland's most authentic traditionally built folk museums, with thatched cottage dwellings furnished to depict the lives of people who lived here from 1700 to the 1900s. Guided tours explain the workings of each cottage. The home of a 1720 cotter is earthen-floored, and its open hearth has no chimney; by the 1820s the cotter's home has a flagstone floor, chimney and oil-lamp lighting; the 1920 cottage is like many you'll see in today's Irish countryside. The Old National Schoolhouse from a century ago and a country pub, or *sheebeen* (where the drink on sale was often illegal poteen), complete the picture of the village.
✚ A2

Tourist information ✉ Quay Street ☎ 074 97 21148

🕐 Mon.–Sat. 9–6, Sun. 10–4, Jul.–Aug.; Mon.–Sat. 10–5, rest of year

Donegal Castle ✉ Donegal (located beside the River Eske) ☎ 074 97 22405; fax 074 97 22405 🕐 Daily 10–5:15, mid-Mar. to Oct.; Thu.–Mon. 9:30–4:30 (last admission 3:45), Nov. to mid-Mar. 🎟 $$

Donegal Railway Heritage Centre ✉ Tyrconnell Street ☎ 074 972 2655 🕐 Daily 9–5 🎟 Free

Belleek Pottery ✉ Belleek, Co. Fermanagh (just across the Donegal border) ☎ 028 6865 9300; www.belleek.ie 🕐 Mon.–Fri. 9–6, Sat. 10–6, Sun. noon–6, Mar.–Oct.; Mon.–Fri. 9–5:30, Sat. 10–5:30, Nov.–Dec.; Mon.–Fri. 9–5:30, rest of year (times can vary, telephone to check) 🍴 Restaurant 🎟 $$

Glencolumbkille Folk Village ✉ Glencolumbkille Co. Donegal (on outskirts of village) ☎ 074 97 30017; fax 074 97 30334 🕐 Daily 10–6, Easter–Sep. 30; Mon.–Fri. 10–6 in Oct. 🍴 Tearoom 🎟 $$

St. Patrick's birthplace is uncertain, but it was probably Scotland or Wales. Son of a Roman centurion, he was taken into slavery while still a young boy. After six years of tending sheep on Slemish mountain in County Antrim, he escaped and studied for several years with Martin of Tours in Gaul before fulfilling his deep wish to bring the message of Christianity to Celtic Ireland.

Legend says that his arrival in County Down was quite by accident – his destination was the Antrim coast farther north, but Strangford Lough's strong tidal currents drew his boat through the narrows and he was deposited where the River Slaney flows into the lough (the Slaney is now a stream near Ringbane townland, north of the village of Saul).

Undaunted, he quickly converted Dichu, a local chieftan, who gave Patrick a barn in which to hold services. For the next 30 years, he traveled the length and breadth of Ireland preaching the gospel to Celtic chieftains and peasants while generating hundreds of legends – there are many "St. Patrick slept here" stories in Ireland. At the end of his life, he returned to his abbey at Saul, northeast of Downpatrick, the place his Irish ministry began, and where he died in AD 461.

A round tower adjoining the chancel of a Celtic-revival church of Saul marks the place where St. Patrick preached his first sermon to the Irish. He was reputedly buried in Down cathedral graveyard (see page 183), where pilgrims bring daffodils each St. Patrick's Day (March 17).

Ireland's patron saint

In St. Patrick's Footsteps

County Down, especially in the Downpatrick area, is strewn with reminders of St. Patrick. Perhaps the best introduction to his history is the excellent St. Patrick Centre close to Down County Museum, next door to Down cathedral, where his life story is recounted in his own words. In the cathedral graveyard, pause by the grave that is said to be his and you'll find an overwhelming sense of reverence that will dispel any importance you may have placed on whether or not the saint's remains actually lie there.

He is also linked with nearby Struell Wells, which is said to have healing properties. Fed by an underground spring, it continues to draw those afflicted with eye ailments and other infirmities to collect their waters in hope of a cure. Near the site there are ruins of an 18th-century church and bath houses for bathing in the holy waters.

As you travel around County Down, it may come as a surprise to learn just how many places have associations of one sort or another with St. Patrick, some marked with historical plaques, others recorded only in the verbal history of a locality. Visit Saul, a place that meant so much to him during his lifetime, and you may discover that the very earth itself seems to be imbued with his spirit even today.

Saul ✉ About halfway between Downpatrick and Strangford on A25

Struell Wells ✉ 1.5 miles east of Downpatrick off the B1

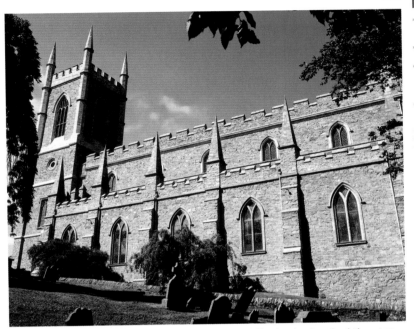

Downpatrick's Church of Ireland cathedral contains traces of earlier churches from the sixth century

Downpatrick

Radiating from the center of Downpatrick are three streets – English Street, Irish Street and Scotch Street – which recall the Elizabethan system of dividing settlements by nationality. Fine Georgian and Victorian buildings line these streets, notably the High Victorian Gothic Assembly Rooms, with a large clock tower and an arcaded first floor, the Regency-style Judge's House, the Court House of 1834, and Southwell Charity Schools and Almshouses, about 100 years older. Northwest of the town are the ruins of the Cistercian Inch Abbey, founded in the late 1180s by John de Courcy on a strategic island in the Quoile Marshes within sight of the Hill of Down. Now reached by a causeway, the monastic ruins include an interesting pointed triple window.

Downpatrick, as its name suggests, has links with Ireland's patron saint (see opposite). The present Down cathedral is a reconstruction of its 13th- and 16th-century predecessors, and a large stone in the churchyard purports to mark St. Patrick's grave (it's the one under a gigantic weeping

willow tree). The gravestone is actually a granite monolith placed on the holy spot in 1901 to protect it from pilgrims who persisted in taking away scoops of earth from the grave. It is said that the bones of SS. Columbanus and Bridgit were transferred here in the 12th century.

St. Patrick's first stone church is thought to have been erected on the historic Mound of Down site that held a Bronze Age fortification. The St. Patrick Centre, an interpretative exhibition center close to the Down County Museum premises, explores the legacy of the good saint and the work of Irish missionaries in the Dark Ages.

Other attractions of the town include the Railway Museum with working engines and steam locomotives, and where on July and August Sunday afternoons the steam locomotive *Guinness* runs trips over a restored half-mile section of the Belfast–Newcastle main line railway to the grave of a Viking king, Magnus Barefoot.

Downpatrick is popular for its access to Strangford Lough (see drive page 169), a beautiful inlet of the sea separating the

Ards Peninsula (see page 172) and the rest of County Down. Dotted with numerous islands formed by submerged drumlins, it was named Strang Fiord (Violent Inlet) by the Vikings because of the tidal surges up and down the Narrows between the lake and the open sea. The lough extends for about 12 miles to the north and measures up to 5 miles wide. It's a serene landscape with gleaming white farmhouses, and several nature reserves, including Delamont Country Park, which has Ireland's longest miniature railway. Across the lough is Portaferry Castle, a 16th-century tower house, now just a ruin, and one of a cluster of strongholds built at strategic points on the lake.

➕ C2

Tourist information ✉ 53a Market Street ☎ 028 4461 2233 🕐 Mon.–Fri. 9–6, Sat. 9:30–6, Sun. 2–6, Jul.–Aug.; Mon.–Fri. 9–5, Sat. 9:30–5, rest of year

Downpatrick Cathedral ✉ The Mall, English Street ☎ 028 4461 4922; www.downcathedral.org 🕐 Mon.–Sat. 9:30–4:30, Sun. 2–4:30 💷 Donations

Down County Museum ✉ English Street ☎ 028 4461 5218; www.downcountymuseum.com 🕐 Mon.–Fri. 10–5, Sat.–Sun. 1–5 🍴 Café 💷 Free

St. Patrick Centre ✉ 53A Market Street ☎ 028 4461 9000; www.saintpatrickcentre.com 🕐 Mon.–Sat. 9:30–6, Sun. 10–6, Jun.–Aug.; Mon.–Sat. 9–5:30, Sun. 1–5:30, Apr.–May and in Sep.; Mon.–Sat. 10–5, rest of year 💷 $$

Downpatrick Railway Museum ✉ Railway Station, Market Street ☎ 028 4461 5779; www.downrail.co.uk /steam 🕐 Call for ride schedules and fares

Inch Abbey ✉ Northwest of Downpatrick, off A7 ☎ 028 9054 6552 🕐 Free access all year 💷 Free

Portaferry Castle ✉ Castle Street, Portaferry ☎ 028 9054 3083 🕐 Closed for renovation until 2007 💷 Free

Delamont Country Park ✉ Downpatrick (on A22, 3 miles north of Downpatrick) ☎ 028 4482 8333; www.delamontcountrypark.com 🕐 Daily 9–dusk 🍴 Tearoom and restaurant 💷 Car $$

Dungannon

The county town of Tyrone, Dungannon is a large, attractive place, built on several hills. It occupies the site of the ancient seat of the O'Neill chieftains, and there are remains of O'Neill Castle, an 18th-century house on the site of 16th-century fortifications. Dungannon prospered on the linen industry,

and this and other town history can be explored in the Donaghmore Heritage Centre.

There's a 200-year tradition behind the fine crystal produced at Killybrackey's Tyrone Crystal factory. Visitors can follow the process from the time the glass is blown until the finished product is engraved.

The town has many fine buildings, including the former Northern Bank building in Market Square, Dungannon Royal School, founded by Charles I in 1628, and the elaborately designed police station in Market Square, which has been known as the "Khyber Pass" since its plans were mistaken for a fortress in India by a clerk in Dublin.

West of Dungannon is the ancestral home of Ulysses S. Grant, victorious Civil War general and 18th U.S. president (1869–77). The maternal great-grandfather of Grant left this two-room farm cottage in 1738 and settled in Pennsylvania. The mud-floor cottage has been restored, and its period furnishings include a settle bed and dresser.

East of Dungannon is Peatlands Park. Peat has been vital in the Irish home for centuries and this park in the southwest corner of the Lough Neagh basin is the place to learn the fascinating 10,000-year history of the peat bogs. Wooded drumlins (rounded hills) break through the surface, and small lakes have been formed in boglands that have been cut over. The rides into the bog on the narrow-gauge railroad uses a locomotive that once transported the peat.

➕ B2

Tourist information ✉ Kilmaddy Centre, 190 Ballygawley Road ☎ 028 8776 7259 🕐 Mon.–Thu. 9–6, Fri. 9–7, Sat.–Sun. 9–5, Jul.–Aug.; Mon.–Fri. 9–5, Sat.–Sun. 10–4, rest of year

Tyrone Crystal ✉ Coalisland Road, Killybrackey (2 miles east of Dungannon) ☎ 028 8772 5335; www.tyronecrystal.com 🕐 Mon.–Sat. 9–5. Tours Mon.–Fri. 11, noon and 2 🍴 Restaurant 💷 $$

U.S. Grant Ancestral Homestead
✉ Dergina, Ballygawley (off A4, 13 miles west of Dungannon) ☎ 028 8555 7133 🕐 Daily 9–5 💷 Free

Peatlands Park ✉ 7 miles east of Dungannon, exit 13 from M1 ☎ 028 3885 1102 🕐 Park: daily 9–9, Easter–Sep. 30; 9–dusk, rest of year; center: daily noon–5, Jun.–Aug.; Sat.–Sun. noon–5, Easter–Sep. 30 💷 $

Enniskillen and Lough Erne

This appealing little town owes much of its attractiveness to its setting on an island where the two sections of Lough Erne constrict to their narrowest point. Overlooking the lough is Enniskillen Castle, a magnificent 15th-century stone fortress sporting a unique two-turret water gate. Down in the vault, lifesize figures depict castle life. Surrounded by great stone barracks, the keep now houses the Museum of the Royal Inniskillin Fusiliers, which features battle trophies of the Dragoons and Fusiliers from the Napoleonic Wars, arms and a host of colorful uniforms.

The county museum features exhibits on the history, wildlife and landscape of this area. Beautiful delicate handmade lace for which Ulster is renowned is attractively displayed in the Sheelin Lace Museum, with some items dating from 1850 to 1900.

The River Erne and its Upper and Lower Loughs are linked to the Shannon river as part of a 500-mile leisure waterway. Video presentations at the Explore Erne Exhibition explain how the lough was formed, its part in the most extensive inland waterway in western Europe, and the effects its history and customs have had on the people who live and work on its shores. The river and the loughs are dotted with 154 intriguing and historical islands, many with ancient monastic ruins (see drive page 186). In summer, two-hour waterbus cruises ply the Lower Lough, departing Enniskillen Round O pier and calling at Devenish Island. Cruising trips of several days are popular – ask at the tourist office.

You can take the 7-mile drive through Lough Navar Forest for a marvelous panoramic view of Lower Lough Erne. Or follow marked trails to viewpoints, the best (and steepest walk) leads to a view across the lough to Donegal and Sligo. Stay alert, whether you're walking or driving, and you might be lucky enough to see one of the red deer or wild goats that roam the forest.

⊞ B2 and A2

Tourist information ✉ Wellington Road ☎ 028 6632 3110 🕐 Daily 9–7, Jul.–Aug.; Sat. 10–6, Sun. 11–5, Easter–Sep. 30; Sat.–Sun. 10–2 in Oct.

Enniskillen Castle ✉ Castle Barracks ☎ 028 6632 5000 🕐 Sat.–Mon. 2–5, Tue.–Fri. 10–5, Jul.–Aug.; Mon. 2–5, Tue.–Fri. 10–5, Sat. 2–5, May–Jun. and Sep.; Mon. 2–5, Tue.–Fri. 10–5, rest of year 🖐 $

Sheelin Lace Museum ✉ Bellanaleck (5 miles south of Enniskillen on A509) ☎ 028 6634 8052; www.irishlacemuseum.com 🕐 Mon.– Sat. 10–1 and 2–6, Mar.–Oct.; by appointment rest of year 🖐 $

Explore Erne Exhibition ✉ Erne Gateway Centre, Corry, Belleek ☎ 028 6865 8866 🕐 Daily 11–5, Jul.–Sep. (last admission at 4:30) 🖐 $

Lough Erne Cruises ☎ 028 6632 2882 🕐 Call for sailing schedules and fares

Lough Navar Forest ✉ 5 miles northwest of Derrygonnelly, signposted off A46 🕐 Daily 10–dusk 🖐 Car $$

Enniskillen Castle reflected in Lough Erne

Drive: **Fermanagh Lakeland**

Duration: 1 day

This 84-mile drive explores the major monastic sites in Ulster, the awesome Marble Arch Cave and a magical boat ride through 300 million years of history.

Start this drive at the tourist center in Enniskillen. Take the A32 toward Omagh for 2 miles until you reach the signpost for the ferries to Devenish. Take a ferry from Trory to get to Devenish Island.
The sixth-century Augustinian abbey founded by St. Molaise is a noteworthy monastic ruin. There is also a 12th-century round tower that has survived the centuries in perfect condition and is regarded as one of the finest in Ireland. Beautifully proportioned with finely cut stones and precise lines is the intricately carved 15th-century high cross in the graveyard. The small museum focuses on the monastic history of the island. The great treasure of Devenish, the book shrine of Molaise, a masterpiece of early Christian art, is kept at the National Museum in Dublin.
Take the B82 for 7 miles for Castle Archdale and Kesh.

In the old estate of the Archdale family is an arboretum, butterfly park and farm with rare breeds. The ruins of the old castle, burned in the Williamite wars of 1689, can be seen in the forest. Castle Archdale is one of the busiest places around Lough Erne. The focus is the marina, where concrete jetties and slipways, built for flying boats taking off for the Battle of the Atlantic in 1941, have been turned to more peaceful use. Here you can hire a boat with a gillie (a fishing guide).
It is possible to reach White Island from here to see the enigmatic carved stones that for centuries have puzzled experts. In the 12th-century church, they seem to represent biblical figures, with the exception of Sheil-na-gig, a female fertility figure, a strange meeting of Celtic pagan art and Christianity.
Turn left onto the B82. After 2 miles, turn left for Kesh via the scenic route for 4 miles. At Kesh turn left for Belleek, onto the A35, then after 1 mile turn on to the A47 and drive for 8 miles to Boa Island (pronounced "Bo").
Two bridges connect Boa Island to the mainland. Just before the bridge at the west end is a track on the left to Caldragh graveyard, where there are two pagan idols in stone. One is called a Janus figure because it is double-faced and could be 2,000 years old; the other, a small, hunched figure, was moved here from Lusty Beg Island. Long

The carved stone figure of Janus in Caldragh churchyard

before Christianity began to populate the islands of Lough Erne, the Celts recognized their mystical qualities. Boa Island, with its echoes of pre-Christian Ireland, is said to be named after Badhbh, the Irish goddess of war.

Continue on the A47 for 5 miles to Castle Caldwell.

The Fiddler's Stone at the entrance to Castle Caldwell is in memory of the fiddler Dennis McCabe, who fell out of Sir James Caldwell's family barge in August 1770 and was drowned. The obituary ends: "On firm land only exercise your skill that you may play and safely drink your fill." The castle, now in ruins, had the reputation of enjoying one of the most beautiful locations of all Irish houses. The fine views are still the same, across water rich in wildlife, with bird hides that allow an opportunity to catch sight of many ducks, geese and grebes.

Continue on the A47 to Belleek (see page 180). Take the A46 for Enniskillen. After 13 miles turn right on the Slavin scenic route. Rejoin the A46 and after 6 miles, turn right and follow signs to Monea.

The ruins of this superb plantation castle (pronounced "Mon-ay"), built in 1618, sit at the end of a long avenue of beech trees. Its builder, Malcolm Hamilton, became Archbishop of Cashel. Surrounded by bog and overlooking a lake, the castle has an impressive entrance, twin circular towers with square turrets and interesting Scottish-type corbels. Occupants came and went until

The ruined tower of a 13th-century priory on Devenish Island

1750, when a fire made it uninhabitable and it was abandoned. There are still remnants of the old wall that surrounded the castle, and an ancient crannóg, or artificial island dwelling, can be seen in front of Monea.

Turn left leaving Monea, then left for Enniskillen. Turn right, following signs to Boho for 5 miles, then right again for Belcoo.

Belcoo sits neatly between the two Lough Macneans, surrounded by mountains and adjacent to its neighboring village, Blacklion. The two loughs are large and very beautiful.

To the south of Lower Lough Macnean is the limestone cliff of Hanging Rock, and by the road is the Salt Man, a great lump of limestone, which, it is said, fell off the cliff and killed a man pulling a load of salt. Just north of Belcoo is the Holywell, traditionally visited by pilgrims in search of the curative powers of St. Patrick's Well.

From Belcoo, cross the border into the Republic and Blacklion for a very short distance, then cross back into Northern Ireland, taking the road along the south shore of Lower Lough Macnean. Turn right along Marlbank Scenic Loop and drive for 3 miles to Marble Arch.

The highlight of Fermanagh is one of the most awesome sights in all of Europe. The impressive great houses. A three-story 18th-century mansion, with pavilions connected to the house by open, arched walkways, the interior is especially notable for its fine rococo plasterwork. The mountainous woodland setting is as dramatic as the house, and is now Florence Court Forest Park, with a landscaped "pleasure" garden as well as the original Irish yew, from which cuttings were first taken to propagate the species, and oaks that were planted some 200 years ago.

From Florence Court, turn right. After a mile turn left on the A32, then after 2 miles turn right for Bellanaleck.
A base for cruising, Bellanaleck gives a glimpse of the winding ways of Upper Lough Erne, as its waters thread through 57 islands between Enniskillen and Galloon Bridge to the southeast. Here are hidden remote treasures such as ruins of Castle Balfour and the 1,350-acre estate at Crom, a conservation area rich in history and rare wildlife.

Return to Enniskillen via the A509.

Devenish Island ✉ 1.5 miles north of Enniskillen, embark at Trory Point, down a lane to the lough shore from the junction of A32 and B82 🕐 Tue.–Sat. 10–6, Sun. 2–6, Apr.–Sep. 💲$, includes ferry crossing and admission to round tower and museum

Castle Archdale Country Park ✉ 3 miles south of Kesh on B82 ☎ 028 6862 1588 🕐 Park: daily 9–dusk; center: Tue.–Sun. 11–7, Jul.–Aug.; Sat.–Sun. noon–6, Easter–Jun. 30; visits by request at other times 💲Free

Marble Arch Caves and Marble Arch Forest
✉ Caves: Marbank Scenic Loop Road, Florence Court (off A4/A32, 12 miles southwest of Eniskillen); forest: near Marble Arch Caves, entrance off main Florence Court–Blacklion road ☎ 028 6634 8855 🕐 Daily 10–5, Jul.–Aug.; 10–4.30, Mar.–Jun. and in Sep. 🍴 Café 💲$$$

Florence Court and Florence Court Forest Park
✉ 8 miles southwest of Enniskillen via A4 and A32 ☎ 028 6634 8249; www.nationaltrust.org.uk 🕐 House: Daily noon–6, Jul.–Aug.; Wed.–Mon. 1–6 in Jun.; Sat.–Sun. 1–6, mid-Mar. through May 30 and in Sep. Park: Daily 10–8, Apr.–Oct.; 10–4, rest of year 🍴 Restaurant 💲$$

Crom Estate ✉ 3 miles west of Newtownbutler off A34 ☎ 028 6773 8118 🕐 Center: daily 10–6, May–Sep.; Sat.–Sun. 10–6, mid-Mar. through Jun. 30 and in Sep. 🍴 Tearoom 💲$$ (car or boat $$)

mysterious beauty of Marble Arch Cave is enhanced by a ride on a quiet, flat-bottom boat through still, dark waters. More than 300 million years of history are here: the boat travels through a spectacular underground world of rivers, waterfalls, lakes, lofty chambers and winding passages with superb stalagmites and stalactites. It's chilly down there, so take a sweater, plus good walking shoes. Nearby Marble Arch Forest, laced with nature trails, includes a walk along the Claddagh Glen and a beautiful waterfall.

Turn left, then right and drive for 4 miles to Florence Court.
Home of the Enniskillen family, Florence Court is one of Northern Ireland's most

Climb to the summit of Mount Errigal, Donegal's highest peak – tough, but rewarding

Letterkenny

Overlooking the River Swilly, which is said to be named after a 400-eyed monster, Suileach, killed by St. Columcille, is the cathedral town and commercial center of north Donegal. Letterkenny claims to have the longest main street in the country, which Letterkenny is overlooked by the Cathedral of St. Eunan. This turn-of-the-20th-century cathedral has a lofty spire, one of the tallest in the country, and stands on Sentry Hill, where secret Masses were held during penal times. Letterkenny is also the home of the Donegal County Museum which, housed in a section of what was the local workhouse back in sadder times, displays artifacts from the prehistoric to the early medieval periods in addition to the folklife of the county and the story of Donegal railways. Temporary exhibitions cover a wide range of subjects.

If you are using Letterkenny as a base for the countryside of north County Donegal, don't miss the splendors of Atlantic Highlands, a landscape of jagged, cliff-filled coastline, rocky mountain pastures and breathtaking mountain passes. Mount Errigal (An Earagait), Donegal's highest at 2,466 feet, is an almost straight climb up to the summit that overlooks spectacular views.

Nearby in Dunlewy (Dun Lúiche), there is something for all the family at Ionad Cois Locha, a charming cottage center beside Dunlewy Lake. There are demonstrations of carding, spinning and weaving of wool, tours, storytelling and boat trips on the lake.

At some point in your Donegal rambles, take in the deeply wooded reaches of Glenveagh National Park. Set between the Derryveagh (Sléibhte Dhoire Bheatha) and Glendowan (Gleann Domhairn) mountain ranges, the park covers 25,000 acres of wilderness, set like a jewel on the edge of Lough Veagh. At the main entrance near Churchill Village, the Regency-style Glebe Gallery houses the collection of the noteworthy painter Derek Hill, who died in 2000, and includes works by Picasso, Bonnard and Kokoshka, together with works by Irish and Italian artists.

➕ B3

Tourist information ✉ Derry Road, Letterkenny ☎ 074 91 21160 🕐 Daily 9–5, Jul.–Aug.; Mon.–Sat. 9–5, Jun.; Mon.–Fri. 9–5, rest of year

Donegal County Museum ✉ High Road (turn right at Courthouse in town center) ☎ 074 91 24613; fax 074 91 26522 🕐 Mon.–Fri. 10–4:30, Sat. 1–4:30 🎟 Free

Glebe Gallery and Glenveagh National Park and Castle ✉ Churchill, about 18 miles northwest of Letterkenny on the Churchill road (R251) ☎ Park: 074 913 7090; gallery: 074 91 37071 🕐 Park and castle: daily 10–6:30, mid-Mar. to Nov.; gallery: Sat.–Thu. 11–6:30, Easter and mid-May to Sep. 🍴 Restaurant and tearoom in castle 🎟 Park: free; castle $$; gallery $

Ionad Cois Locha (Lakeside Centre) ✉ Dunlewy. From Letterkenny take N56 and turn left at Termon on to R251 ☎ 074 91 31699; fax 074 95 31698 🕐 Mon.–Sat. 10:30–6, Sun. 11–6, mid-Mar. to early Nov. 🍴 Tearoom, restaurant 🎟 Cottage tour: $$; boat ride: $$; combination ticket: $$$

Londonderry

Londonderry is widely known by its original name of Derry, especially by its mostly Catholic population. Derry's notorious Bogside district has seen much unrest, for it is here that Catholic and Protestant factionalism is most sharply polarized. Catholics, stranded on the Republic's border, suffered much discrimination during the time of Protestant control. However, for all its political ill-feelings, Derry is a fascinating city, retaining intact the 17th-century walls that played a significant role in its history.

The walls are about a mile in circumference and a walk around them is recommended. They are the only unbroken city walls in the British Isles, and this was the last city in Europe to build protective wall fortifications. The walls measure 20 to 25 feet high and 14 to 30 feet thick, with seven gates. The old, walled section of modern-day Londonderry is west of the River Foyle, with ancient winding lanes and rows of charming Georgian and Victorian buildings. In the northeastern walls, Shipquay Gate is only two blocks from the river, and the historic old Guildhall with its turrets and tower clock is midway between river quays and this gate.

Most of what you'll want to see will be within a short walk of these points. Walk them on your own, or join a guided tour from the tourist information center.

Derry's St. Columb's Cathedral was built in the mid-1600s. It's a splendid neo-Gothic structure, but much of what you'll see today has been added since. One of its most important features is the memorial window showing the relief of the siege in 1689.

Learn more about Derry's history at the Tower Museum. Exhibitions and audiovisuals are presented in an exemplary manner and portray the dark ages of the "Troubles." An "Armada Shipwreck" exhibition tells the story of *La Trinidad Valencera*, one of the largest ships of the Spanish Armada. The Tower was built by Paddy O'Doherty as an act of faith of better times to come.

A small cottage in Ballyarnet (2 miles from the center of Londonderry) is dedicated to the memory of Amelia Earhart, the first woman to fly solo across the Atlantic. She landed in an adjacent field in May 1932, and there's a commemorative sculpture at the landing site. The cottage holds exhibitions centered around the famous American aviatrix and is set in beautiful grounds.

Londonderry's *Peace* statue symbolizes hope for a land where politics and religion divide

✚ B3 (regional map on page 152)

Tourist information ✚ B2 ✉ 44 Foyle Street ☎ 028 7126 7284 ⏰ Mon.–Fri. 9–7, Sat. 10–6, Sun. 10–5, Jul.–Sep.; Mon.–Fri. 9–5, Sat. 10–5, mid-Mar. through Jun. 30 and Oct.; Mon.–Fri. 9–5, rest of year

City Walls ✚ B2 ✉ Tours: 44 Foyle Street ☎ 028 7126 7284 ⏰ Tours: contact tourist information for details of times 🚶 $$

St. Columb's Cathedral ✚ B1 ✉ London Street (near Bishop's Gate) ☎ 028 7126 7313 ⏰ Mon.–Sat. 9–5, Apr.–Sep.; 9–1 and 2–4, rest of year 🚶 $

Tower Museum ✚ B2 ✉ Union Hall Place ☎ 028 7137 2411 ⏰ Mon.–Sat. 10–5, Sun. 11–3, Jul.–Aug.; Mon.–Sat. 10–5, Sep.; Tue.–Sat. 10–5, rest of year 🚶 $$

Earhart Centre ✚ Off the map ✉ Ballyarnet Country Park, 1.5 miles beyond Foyle Bridge, off B194 ☎ 028 7135 4040 ⏰ Mon.–Thu. 10–4, Fri 10–1, Jul.–Aug.; by appointment, rest of year 🚶 Free

Mountains of Mourne

The Mourne Heritage Trust at Newcastle provides lots of information and guided walks. One of the nature trails follows the "Brandy Pad," a notorious smugglers' route that links Hilltown, notable for its many pubs, with the coast south of Newcastle.

There is more woodland in the Tollymore and Castlewellan forest parks. Castlewellan is an outstanding feature with a 3-mile trail around the lake that features sculptures created from the park's natural materials. There are also gardens and the Peace Maze, tropical birds and the world's longest and largest hedge. To the south the stone-walled countryside is evocatively named Silent Valley.

Slieve Donard, at 2,800 feet, is the highest mountain, and clothing its slopes is the Donard Forest Park. It's a gorgeous 8-mile drive up to and around the thickly wooded Slieve Gullion Forest Park. Walkers who follow the mountaintop trail will be rewarded by views of the Ring of Gullion and both the Mourne and Cooley mountains. Two dams form the Silent Valley and Ben Crom reservoirs, which supply 30 million gallons of water daily to County Down and Belfast. This is worth a visit just for the scenery, which includes lovely parkland before the dams. During July and August, a shuttle bus runs from the information center to the top of nearby Ben Crom.

Eastern coastal resorts of Dundrum, Annalong and Kilkeel provide alternative bases to Newcastle. Dundrum Castle, built by John de Courcy about 1177, is one of Northern Ireland's finest Norman castles. From its hilltop perch, the castle overlooks Dundrum Bay, with splendid views of the sea and the Mourne mountains. Bird-watchers should visit Murlough Nature Reserve where sea birds and a wide variety of botanical specimens flourish in an outstanding habitat of woodland and heath surrounded by the estuary and the sea. You can opt for organized guided walks or follow a self-guiding marked trail.

The wild, steep granite hills of the Mountains of Mourne present an unforgettable aspect when seen across Carlingford Lough from the Republic. One of several fortifications guarding the entrance to the lough is Greencastle, and it has not had an easy time over the centuries. It was besieged by Edward the Bruce in 1316, sacked twice in the 14th century, later garrisoned for Elizabeth I, fell to Cromwell in 1652 and then fell into disuse. In today's more peaceful climate, the castle offers terrific views of the lough and the mountains.

There are a number of literary associations in this area too. Before moving to Yorkshire, Patrick Brontë, father of the Brontë novelist sisters, taught at Drumballyroney school and preached in the local church; both structures have been preserved. Brontë was born in 1777 at Emdale, and the 8-mile Brontë Homeland Drive starts from this point.

If you are visiting the Mountains of Mourne, cross over into Inniskeen, in the next-door county of Monaghan, to the birthplace in 1904, of Patrick Kavanagh, one of Ireland's greatest poets, who was often inspired by its rich heritage of legends and myths, as well as the physical demands the stony land made on rural life in the county. The old parish church that was frequented by Kavanagh, is now the Patrick Kavanagh Centre, with displays on local history, Kavanagh memorabilia, an audiovisual theater and research library. Paintings depict the epic poem *The Great Hunger*.

➕ C2

Mourne Heritage Trust ✉ 87 Central Promenade,

Annalong's deep-water harbor sits beneath the Mountains of Mourne

Newcastle, Co Down ☎ 028 4372 4059; www.mournelive.com ◷ Mon.–Fri. 9–5 ✋ Free

Castlewellan Forest Park ✉ Main Street, Castlewellan ☎ 028 4377 8664 ◷ Daily 10–dusk ✋ $; parking $$

Slieve Gullion Forest Park ✉ 5 miles southwest of Newry on B30 ☎ 028 3755 1277 ◷ Daily 10–dusk, Easter–Sep. 🍴 Café ✋ Car: $$

Silent Valley Mountain Park ✉ Head Road, Annalong, Co. Down ☎ 028 4176 4753 ◷ Daily 10–6:30, Apr.–Sep.; 10–4, rest of year 🍴 Restaurant ✋ Parking $$

Dundrum Castle ✉ 5 miles north of Newcastle, Co. Down ☎ 028 9054 6518 ◷ Tue.–Sat. 9–6, Sun. 1–6, Apr.–Sep.; Sat. 10–4, Sun. 2–4, rest of year ✋ Free

Murlough Nature Reserve ✉ 2 miles south of Dundrum on A24, Co. Down ☎ 028 4375 1467 ◷ Reserve always open; center: daily 10–6 (weather permitting), Jun. to mid-Sep.; Sat.–Sun. 10–6, mid-Mar.–May ✋ Parking $

Greencastle ✉ Kilkeel, Co. Down ☎ 028 9054 3037 ◷ Tue. and Fri.–Sat. 2–6, Wed. and Thu. 10–1, Sun. 2–6, Jul.–Aug. ✋ Free

Brontë Homeland Interpretative Centre ✉ Drumballyroney, Rathfriland, Co. Down ☎ 028 4062 3322 ◷ Fri.–Sun noon–4:30, Apr.–Sep.; by appointment rest of year ✋ $$

Patrick Kavanagh Rural and Resource Centre ✉ Innishkeen, Co. Monaghan ☎ 042 937 8560 ◷ Tue.–Sun. 11–4:30, Dec.–May; by appointment, rest of year ✋ $$

Omagh

Omagh has long been an important center for the extensive agricultural area which surrounds it. High Street is the undisputed heart of the town, with the best shops and architecture, but the Strule River is a major artery, with some fine old bridges and excellent views of the city. The best townscapes include a group of four churches, the most prominent being the Church of the Sacred Heart with its twin asymmetric towers. To the north of the town are two attractions to give you a taste of the history of Northern Ireland. The well-known Ulster American Folk Park is a unique outdoor museum that has as its main theme the history of 18th- and 19th-century emigration from Ulster to North America. Rural Ulster thatched cottages contrast with log cabins in the New World, and there's a full-scale replica of an emigrant ship at a dock surrounded by buildings from the Ulster ports of Londonderry, Belfast and Newry. Reconstructions include the ancestral home of the Mellon family of Pittsburgh, whose forefathers were from Ulster. They endowed the folk park, as well as the home of John Joseph Hughes, the first Catholic archbishop of New York, who was instrumental in building St. Patrick's Cathedral in New York City. The An Creagan Visitor Centre is designed to re-create the archeological sites of the area. An interpretative exhibition and museum offer information and well-known local stories to transport you back to the Stone Age. Route guides allow you to explore archeological, cultural and environmental sites of the area.

When you have had your fill of history, take a 5-mile drive through the woodlands of Gortin Glen Forest Park, with its off-the-road scenic viewing points. En route, keep an eye out for wildfowl and an unusual herd of Japaneese Sika deer who inhabit this forest park. The visitor center supplies informative booklets. Alternatively, given Ireland's unpredictable weather, Aladdin's Kingdom, an indoor children's adventure playground, can be a welcome alternative if you have little ones. There are pendulum swings, a spiral glide, crawl tunnels, a mountain climb, rope bridges and even a haunted house.

Omagh's other attractions lie east toward Cookstown. You'll hear all about "scutching," "hackling," "weaving" and "beetling" at the linen-making demonstrations at Wellbrook Beetling Mill. Beetling, the final part of the process, is when the cloth is beaten unmercifully with wooden hammers, or beetles, to produce a sheen. "Linen-speak" has been used in this water-powered hammer mill since the 18th century, when the

Ulster American Folk Park has fascinating models of hide huts, ancient farms and stockades
Inset: Small tortoiseshell butterfly

phenomenal noise must have been literally deafening for the employees.

Nearby is Drum Manor Forest Park, a haven for nature lovers, featuring a shrub garden, an arboretum, a lake, a heronry, a walled butterfly garden and a self-guided nature trail.

✠ B2

Tourist information ✉ Strule Arts Centre, Townhall Square ☎ 028 8224 7831 🕓 Mon.–Sat. 10–6

Ulster American Folk Park ✉ Castletown, north of Omagh on A5 ☎ 028 8224 3292; www. folkpark.com 🕓 Mon.–Sat. 10:30–4:30, Sun. 11–5, Apr.–Sep.; Mon.–Fri. 10:30–3:30, rest of year 🍴 Café 🖐 $$

An Creagan Visitor Centre ✉ Creggan, Omagh (13 miles east of Omagh on A505) ☎ 028 8076 1112; www.an-creagan.com 🕓 Daily 11–5, Apr.–Sep.; Mon.–Fri. 11–5, rest of year (craft shop open at weekends) 🖐 $

Gortin Glen Forest Park ✉ 7 miles north of Omagh on B48 ☎ 028 8167 0666 🕓 Daily 10–dusk 🍴 Café 🖐 Parking: $$

Aladdin's Kingdom ✉ Mountjoy Road, north out of Omagh ☎ 028 8225 1550 🕓 Mon.–Fri. 2:30–7, Sat. 10:30–6:30, Sun. 2–6:30 🖐 $ (varies for activities)

Wellbrook Beetling Mill ✉ 23 miles east of Omagh off A505 ☎ 028 8674 8210; www.nationaltrust.org.uk 🕓 Daily 2–6, Jul.–Aug.; Sat.–Sun. 2–6, mid-Mar. through Jun. 30 and in Sep. 🖐 $$

Drum Manor Forest Park ✉ 23 miles east of Omagh on A505 ☎ 028 8676 2774 🕓 Daily 10–dusk 🖐 Parking $$

The Sperrin Mountains

Nobel Prize-winning poet Seamus Heaney grew up on the edge of the Sperrin Mountains, and their softly rounded beauty figures in much of his work. The range, bounded by the towns of Magherafelt, Omagh, Cookstown and Strabane, runs about 40 miles east to west, and the highest point rises only 2,240 feet at Sawel. The hillsides tend to be a bit bare, but you can drive through the wooded valleys for 200 miles.

The tourist office at Strabane has useful information abut the Sperrins and has a series of 10 circular-walks leaflets giving information about the region's geology, archeology and folklore. The long-distance Ulster Way takes in part of the Sperrins.

South of the mountain range is the mysterious complex of stone circles at Beaghmore. The three pairs of circles, a single circle, and stone rows known as "alignments" were discovered in AD 130, but are believed to date from the Bronze Age or earlier.

West of the mountains, near Strabane, is the Wilson Ancestral Home. Judge James Wilson, grandfather of Woodrow Wilson,

Discovered beneath a peat layer, the origins of the Beaghmore Stone Circles are still unknown

28th president of the United States and an early winner of the Nobel Prize, left for America in 1807 from this small thatched whitewashed cottage. Members of the Wilson family still live next door in a modern farmhouse. The cottage, with its traditional hearth fire, holds some of the original furniture, including a portrait of James Wilson and large curtained beds.

To the northern boundary of the Sperrins, just 3 miles south of Dungiven, is Banagher Glen and Forest, a National Nature Reserve and Special Area of Conservation. There are some superb walks here and the chance to see buzzards, wild flowers and butterflies.

➕ B3

Tourist information ✉ The Alley and Conference Centre, 1a Railway Street, Strabane ☎ 028 7138 4444 🕐 Mon.–Sat. 9–5:30, Jul.–Aug.; Mon.–Sat. 9–5, rest of year

Banagher Glen ✉ 3 miles south of Dungiven off the B74 ☎ 028 776 0307 (Limavady Tourist Office) 🕐 Open for pedestrians all year round. Parking lot daily 9–9 Jul.–Aug.; Sat.–Sun. 9–9, Jun., Sep. ✋ Free

Beaghmore Stone Circles ✉ Between Cookstown and Gortin, Co. Tyrone (signposted off A505) ✋ Free

Wilson Ancestral Home ✉ Dergalt, 2 miles southeast of Strabane, off Plumbridge road ☎ 028 7138 2204 🕐 Tue.–Sun. 2–5, Jul.–Aug., or by arrangement ✋ Free

The bewitching coastline at Ineuran Bay on the Inishowen Peninsula

The Inishowen Peninsula

The Inishowen Peninsula stretches north for 26 miles between loughs Swilly and Foyle, and culminates in Malin Head, Ireland's northernmost point. It's an area of both scenic beauty and ecological importance, and the peninsula's heritage reaches back beyond recorded history, leaving relics of those distant days scattered across its face.

On the 800-foot-high Greenan Mountain sits the Grianan of Aileach, an ancient stone circular fort (*cashel*) affording spectacular panoramic views of this part of Ulster. As far as archeologists can determine, the dry-stone structure was built about 1700 BC and during the Iron Age served as a temple of the sun. High kings of Ireland regarded it as a sacred spot. At the foot of the access road, Burt church's circular design follows that of the fort itself.

A few miles farther to the north, at the pretty little resort town of Fahan, the old graveyard holds a flat, two-faced cross from the seventh century and two rather curious carved stones.

Buncrana is the principal town of Inishowen. The ruins of 16th-century Buncrana Castle, where Wolfe Tone was imprisoned after his capture in 1798, overlook the Crana River. Close by are the ruins of O'Doherty's Castle. North of Buncrana is Dunree Head and Fort Dunree, a restored coastal defense battery that commands superb views of Lough Swilly, and was in use from the Napoleonic era to the departure of the British militia in 1938.

Magheramore Hill near Clonmany is the home of the huge capstone of a Bronze Age dolmen and is reputed to have been thrown by Ireland's legendary giant hero, hence its local name of "Finn McCool's Finger Stone." North of Clonmany in the delightful seaside resort of Ballyliffin. Irish music nights are often held in local hotels and pubs.

The prosperous town of Carndonagh has been an important ecclesiastical center since the fifth century. The striking 1945 Church of the Sacred Heart holds exceptionally fine statuary by the famous sculptor Albert Power, and the nearby Church of Ireland occupies a site on which St. Patrick founded one of his churches. If you're picnicking, there's a picnic area in lovely woods on the outskirts of town, on the Ballyliffin side.

A drive to Malin Head takes you as far north as you can go on Ireland's mainland. While this northerly point lacks the spectacular clifftop heights you've seen en route, it provides marvelous panoramic views of the peninsula and the sea. Southwards takes you through the picturesque village of Culdaff, with lovely sandy beaches, to Moville. This coast is popular with divers although the unpredictable tides mean you need to be experienced. The area is also a favorite for fishing and bird watching.

Grianan of Aileach ☒ Signposted from Burt, 3 miles south of Bridgend, 10 miles south of Buncrana on N13 Letterkenny/Londonderry road (main access to Inishowen peninsula) Ⓒ Free access

If there's anything the Irish love it's a good story. It seems only natural, then, that gaps in their long history are quickly filled with stories that evolve into legends. At the top of the list is the legend of Fionn MacCumhaill, "The Fair One," whose name has several spellings, the easiest of which is simply Finn MacCool. Was he a real man who lived in the third century, or a figment of the lively Irish imagination whose exploits were first written about in the seventh and eighth centuries? That weighty question matters not one whit to the Irish – he is their hero, real or fanciful fiction, and that is that.

Ireland's legendary hero

Finn MacCool

Decended from the gods through his mother, he was of gigantic stature, noble of nature, and fearless in battle. He also possessed infinite wisdom and accumulated the knowledge of the ages. The story goes that while cooking the Salmon of Knowledge, Finn burned his thumb and stuck it in his mouth to ease the pain, whereupon the salmon's wisdom became his own. From that time forward, he had only to put his thumb in his mouth to find the answer to any perplexing matter.

Finn was also a romantic who rescued his beloved wife Saba from an enchantment that had turned her into a fawn. They had seven supremely happy years together before she fell victim to a wicked spell while she was carrying Finn's son Oisin, and the story of the boy's birth and return to his father through a magical sequence of events forms an important element of Finn's legend.

One of his most significant acheivements was the gathering of his Fianna band of faithful and skilled warriors (this is where the modern-day Fianna Fail political party gets its name) of the highest moral character and courage. Even today you may run across a huge stone in a field believed by locals to have been flung there by Finn or one of the Fianna, and there are those who will tell you that the Isle of Man is actually a sod of Irish soil hurled by Finn MacCool, leaving a great hole that became the largest of Glendalough's sparkling lakes.

His stories are legend, but by far the most widely told (and half believed) is the one of the Giant's Causeway. Forget the scientific theory behind its creation (see page 178), as far as the Irish are concerned, the causeway would still be above water all the way across had it not been for a ferocious tiff between the Ulster giant, Finn MacCool, and his Scottish counterpart, Finn Gall. Finn MacCool actually built the causeway, but when he went home to rest, the wily Scotsman tripped across, club in hand, to catch his foe unawares. When Finn Gall burst into Mrs. MacCool's kitchen and demanded to know if the sleeping giant was her husband, she – in a master stroke of quick thinking – assured him that it was only her wee baby. Imagining the father of such a gigantic babe put such a fright into the Scotsman that he hightailed it back across the water, destroying the causeway behind him to keep Finn MacCool in Ireland where he belonged. Fact or fiction, either way you'll agree, it is one whale of a story!

To learn more about Ireland's intriguing, legendary figures, look for Lady Gregory's fascinating book *Gods and Fighting Men*, published by Colin Smythe and with an introduction by W.B. Yeats, available in bookshops specializing in Irish publications.

Hotels and Restaurants

The hotels and restaurants in this book were selected by local specialists and include establishments in several price ranges. Since price is often the best indication of the level of facilities and quality of service, a three-tiered price guide appears at the beginning of the listings. Because variable rates will affect the amount of foreign currency that can be exchanged for dollars (and therefore affect the cost of the room or meal), price ranges are given in the local currency.

Although price ranges and operating times were accurate at press time, this information is always subject to change without notice. If you're interested in a particular establishment, it is always advisable to call ahead to book.

Facilities suitable for travelers with disabilities vary greatly, and you are strongly advised to contact an establishment directly to determine whether it can meet your needs. Older buildings may not be adequately designed or equipped for visitors with limited or impaired mobility.

Accommodations

Accommodations have been selected with two considerations in mind: a particular sense of character or sense of local flavor, or a central location that is convenient for sightseeing. Remember that centrally located hotels fill up quickly, especially during busy summer vacation periods; make reservations well in advance. In-room bathrooms (sometimes referred to as "en-suite bathrooms") may not be available in budget hotels. Room rates normally include a full hot breakfast meal of bacon, sausage, eggs, fried potatoes and toast that should leave you feeling well-fed most of the day. Some hotels offer a price for overnight accomodations that includes an evening meal (known as "half-board" in Ireland).

Eating Out

Listed restaurants range from upscale places suitable for an elegant evening out to small cafés where you can stop and take a leisurely break from a busy day of sightseeing. Most Irish meals are meat based, although some enticing vegetarian alternatives are now finding a place on the menus in town and city restaurants A delicious tradition not to be missed is the popular plate of oysters accompanied by a pint of Guinness. You can sample epicurian seafood delights in Kinsale, often considered to be Ireland's gourmet capital.

Different tastes are catered to in Ireland's hotels

KEY TO SYMBOLS

	hotel
	restaurant
	address
	telephone number
	days/times closed
AX	American Express
DC	Diners Club
MC	MasterCard
VI	VISA

Hotel
Price guide: double room with breakfast for two people:
$$$ over €180
$$ €110– €180
$ up to €110

Restaurant
Price guide: dinner per person, excluding drinks
$$$ over €50
$$ €25–€50
$ up to €25

Three Square a Day

Traditionally, the Irish have always had their heartiest meal at midday. That's primarily because, as an agricultural nation, those working in the fields felt the need for sustenance to see them through a long afternoon. Lunch ("dinner" to the Irish) was the main meal, and the early evening "tea" was often as light as soup and brown bread or sandwiches. That still holds true today, and a full restaurant or pub lunch will provide as much to eat as most dinners. However, Irish eating habits have changed, and if you are simply not ready for a full meal at noon after that sumptuous breakfast, just look for the nearest pub offering "pub grub," order a cup of hearty soup to go with a sandwich or leafy salad plate and save your main meal for the evening.

Connacht

BALLINASLOE, CO. GALWAY

Hayden's Gateway $–$$
Built around 1803, this fine hotel offers excellent service. Meals are served throughout the day, either in the Garbally Restaurant or the award-winning coffee shop.
On the N6, Dublin–Galway road 090 96 42347; fax 090 96 42347 Closed Dec. 25 AX, DC, MC, VI

BALLYNAHINCH, CO. GALWAY

Ballynahinch Castle $$$
The castle stands at the foot of Ben Lettery on the banks of the famous salmon river, the Ballynahinch. The extensive grounds offer woodlands and scenic walks. The individually designed bedrooms are spacious and comfortable, and game and fresh local produce are a treat in the charming restaurant. Other facilities include tennis, fishing, croquet, and river and lakeside walks.
From N59, take Roundstone exit – the hotel is 3 miles from turnoff 095 31006; fax 095 31085; www.ballynahinch-castle.com Closed Dec. 15–27 and Jan. 29–Feb. 23 AX, DC, MC, VI

CASHEL BAY, CO. GALWAY

Zetland Country House $$$
In gardens featuring an unusual set of rock formations, flowers shrubs and woodland, this country house overlooking Cashel Bay is enhanced by attractive furnishings.There is a lounge and cocktail bar; many rooms have a sea or garden view.
Cashel Bay. N59 from Galway–Clifden, turn right towards Recess on the R340. After about 4 miles turn left onto R341, hotel is 1 mile ahead on the right 095 31111; fax 095 31117; www.zetlandcountryhouse.com AX, DC, MC, VI

CASTLEBAR, CO. MAYO

Welcome Inn $$
This town-center hotel offers a range of modern facilities behind its Tudor frontage. The bedrooms are spacious and well equipped and you can enjoy excellent cuisine in Reynards restaurant and there is also a nightclub.

N5 to Castlebar; the hotel is just past the Church of the Holy Rosary 094 902 2288; fax 094 903 21766 Closed Dec. 24–27 AX, MC, VI

CLIFDEN, CO. GALWAY

Alcock and Brown $$
The bar and restaurant are very inviting in this comfortable town-center hotel. The menu offers fish specialties and service is friendly.
N59 Galway–Clifden road via Oughterard 095 21206; fax 095 21842; www.alcockandbrown-hotel.com Closed Dec. 22–26 AX, DC, MC, VI

Mitchell's $$–$$$
A good choice of quality food is available throughout the day from this popular Clifden restaurant. Hearty Irish stew is a specialty, with good portions of seafood and steaks.
Market Street 095 21867; fax 095 21770 Closed Nov–Feb. AX, DC, MC, VI

Quay House $$
The Quay House is Clifden's oldest building, constructed around 1820. It has 14 individually furnished rooms, some with balconies and working fireplaces. It also has a wonderful collection of Georgian furniture and family portraits. Just seven minutes walk into town. Fishing, golf and pony-rides are all nearby.
Beach Road 095 21369; fax 095 21608; www.thequayhouse.com Closed early Nov. to mid-Mar. MC, VI

COLLOONEY, CO. SLIGO

Markree Castle $$–$$$
This magnificent castle dates back to 1640. Restoration work has transformed this grand building into a hotel with the imposing Knockmuldowney Restaurant. Facilities include horseback riding.
Off N4 at Collooney crossroads just north of the N17 exit, 7 miles south of Sligo. Hotel gates on right side after half a mile 071 916 7800; fax 071 67840; www.markreecastle.ie Closed Dec. 24–27 AX, DC, MC, VI

GALWAY, CO. GALWAY

Galleon $
Small, cozy restaurant with widely varied menu emphasizing seafood,

grills, and Irish and vegetarian dishes at reasonable prices.
✉ Salthill ☎ 091 522 963 MC, VI

🏨 Glenlo Abbey $$$
Standing in a landscaped 138-acre estate, this restored 18th-century abbey overlooks a beautiful loch. The bedrooms are in a modern wing along with a library, restaurants, cocktail and cellar bars. Leisure facilities are situated in the grounds and include golf, fishing, boating and clay-pigeon shooting.
✉ Bushypark – 2.5 miles from Galway city center on N59 ☎ 091 526 666; fax 091 527 800; www.glenlo.com ⓒ Closed Dec. 24–26 AX, DC, MC, VI

🍴 Kirwan's Lane $$
Popular with locals. The chef-proprietor features bistro-style grills and Asian-influenced dishes.
✉ Kirwan's Lane ☎ 091 568 266 ⓒ Closed Sun. lunch AX, MC, VI

🍴 The Malt House $$–$$$
Traditional fare plus vegetarian menu. Hot seafood dishes such as pan-fried crab claws and garlic mussels are outstanding.
✉ Old Malt Shopping Mall, High Street (in quiet deadend) ☎ 091 567 866 ⓒ Closed Sun. AX, DC, MC, VI

🍴 Pierres Restaurant $$
This popular French restaurant in the heart of town uses local ingredients in its traditional cooking offerings. Helpful staff create an informal atmosphere for customers. Fixed-price menu.
✉ 8 Quay Street ☎ 091 566 066 ⓒ Dinner only AX, MC, VI

🏨 Victoria $$
Bedrooms are well equipped; facilities include 24-hour room service, a good bar and pleasant restaurant. Friendly atmosphere.
✉ Beside railroad station, Victoria Place, off Eyre Square
☎ 091 567 433; fax 091 565 880; www.victoriahotelgalway.com AX, MC, VI

KILCOLGAN, CO. GALWAY

🍴 Moran's Oyster Cottage $$$
Internationally famed seafood restaurant in a 200-year-old thatched cottage. Oysters are a specialty, with smoked salmon and

mussel soup another hot favorite with visitors and locals.
✉ The Weir, about 10 miles south of Galway town, signposted from N18 (Galway–Limerick road) ☎ 091 796 113 ⓒ Closed Good Friday and Dec. 24–26 AX, MC, VI

ROSCOMMON, CO. ROSCOMMON

🏨 Abbey $$
Set in its own grounds just outside Roscommon, this fine manor house dates back more than 100 years. The bedrooms are well decorated, with a choice of period-style rooms in the original house; those in the newer wing are more contemporary. Service is attentive and the hotel has a friendly atmosphere. The popular brasserie-style restaurant serves traditonal meals that feature local ingredients.
✉ Just outside Roscommon on N63 Galway Road, opposite railroad station ☎ 090 662 6240; fax 090 662 6021; www.roscommonabbeyhotel.com ⓒ Closed Dec. 24–27 AX, DC, MC, VI

ROUNDSTONE, CO. GALWAY

🏨 Eldons $$
This distinctive building stands on the main street of a picturesque fishing village. Guests receive a warm welcome and good service. The seafood restaurant, Beola, also serves a good choice of dishes.
✉ Off N59 through Toombedla to Roundstone village ☎ 095 35933; fax 095 35722; www.eldons.ie ⓒ Closed Jan. AX, DC, MC, VI

SLIGO, CO. SLIGO

🍴 Bistro Bianconi $–$$
Pleasant informal restaurant with emphasis on Italian and spicy international dishes.
✉ 44 O'Connell Street (on main street) ☎ 071 91 41744 ⓒ Closed Sun., Good Friday and Dec. 2–26 DC, MC, VI

🏨 Sligo Park $$–$$$
Set on 7 acres of parkland to the south of Sligo, this hotel is ideal for exploring Yeats country. Offering excellent "executive" rooms, there are good beaches, an indoor heated pool, tennis, aerobics, sauna, solarium and hot tub.

✉ Pearse Road, on N4 ☎ 071 91 90400; fax 071 91 69556; www.sligoparkhotel.com ⓒ Closed Good Friday and Dec. 23–26 AX, DC, MC, VI

WESTPORT, CO. MAYO

🏨 Ardmore Country House $$$
A picturesque country house hotel ideally placed above the quay yet close to the heart of town. Most of the large individually decorated bedrooms have great views over Clew Bay. No children under 12.
✉ The Quay ☎ 098 25994 ; www.ardmorecountryhouse.com AX, MC, VI

🏨 Knockranny House $$$
Overlooking Westport with Clew Bay in the distance, this family-run hotel offers a spa, luxurious lounge, bar and the restaurant, La Fougèré, offers excellent seafood.
✉ N5 Westport–Castlebar Road, close to Westport ☎ 098 28600; fax 098 28611; www.khh.ie ⓒ Closed Dec. 22–27 AX, MC, VI

🍴 Quay Cottage $–$$
Charming quayside restaurant known for its seafood chowder, choice fish dishes, mountain lamb and steaks. Excellent vegetarian choices, too.
✉ The Harbour (beside gate to Westport House) ☎ 098 26412 ⓒ Dinner only. Closed Sun. and Mon. in winter, Dec. 24–26, all Jan. AX, MC, VI

Leinster

ARTHURSTOWN, CO. WEXFORD

🏨 Dunbrody Country House and Restaurant $$–$$$
Surrounded by parkland, you'll find tranquility and hospitality in this elegant Georgian manor house. The bedrooms are individual and there is an award-winning restaurant, golf, horseback riding, clay-pigeon shooting, a spa, and beaches nearby.
✉ From N11 follow signs for Duncannon and Ballyhack (R733). Hotel is 20 miles on from the turnoff. Turn left at gate lodge on approaching Arthurstown
☎ 051 389 600; fax 051 389 601; www.dunbrodyhouse.com ⓒ Closed Dec. 25–26 AX, DC, MC, VI

KEY TO SYMBOLS

🏨 hotel
🍴 restaurant
✉ address
☎ telephone number
🕐 days/times closed
🚆 nearby train or bus route(s)
AX American Express
DC Diners Club
MC MasterCard
VI VISA

Hotel

Price guide: double room with
breakfast for two people:
$$$ over €180
$$ €110–€180
$ up to €110

Restaurant

Price guide: dinner per person,
excluding drinks
$$$ over €50
$$ €25–€50
$ up to €25

Changing Tastes

There is little doubt that tourism
has had a notable impact on the
cuisine in Ireland. Until recently
there was hardly any tradition
of eating out, except on rare
occasions at a local hotel.
Patterns of diet were
conservative, based on "meat
and two veg" (somewhat
overcooked), potatoes (of
course) and large quantities of
dairy fat. Now demands for
predictable, inexpensive fast
food are met, as everywhere,
with burgers and pizzas – a
better bet being fish and chips
(fries). The restaurant scene
reflects the country's
broadening cosmopolitan
population, and French, Italian,
Chinese, Russian and Indian
restaurants have blossomed
throughout the country.
Sophisticated tastes have also
introduced organic and
vegetarian restaurants – once
unheard of. In fact it seems hard
to imagine the grim days of the
19th century when so many of
the population were starving
and food preparation amounted
to little more than boiling a
potato!

BETTYSTOWN, CO. MEATH

🏨 **Neptune Beach Hotel and
Leisure Club $$$**
Overlooking the sea with access to a
sandy beach. Many bedrooms enjoy
sea views; facilities include a gym,
indoor pool, sauna and solarium.
✉ Bettystown. Off N1
Dublin–Belfast Road ☎ 041 982
7107; fax 041 982 7412
www.neptunebeach.ie   AX, MC, VI

DUBLIN, CO. DUBLIN

🏨 **The Clarence $$$**
The hotel is in the heart of Dublin city
center within walking distance of
many restaurants and theaters. This
is an individual and very tasteful
establishment with richly furnished
bedrooms. For sheer luxury, the two-
bedroom penthouse suite is
outstanding. The public areas have a
long gallery, smart bar and the fine
restaurant serves excellent cuisine.
✉ 6–8 Wellington Quay
☎ 01 407 0800; fax 01 407 0820
www.theclarence.ie   🕐 Closed Dec.
24–26 AX, DC, MC, VI

🍴 **L'Ecrivain $$$**
Fine restaurant with emphasis on
superb classic French cuisine.
Excellent desserts. Good wine list.
Reservations recommended.
✉ 109A Lower Baggot Street (near
Merrion Square) ☎ 01 661 1919
🕐 Closed Sat. lunch and all Sun.
AX, DC, MC, VI

🏨 **Harding $**
At the heart of the fascinating
Temple Bar area of Dublin, this
friendly, renovated hotel offers
simple bright rooms. Darkey Kelly's
Bar & Restaurant features traditional
Irish and contemporary music.
✉ Copper Alley, Fishamble Street,
Temple Bar ☎ 01 679 6500; fax 01
679 6504; www.hardinghotel.ie
🕐 Closed Dec. 23–26 AX, MC, VI

🍴 **Juice $**
This cool and clean-cut restaurant is
perfect for a healthy option. Juices,
smoothies and vegetarian food
inspired by cuisine from Japan to
Mexico and the Caribbean.
✉ 73–83 South Great George's
Street ☎ 01 475 7856 AX, MC, VI

🍴 **Locks Restaurant $$**
Canalside place in a Scandinavian
style, with a sophisticated vibe.

The classical French cuisine includes
potato and black bacon soup and
braised venison shank with root
vegetables, port and orange.
✉ 1 Windsor Terrace, Portobello
☎ 01 454 3391 🕐 Closed Sat.
lunch and Sun. and Dec. 24–Jan. 6
AX, DC, MC, VI

🏨 **Longfield's $$$**
This intimate townhouse hotel lies
close to the city center and serves
good food in the No. 10 Restaurant.
✉ 10 Fitzwilliam Street. Take
Shelbourne Hotel exit from
St. Stephens Green, continue down
Baggot Street for half a mile, turn
left at Fitzwilliam Street exit. The
hotel is on the left ☎ 01 676 1367;
fax 01 676 1542 ; www.longfields.ie
🕐 Closed Dec. 24–27 AX, DC,
MC, VI

🍴 **The Lord Edward $$–$$$**
This informally elegant, upstairs
restaurant is one of Dublin's oldest,.
The traditional menu features
seafood dishes (their specialty)
balanced by an excellent Irish stew,
and corned beef and cabbage.
✉ 22 Christchurch Place (in the
Liberties, near Christ Church
Cathedral) ☎ 01 454 2420
🕐 Closed Sat. lunch, Sun. and Dec.
24–Jan. 2 AX, DC, MC, VI

🏨 **Marine $$$**
On the north shore of Dublin Bay
with attractive gardens and
seashore walks, this hotel features
spacious public rooms and well-
equipped bedrooms. It is near the
Sutton rapid railroad into the city
center and Portmarnock Golf Course;
there is an indoor pool and sauna.
✉ Sutton Cross. Take the road from
M1 toward Dublin city center, turn
off at 2nd exit for Coolocil, then
continue until T-junction and turn
left; after 1 mile the hotel is on
right ☎ 01 839 0000, fax 01 839
0442; www.marinehotel.ie
🕐 Closed Dec. 25–26 AX, DC,
MC, VI

🏨 **The Merrion $$$**
Four Georgian townhouses, with a
modern garden wing, include an
indoor pool, gym and steam room.
✉ Upper Merrion Street, on the
east side, beyond government
buildings on the right side
☎ 01 603 0600; fax 01 603 0700;
www.merrionhotel.com AX, DC,
MC, VI

🏨 Parliament Hotel $

A City-center hotel with an eye-catching Edwardian facade in a central position on the edge of TempleBar. The 63 en-suite bedrooms are decorated in bright, contemporary style and The Forum and the Senate Room restaurants serve good international cuisine. ✉ Lord Edward Street, opposite Dublin Castle ☎ 01 670 8777; fax 01 670 8787; www.regencyhotels.com 🕐 Closed Dec. 25-27 MC, VI

🍴 Patrick Guilbaud $$$

Said to serve the best French cuisine in Dublin using the finest seasonal Irish produce, all presented with flair and innovation. The set lunch is a good value. The restaurant is accessed via Merrion Hotel or own street entrance. ✉ Merrion Hotel, 21 Upper Merrion Street ☎ 01 676 4192; fax 01 661 0052 🕐 Closed Sun., Mon., Dec. 25–Jan. 6 AX, DC, MC, VI

DUNDALK, CO. LOUTH

🏨 Ballymascanlon House $$–$$$

A Victorian mansion whose 130-acre grounds include an 18-hole golf course. Use the elegant restaurant and spacious lounge. There is a new wing of luxurious bedrooms, an indoor heated pool, tennis, sauna, gym and hot tub. ✉ North of Dundalk take T62 to Carlingford ☎ 042 935 8200; fax 042 937 1598; www.ballymascanlon.com 🕐 Closed Dec. 24–27 AX, DC, MC, VI

ENNISCORTHY, CO. WEXFORD

🏨 Riverside Park $$

In a picturesque setting beside the River Slaney, the hotel is easily distinguished by its terracotta and blue color scheme. Public areas, including the dramatic lobby, take full advantage of the views. The spacious, attractive bedrooms are equipped with every convenience. ✉ The Promenade. One third mile from Newbridge, center of Enniscorthy, N11 Dublin–Rosslare Road ☎ 05392 37800; fax 05392 37900; www.riversideparkhotel.com 🕐 Closed Dec. 24–26 AX, DC, MC, VI

GOREY, CO. WEXFORD

🏨 Marlfield House $$$

This Regency house was once the residence of the Earl of Courtown. Bedrooms are in keeping with the luxurious and well-proportioned day rooms, which include a library, drawing room, dining room and conservatory. Druids Glen and several golf courses are nearby. ✉ 1 mile outside Gorey on the Courtown Harbour Road ☎ 053 942 1124; fax 053 942 1572; www.marlfieldhouse.com 🕐 Closed Dec. 16–Feb. AX, DC, MC, VI

HOWTH, CO. DUBLIN

🍴 Abbot Restaurant $$

Adjacent to a 16th-century pub, the decor features fires, gas lights and original stone walls. Excellent range of seafood and traditional Irish meals. Try the seafood chowder and brown bread. Irish music every night. ✉ Abbey Street (9 miles from Dublin city center) ☎ 01 839 0307 🕐 Closed Sun. and Mon., Good Friday and Dec. 25 🚆 DART, north of Dublin AX, DC, MC, VI

KILKENNY, CO. KILKENNY

🏨 Club House $$–$$$

This 200-year-old hotel offers private parking and the suites have all been refurbished. Supervised by the owner, this is a comfortable and friendly hotel, with an open fire, Georgian dining room and gym. ✉ Patrick Street, city center, near Kilkenny Castle. ☎ 056 77 21994; fax 056 77 71920; www.clubhousehotel.com 🕐 Closed Dec. 24–27 AX, DC, MC, VI

🏨 Kilkenny $$$

Set on 5 acres of wooded land on the outskirts of Kilkenny, this hotel has refurbished bedrooms and an Italian restaurant with views of the landscaped gardens. There is also a nice bar and conservatory lounge. Health club and pool. ✉ College Road. Follow ring road to Callan and Clonmel traffic circle, hotel is on the right ☎ 056 77 62000; fax 056 77 65984; www.hotelkilkenny.ie AX, DC, MC, VI

🍴 Langton Room $$

One of Kilkenny's favorite restaurants and a member of the "Kilkenny Good Food Circle," this

spot serves classic, wholesome dishes, some with an Oriental twist. The spacious dining room has a rather impressive glass roof. ✉ Langton House Hotel, 69 John Street ☎ 056 77 65133 🕐 Closed Dec. 25 AX, DC, MC, VI

LUCAN, CO. DUBLIN

🏨 Lucan Spa $$

Set on its own grounds, the Lucan Spa is a fine Georgian House that provides Old World charm and relaxation. Golf courses are nearby. ✉ On N4, about 7 miles from city center, 20 minutes from Dublin airport ☎ 01 628 0494; fax 01 628 0841; www.lucanspahotel.ie 🕐 Closed Dec. 25 AX, DC, MC, VI

NEWBRIDGE, CO. KILDARE

🏨 Keadeen $$$

A family-owned hotel set on 9 acres of landscaped gardens and well placed for Dublin airport and the Mondello racing circuit. The hotel has an indoor pool, sauna, solarium, gym, hot-tub and massage. Public areas include a spacious drawing room, and two bars. Only one mile from the Curragh racecourse. ✉ M7 exit 10 Newbridge, Curragh, towards Newbridge. Hotel is on left, half a mile from traffic circle ☎ 045 431 666; fax 045 434 402; www.keadeenhotel.ie 🕐 Closed Dec. 24–27 AX, DC, MC, VI

ROSSLARE, CO. WEXFORD

🏨 Kelly's Resort $$

This popular seafront hotel offers a leisure center, tennis courts, a children's play room and spacious gardens. Choose between La Marine Bistro and the main award-winning restaurant. Public rooms are adorned with contemporary Irish art. ✉ Town center on seafront ☎ 05391 32114; fax 053 913 2222; www.kellys.ie 🕐 Closed mid-Dec. to mid-Feb. AX, MC, VI

SLANE, CO. MEATH

🏨 Conyngham Arms $$

In the picturesque village near the famous prehistoric tombs of Newgrange, this hotel is ideal for exploring the historic area of Tara and the Boyne Valley. Fishing,

KEY TO SYMBOLS

🏨	hotel
🍴	restaurant
✉	address
☎	telephone number
🕐	days/times closed
AX	American Express
DC	Diners Club
MC	MasterCard
VI	VISA

Hotel
Price guide: double room with
breakfast for two people:
$$$ over €180
$$ €110–€180
$ up to €110

Restaurant
Price guide: dinner per person,
excluding drinks
$$$ over €50
$$ €25–€50
$ up to €25

Irish Cuisine

You may be surprised to learn
that the hallowed "corned beef
and cabbage" is wholly a
figment of the Irish American
image of Ireland. The Irish
tradition is boiled bacon and
cabbage, along with Irish stew,
made with lamb and absolutely
delicious. The equally hallowed
potato is still high on the list of
Irish culinary preferences, but
these days the old spud comes
to the table roasted, baked,
boiled, mashed or as french
fries (call them "chips," potato
chips are "crisps"). And far from
being the main dish as it was
for generations, your potato is
accompanied by local beef,
lamb, chicken (often a curry),
prawns or fish. Salads often
include cold meats such as
turkey, chicken or ham, and
vegetables complete the
heaping plates of "mains."
Don't-miss foods include locally
made cheddar, blue or herb soft
cheese. Fish (trout and salmon)
can be found throughout the
country: Dublin Bay prawns and
plaice, a lovely saltwater fish,
are specialties and you don't
have to be rich to enjoy oysters.

horseback riding and tennis are
available locally.
✉ From N2 turn onto N51, hotel is
just on the left ☎ 041 988 4444;
fax 041 982 4205;
www.conynghamarms.com
AX, DC, MC, VI

STRAFFAN, CO. KILDARE

🏨 The K Club $$$
You will stay in elegant bedrooms
overlooking the gardens, river or golf
course at this beautiful, luxury hotel.
Facilities include a Ryder Cup golf
course, fishing, horseback riding
and more.
✉ From Dublin city center (17 miles
take N4 exit R406 and hotel
entrance is on right in Straffan
☎ 01 601 7200; fax 01 601 7297;
www.kclub.com   AX, DC, MC, VI

🍴 Barberstown Castle $$$
For that extra special occasion, dine
by candlelight in this original
13th-century castle. The confident
modern French and Irish cooking
includes main courses such as baked
wild salmon with pan-fried oysters.
✉ Clan Celdridge Road, just outside
Straffan   ☎ 01 628 8157;
www.barberstown.ie   🕐 Dinner
only. Closed Sun.–Tue., Jan. and
Dec. 24–25 AX, MC, VI

WEXFORD, CO. WEXFORD

🍴 Forde's Restaurant $$
Fresh flowers and candles create a
romantic atmosphere at this modern,
informal restaurant on the first floor
overlooking the harbor. The menu
leans towards local seafood, with
some vegetarian options. Moules
marinière with toasted garlic rye
bread followed by rack of lamb is a
popular choice.
✉ Crescent Quay   ☎ 053 912 3832
🕐 Closed Dec. 22–25
DC, MC, V

🏨 Talbot $$$
The Talbot is a contemporary style
hotel created from a renovated 1905
grain mill which enjoys panoramic
views of Wexford Harbour and the
River Slaney. Facilities include a
pool, and health and beauty spa.
Good restaurant and bar snacks.
✉ The Quay. Take N11/N25 to
Wexford, hotel on waterfront
☎ 053 912 2566; fax 053 912 3377;
www.talbothotel.ie   🕐 Closed Dec.
24–25 AX, DC,MC, VI

WOODENBRIDGE, CO. WICKLOW

🏨 Best Western Woodenbridge $
This is a comfortable hotel in the
Vale of Avoca, about an hour's drive
from the ferry ports of Dun
Laoghaire and Rosslaire and close to
the N11. Renovations have given
this hotel a new lease on life.
Hospitality and good food are their
goal. Golf and fishing are on the
doorstep.
✉ Vale of Avoca. Between Avoca
and Arklow ☎ 0402 35146;
fax 0402 35573; www.
woodenbridge.com   MC, AX, VI

BALLYLICKY, CO. CORK

🏨 Sea View House $$–$$$
Sample Irish hospitality at this
country house overlooking Bantry
Bay. Set in gardens, it has cozy
lounges with turf fires, and pleasant
bedrooms. Award-winning food is
served in plush surroundings. Local
seafood, lamb, beef and veal feature
on the menu. This is a good touring
base for west Cork and Kerry.
✉ 3 miles from Bantry, 8 miles from
Glengarriff on N71 ☎ 027 50073 or
027 50462; fax 027 51555;
www.seaviewhousehotel.com
🕐 Closed mid-Nov.–mid-Mar.
AX, DC, MC, VI

BALLYVAUGHAN, CO. CLARE

🏨 Gregans Castle $$–$$$
Overlooking Galway Bay, this hotel
is in an area rich in archeological,
geological and botanical interest.
The emphasis here is on good food
using fresh local produce.
✉ 3.5 miles south of Ballyvaughan
on N67 ☎ 065 7077 005; fax 065
7077 111; www.gregans.ie
🕐 Closed Dec. to mid-Mar. AX,
MC, VI

BANTRY, CO. CORK

🍴 O'Connor's Seafood Restaurant $–$$
Cozy restaurant well placed in the
town center where fresh fish and
shellfish are the specialties.
Mussels cordon bleu is good. Live-
lobster tank and excellent meat, too.
✉ The Square ☎ 027 50221
🕐 Closed Sun. and Mon. dinner in
winter MC, VI

BLARNEY, CO. CORK

🍴 Blairs Inn $$
This popular riverside country pub features Irish music on Monday evenings after 9:30 p.m (Jun.–Sep.). Feast on local seafood and lamb and other meats and game in season.
✉ Cloghroe, Blarney (3.5 miles from Blarney on R578) ☎ 021 438 1470 AX, DC, MC, VI

BUNRATTY, CO. CLARE

🏨 Bunratty Shannon Shamrock $$
Set in picturesque Bunratty with its medieval castle, and surrounded by lawns and flowers, this modern ranch-style building has an indoor heated pool, sauna, gym and hot-tub in the Euphoric Fitness Centre.
✉ Take Bunratty bypass, exit off Limerrick–Shannon divided highway ☎ 061 361177; fax 061 364863; www.dghotels.com AX, MC, VI

CAHERDANIEL, CO. KERRY

🏨 Derrynane $$
Halfway around the famous Ring of Kerry, this modern hotel overlooking the sea is ideal for touring.
✉ 2 minutes' walk off the main road ☎ 066 947 5136; fax 066 947 5160 🕐 Closed early Oct. to Easter. AX, DC, MC, VI

CLONAKILTY, CO. CORK

🏨 The Lodge and Spa at Inchydoney Island $$
Chosen as Ireland's hotel of the year in 2006, this luxurious place sits on the stunning coastline, near a sandy beach. Bedrooms are contemporary in style, and many have sea views. Healthy options are available at the Gulfstream Restaurant, and treatments such as thalassotherapy in the spa.
✉ N71 West Cork Road to Clonakilty. Take second exit at the traffic circle and follow signs to Lodge and Spa ☎ 023 33143; www.inchydoneyislandhotel.com AX, MC, VI

CLONMEL, CO. TIPPERARY

🏨 Minella $$
This mansion on 9 acres of grounds on the banks of the River Suir has comfortable bedrooms with good views; some of the bathrooms are more luxurious and have hot tubs.
✉ Coleville Road ☎ 052 22388; fax 052 24381; www.hotelminella.ie 🕐 Closed Dec. 21–27 AX, DC, MC, VI

CORK, CO. CORK

🏨 Best Western Ambassador $$
This distinguished sandstone and granite 19th-century building is a fine hotel with city views. Some bedrooms have balconies. There is a cocktail lounge, bar, restaurant and health spa center.
✉ Militry Hill, St. Lukes, just off Wellington Road ☎ 021 453 9000; fax 021 455 1997; www.ambassadorhotel.ie 🕐 Closed Dec. 24–25 AX, DC, MC, VI

🍴 Four Liars Bistro $$
An intimate restaurant where the walls display the head chef's own artwork. The innovative food is put together with flavors from all the over the world, while using quality local ingredients. Notable main courses include pan-fried black sole in a cream lobster sauce and loin of pork in wild mushroom sauce.
✉ The Butter Exchange, Shandon ☎ 021 4394040 🕐 Closed Mon.–Sat. lunch AX, MC, VI

🏨 Hayfield Manor Hotel $$$
Although built in the mid-1990s, this splendid, secluded hotel in the university area has the feel of a large period house. The bedrooms are very comfortable and the public rooms elegant, with real fire places.
✉ Perrott Avenue, College Road ☎ 021 484 5900; www.hayfieldmanor.ie AX, DC, MC, VI

🍴 Isaacs $–$$
Informal restaurant in an 18th-century warehouse. Mediterranean and other international influences, traditional Irish cuisine, daily blackboard specials, and vegetarian specialties are offered.
✉ 48 MacCurtain Street ☎ 021 450 3805 🕐 Closed Sun. lunch, Christmas week AX, MC, VI

COURTMACSHERRY, CO. CORK

🏨 Courtmacsherry $
This family-run Georgian house is set in attractive grounds near the beach. Quality meals are served in the kitchen. A riding school is available to all ages.
✉ M71 to Bandon, then R602 to Timoleague – head for Courtmacsherry. Hotel is by the beach at the far end of the town ☎ 023 46198; fax 023 46137 🕐 Closed Oct.–Mar. MC, VI

DOOLIN, CO. CLARE

🏨 Aran View House $–$$
Situated on 100 acres of rolling farmland and commanding panoramic views of the Aran Islands. A welcoming hotel with a convivial atmosphere, attractive accommodations and comfortably furnished.
✉ Coast Road ☎ 065 707 4061 or 065 707 4420; fax 065 707 4540; www.aranview.com 🕐 Closed Nov.–Mar. AX, DC, MC, VI

DUNGARVAN, CO. WATERFORD

🏨 Lawlors $–$$
An ideal touring center, this family-run streetside hotel caters to both leisure and business guests. There is regular live evening entertainment. Davitts Restaurant offers a comprehensive international menu.
✉ Off N25 ☎ 058 41122; fax 058 41000; www.lawlorshotel.com 🕐 Closed Dec. 24–25 AX, DC, MC, VI

ENNIS, CO. CLARE

🏨 Temple Gate $$
This smart hotel incorporates a 19th-century Gothic-style building with attractive bedrooms. The public areas include a lounge library, Preachers Pub and JM's Bistro. It shares the grounds with the Clare Museum and is set back from the center of the historic town of Ennis.
✉ The Square. From Ennis follow signs for Temple Gate ☎ 065 682 3300; fax 065 682 3322; www.templegatehotel.com 🕐 Closed Dec. 25–26 AX, DC, MC, VI

GOUGANE BARRA, CO. CORK

🏨 Gougane Barra $$
Right on the lake shore, this hotel is popular for its cuisine. Its relaxing bedrooms and bathrooms all have mountain or lake views.
✉ Off N22 ☎ 026 47069; fax 026 47226 🕐 Closed late Oct. to mid-Apr. AX, DC, MC, VI

KEY TO SYMBOLS

- 🏨 hotel
- 🍴 restaurant
- ✉ address
- ☎ telephone number
- ⌚ days/times closed
- AX American Express
- DC Diners Club
- MC MasterCard
- VI VISA

Hotel
Price guide: double room with breakfast for two people:
- $$$ over €180
- $$ €110–€180
- $ up to €110

Restaurant
Price guide: dinner per person, excluding drinks
- $$$ over €50
- $$ €25–€50
- $ up to €25

The Best-Value Meal
One thing is certain: You won't leave Ireland hungry. A "traditional Irish breakfast" (or the "Ulster fry" north of the border) is, simply put, overwhelming. Even if you're a coffee-and-toast person at home, you're not likely to resist the repast spread before your eyes every morning that includes a brimming plateful of bacon, eggs, broiled tomatoes with soda and potato breads and butter. Accommodation rates are nearly always quoted with a full breakfast included, so you might as well stoke up for the day!

KENMARE, CO. KERRY

🏨 Landsdowne Arms Hotel $–$$
Historic, elegant 26-room hotel offering good hospitality in the heart of the lovely town of Kenmare. Good bar food served all day and the dining room offers excellent Irish and international cuisine. There is an Irish music nightly in the Bold Thady Quill Bar.
✉ Main Street ☎ 064 41368; fax 064 41114; www.lansdownearms.com ⌚ Closed Dec. 25 MC, VI

🏨 Park Hotel Kenmare $$$
This luxurious country house stands above terraced gardens overlooking the estuary of the Kenmare River, with a fine mountain backdrop. Warm, professional service draws guests back regularly. The restaurant offers good food and fine wines. The world-renowned Samas spa is here; also golf, tennis, and croquet.
✉ On R569, beside golf course ☎ 064 41200; fax 064 41402; www.parkkenmare.com ⌚ Closed Jan. 3 to mid-Feb., Mon.–Fri. mid–Feb to mid-Apr. and in Nov. AX, DC, MC, VI

KILLARNEY, CO. KERRY

🏨 Aghadoe Heights $$$
This hotel is a luxurious and hospitable haven concealed behind an austere facade. The award-winning restaurant continues to receive recognition, and standards of service have brought accolades. Other facilities include an indoor heated pool, tennis, fishing, sauna, solarium, gym, and spa.
✉ 10 miles south of Kerry airport and 3 miles north of Killarney. The hotel is signposted off the N22 Tralee Road ☎ 064 31766; fax 064 31345; www.aghadoeheights.com ⌚ Closed Dec. 31–Jan. 2 AX, DC, MC, VI

🍴 Gaby's $$–$$$
Offering tempting seasonal menus in classic French style: Specialties may include cassolette of shrimps and monkfish in a lightly gingered sauce, Gaby's famous smoked salmon pâté, lobster "Gaby" (a secret recipe), and classics like sole meuniere. Availability of seafood depends on daily landings, but there's always a choice.
✉ 27 High Street ☎ 064 32519

⌚ Closed Sun. and Mon.–Tue. mid-Jan. to mid-Mar. AX, DC, MC, VI

🏨 Killarney Park $$$
On the edge of town, this charming hotel has rich colors, open fires and welcoming staff. Also there's an indoor heated pool, sauna, gym, hot tub, outdoor hot tub and pool.
✉ Kenmare Place. N22 from Cork–Killarney ☎ 064 35555; fax 064 35266; www.killarneyparkhotel.ie ⌚ Closed Nov. 28–Dec. 15 and Dec. 24–26 AX, DC, MC, VI

🏨 Lake $$
This former mansion stands among mountain views and woodland walks. Some bedrooms have balconies and four-poster beds.
✉ Muckross Road. Kenmare Road out of Killarney ☎ 064 31035; fax 064 31902 ⌚ Closed Dec. 16–Jan. 1 AX, DC, MC, VI

KINSALE, CO. CORK

🏨 Actons $$–$$$
Set in attractive gardens overlooking the waterfront and marina, Actons has a bar and bistro, plus the Captain's Table restaurant. The friendly and attentive staff contribute to a visit. Bedrooms and lounge are comfortable.
✉ Pier Road. Hotel faces Kinsale Harbour, close to the Yacht Club ☎ 021 477 9900; fax 021 477 2231; www.actonshotelkinsale.com ⌚ Closed Christmas and Jan. AX, DC, MC, VI

🍴 Man Friday $$
Popular long-established restaurant with a garden terrace. Seasonal à la carte menus feature seafood from local waters, duck, lamb and steak.
✉ Scilly (a 10-minute walk from town center, overlooking harbor, near Spaniard Pub) ☎ 021 477 2260 ⌚ Mon.–Sat. dinner. Closed Sun. AX, DC, MC, VI

🏨 Trident $$–$$$
The Trident Hotel has fabulous views over Kinsale Harbour. There is a good choice of food at the Pier One Restaurant and the Wharf Tavern.
✉ Worlds End. Take the R600 from Cork city to Kinsale; the hotel is just beyond the pier, on the waterfront ☎ 021 477 2301; fax 021 477 4173 ⌚ Closed Dec. 25–26 AX, MC, VI

LIMERICK, CO. LIMERICK

🍴 McLaughlin's Restaurant $$
The restaurant is housed in the Castletroy Park Hotel, which is set on 14 acres of splendid grounds. The dining room features wood accents with art and native crafts on the walls. The chef's contemporary interpretations of local and international dishes always please. The restaurant is named after the inventor of hydroelectric power.
✉ Castletroy Park, Dublin Road
☎ 061 335 566   AX, DC, MC, VI

LISDOONVARNA, CO. CLARE

🏨 Sheedy's Country House Hotel $$
Well-run family hotel with an award-winning restaurant. The hotel is beside a spa complex in well-tended gardens close to the Burren region with its unique flora and fauna. Eight rooms and three junior suites.
✉ Town center, close to the sulphur wells ☎ 065 707 4026; fax 065 707 4555; www.sheedys.com ⏰ Closed Oct.–Mar. AX, MC, VI

LISMORE, CO. WATERFORD

🏨 Ballyrafter House $$
A welcoming country house with a bar and conservatory, where locals and guests gather to discuss the day's events. Most bedrooms are pleasantly furnished in pine with en suite facilities. There is salmon fishing on the Blackwater river, and horseback riding is available locally.
✉ Half a mile from Lismore ☎ 058 54002; fax 058 53050; www.water-fordhotel.com ⏰ Closed Nov.–Feb. AX, DC, MC, VI

MALLOW, CO. CORK

🏨 Longueville House $$$
Set in a wooded estate, this elegant 18th-century Georgian mansion has bedrooms overlooking the river valley and the courtyard maze. Its situation makes it an ideal base for touring. The restaurant has a long-standing reputation for excellence; many ingredients are home-grown. Specialties include roast lamb filled with parsley purèe, blackwater salmon, and gooseberry tart with elderflower ice cream. Dinner reservations recommended.
✉ 3 miles west of Mallow on N72

to Killarney ☎ 022 47156 or 022 47306; fax 022 47459; www.longuevillehouse.ie ⏰ Closed Jan. 6 to mid-Mar. AX, DC, MC, VI

MIDLETON, CO. CORK

🏨 Barnabrow Country House $$
This is a 17th-century family-run country house set in 35 acres of parkland adjacent to the village of Cloyne, near Midleton. A blend of old-world charm and new-world comfort with a good restaurant.
✉ Cloyne, Midleton. Take N25 from Cork to Midleton, then turning for Cloyne village ☎ 021 465 2534; www.barnabrowhouse.ie ⏰ Closed Dec. 23–27   DC, MC, VI

🏨 Midleton Park $$
This purpose-built hotel has fine, spacious suites, while the comfortable restaurant offers good food and attentive service. On-site parking is available.
✉ From Cork, turn off N25, hotel on right. From Waterford, turn off N25, over bridge until T-junction, turn right, hotel on right ☎ 021 463 5100; fax 021 463 5101; www.midletonpark.com ⏰ Closed Dec. 25 AX, DC, MC, VI

ROSCREA, CO. TIPPERARY

🏨 Grant's $
An attractive hotel opposite the 13th-century castle and Heritage Centre. Bedrooms are pleasantly furnished in warm colors and there is an excellent and relaxing oak-paneled lobby lounge with deep leather armchairs and sofas. Restaurant, pub and café-bar.
✉ Castle Street. Off N7 Dublin–Limerick Road. Turn off for town center and follow signs to hotel ☎ 0505 23300; fax 0505 23209 AX, DC, MC, VI

ROSSCARBERY, CO. CORK

🏨 Celtic Ross $$
This hotel overlooks a lagoon on the edge of a peaceful village and is a striking landmark on the west Cork coastline. The spacious, light-filled public areas have richly textured fabrics and highly polished Irish elm, yew, bog oakwood and cherrywood. Facilities include the new Druids Restaurant, Kingfisher Bar, a swimming pool and the new Holistic Suite for therapies and treatments.

✉ On the N71 Bandon–Clonakilty road. Follow signs for Skibbereen ☎ 023 48722; fax 023 48723; www.celticcross.com ⏰ Closed Jan. to mid-Feb. AX, DC, MC, VI

TRALEE CO. KERRY

🏨 The Brandon $$
This modern hotel with excellent leisure facilities is a golfer's paradise, within 30 minutes drive of six superb courses. Other facilities include an indoor heated pool, sauna, solarium, gym and spa.
✉ Prince's Street ☎ 066 712 3333; fax 066 712 5019; www.brandonhotel.ie ⏰ Closed Dec. 22–29 AX, DC, MC, VI

TRAMORE, CO. WATERFORD

🏨 Majestic $–$$
A short distance from the beach, the Majestic has good sea views. Entertainment is held in the lounge during the summer, and there is a recreation center and gardens. Bedrooms are comfortable and are equipped with modern facilities.
✉ Turn off N25 through Waterford onto R675 to Tramore ☎ 051 381 761; fax 051 381 766; www.majestichotel.ie AX, MC, VI

WATERFORD, CO. WATERFORD

🏨 Dooley's $–$$
In the heart of Waterford near the quayside, Dooley's is a comfortable family-run hotel. The smart public areas and bedrooms are stylish, and there is an elevator to all floors. Guests are very well cared for in a warm and friendly atmosphere.
✉ 30 The Quay ☎ 051 873 531; www.dooleys-hotel.ie ⏰ Closed Dec. 25–29 AX, DC, MC, VI

🍴 Fitzpatrick's Restaurant $–$$
Housed in a charming old coach house, this highly recommended restaurant specializes in seafood. There is also Irish beef and a good range of vegetarian dishes. Early-bird menu available.
✉ Manor Court, Cork Road ☎ 051 378 851 MC, VI

🏨 Granville $–$$
This charming quayside hotel has comfortable bedrooms and the

KEY TO SYMBOLS

🏨	hotel
🍽	restaurant
✉	address
☎	telephone number
🕐	days/times closed
AX	American Express
DC	Diners Club
MC	MasterCard
VI	VISA

Hotel

Price guide: double room with breakfast for two people:

$$$ over €180/UK£110
$$ €110–€180/UK£70–£110
$ up to €110/UK£70

Restaurant

Price guide: dinner per person, excluding drinks

$$$ over €50/UK£30
$$ €25–€50/UK£15–£30
$ up to €25/UK£15

Themed Foods

Throughout Northern Ireland, look for the green and white "Taste of Ulster" sign, which guarantees the best of fresh local produce. Special events at the Ulster American Folk Park (page 194) near Omagh often offer the chance to taste various traditional delicacies, either of the Old Country or the New World. At the Frontier Festival Weekends in summer, guests can enjoy pioneer cooking, while at the end of October, Halloween fare accompanies fun and dramatic antics around the park.

public areas and restaurant are appointed to a high standard.
✉ The Quay. Take the N25 to the waterfront city center, opposite the clock tower ☎ 051 305 555; fax 051 305 566; www.granville-hotel.ie 🕐 Closed Dec. 24–26 AX, DC, MC, VI

🍽 La Bohème Restaurant $$$

Housed in the converted vaults of an historic Port of Waterford building, La Bohème combines classic French cuisine with an inviting, intimate atmosphere. Owner/chef Eric Thèze, and wife, Christine – who together restored this Georgian space – offer a tempting menu of modern delicacies and heritage recipes. Chief among La Bohème's specialties is grilled lobster.
✉ 2 George Street ☎ 051 875 645 🕐 Closed lunch. Table d'hôte Tue.–Fri. (Early bird 5:30.7pm); à la carte Tue.–Sat. AX, MC, V

🏨 Waterford Castle Hotel and Golf Club $$$

This hotel is set on the grounds of a private 310-acre island, where access is gained by a private chain-linked ferry. The 16th-century castle is now an elegantly restored, internationally acclaimed 19-bedroom hotel. It has an 18-hole championshp golf course, clay-pigeon shooting, archery and tennis.
✉ The Island, Ballinakill ☎ 051 878 203; fax 051 879 316; www.waterfordcastle.com AX, DC, MC, VI

YOUGHAL, CO. CORK

🏨 Devonshire Arms $

This 19th-century hotel has been restored with considerable attention to detail. It offers good food in both the restaurant and the bar. Known locally as "the Dev;" it is a local institution that has been offering accommodations for over 170 years.
✉ Pearse Square ☎ 024 92827 🕐 Closed Dec. 25 and Good Friday AX, DC, MC, VI

Ulster and Northern Ireland

BALLYBOFEY, CO. DONEGAL

🏨 Kee's Hotel & Leisure Club $$

This former coaching inn is a comfortable hotel with well-

furnished bedrooms and good facilities. There is a bistro as well as a conservatory lounge and popular restaurant, plus indoor heated pool, sauna, gym, and spa bath.
✉ 1 mile northeast on N15, in Stranorlar village ☎ 074 91 31018; fax 074 91 31917; www.keeshotel.ie AX, DC, MC, VI

BALLYCONNELL, CO. CAVAN

🏨 Slieve Russell Golf and Country Club $$$

An imposing hotel on 300 acres of land, which also accommodates a championship golf course. Public areas include lounges, three restaurants and a fitness suite. Bedrooms are tastefully furnished and facilities include the Clúin Spa and Wellness Centre.
✉ From Cavan, head for Enniskillen, at Butlersbridge turn left toward Belturbet. Through village toward Ballyconnell, hotel is on left after 5 miles ☎ 049 952 6444; fax 049 952 6046; www.quinnhotels.com AX, DC, MC, VI

BALLYMENA, CO. ANTRIM

🏨 Adair Arms $$

Public areas in the Adair Arms are spacious and the lounge is inviting. The bedrooms are well presented and the restaurant offers a good choice from à la carte and fixed-price menus. There is a well-stocked bar and lighter meals are available in the Lanyon Grill.
✉ 1 Ballymoney Road ☎ 028 2565 3674; fax 028 2564 0436; www.adairarms.com 🕐 Closed Dec. 25 AX, DC, MC, VI

BANGOR, CO. DOWN

🍽 Genoa Restaurant $–$$

Charming seaside restaurant specializing in seafood, often mixed with international recipes. Try the lamb and traditional dishes often featured on the menu.
✉ 1a Seacliff Road (at Bangor Marina parking lot) ☎ 028 9146 9253 🕐 Closed Sun.–Mon. MC, VI

🏨 Royal $$

This substantial Victorian hotel overlooks the marina and offers modern comfortable bedrooms; the bars have a traditional atmosphere. Quays restaurant provides a more formal dining experience. There is

weekly live entertainment.
✉ Bangor seafront. Turn right at
seafront; hotel overlooks the marina
☎ 028 9127 1866; fax 023 91
467810; www.royalhotelbangor.com
AX, DC, MC, VI

BELFAST, CO. ANTRIM

🍴 Benedicts $$
This lively, atmospheric restaurant
has a cocktail bar downstairs. The
modern and sophisticated cuisine
relies on simple, fresh ingredients.
✉ Benedicts Hotel, 7–21 Bradley
Place ☎ 028 9059 1999; fax 028
9059 1990 AX, DC, MC, VI

🏨 Culloden $$$
An elegant baronial mansion
converted to a modern hotel with
every convenience and excellent
views. The day rooms include a bar
and lounge areas. Facilities include
indoor heated pool, tennis, sauna,
solarium, gym, spa, beauty salon
and aromatherapy. The restaurant
serves accomplished dishes.
✉ Bangor Road, on A2 ☎ 028
9042 1066; fax 028 9042 6777;
www.hastingshotels.com AX, DC,
MC, VI

🍴 The Edge Restaurant $$
Close to the Waterfront Hall, making
it an excellent choice for pre-theater
meals and great riverside views; the
food at the Edge matches the
contemporary décor. Plenty of choice
featuring delicious local ingredients
and beautifully presented dishes.
✉ Mays Meadow, Laganbank Road
☎ 028 9032 2000; fax 028 9032
2111 ⓘ Closed Sat lunch and Sun
AX, MC, VI

🏨 Malmaison $$$
This stunning downtown hotel has
been created from two 1850
warehouses, with the original
Italianate facade retained. It is close
to the city's attractions. Sample the
excellent home-grown menu items.
Bedrooms are well-equipped.
✉ 34–38 Victoria Street. This street
is one way, hotel next to First Trust
building ☎ 028 9022 0200 ; www.-
malmaison.com AX, DC, MC, VI

🍴 Nick's Warehouse $$
This lively air-conditioned, two-story
restaurant makes the most of a
clever warehouse conversion.
Cooking is seasonal and modern but
with a homey feel. International

influences are certainly discernible,
but Irish ingredients and traditonal
themes are not overlooked.
✉ 35–39 Hill Street ☎ 028 9043
9690 ⓘ Closed Sun. and Mon.
evenings AX, DC, MC, VI

CARRICKFERGUS, CO. ANTRIM

🏨 Dobbins Inn $$
Colorful window boxes adorn the
front of this popular inn near the
ancient castle. Public areas are
modern without compromising the
inn's original character.
✉ 6–8 High Street. From Belfast
take M2, keep right at traffic circle
follow A2 to Carrickfergus, turn left
opposite castle ☎ 028 9335 1905;
fax 028 9335 1905;
www.dobbinsinnhotel.co.uk
ⓘ Closed Jan. 1 and Dec. 25–26
AX, DC, MC, VI

CARRICKMACROSS, CO. MONAGHAN

🏨 Nuremore $$$
This Victorian mansion serves as a
quiet retreat, overlooking a lake and
18-hole golf course. Indoor and
outdoor leisure and sporting
facilities are on hand. The restaurant
serves imaginative dishes, and
dedicated staff ensure a pleasant
stay in this friendly hotel.
✉ 2 miles south of Carrickmacross
on Dublin–Londonderry road ☎ 042
966 1438; fax 042 966 1853; www.-
nuremore.com AX, DC, MC, VI

CAVAN, CO. CAVAN

🏨 Kilmore $$
This refurbished hotel set on a
hillside on the edge of Cavan has a
good restaurant. Golfing, fishing,
boating and horseback riding are
available nearby.
✉ Dublin Road. About 2 miles from
Cavan on N3 ☎ 049 433 2288; fax
049 433 2458; www.hotelkilmore.ie
AX, DC, MC, VI

DONEGAL, CO. DONEGAL

🏨 Harvey's Point Country Hotel $$$
An elegant hotel superbly located on
Lough Eske offering spacious public
rooms, excellent cuisine and a range
of facilities including tennis and
fishing. You can expect a warm Irish
welcome at Harvey's.
✉ Lough Eske. From Donegal take

N56 then 1st right signposted Loch
Eske and Harvey's Point. Hotel is
about 10 minutes' drive ☎ 073 97
22208; fax 073 97 22352;
www.harveyspoint.com ⓘ Closed
Sun.–Tue., Nov. 1–Mar. 1 AX, DC,
MC, VI

DUNFANAGHY, CO. DONEGAL

🏨 Arnold's $$$
Set on the coast, overlooking
Sheephaven Bay, this hotel has sandy
beaches on its doorstep. It has been
in the Arnold family for three
generations. Public areas offer
comfortable seating and there is a
good restaurant and comfy bars, and
live music in the summer. Tennis,
fishing and horseback riding are also
available.
✉ On N56 from Letterkenny. Hotel
is on left entering the village
☎ 074 91 36208; fax 074 91 36352;
www.arnoldshotel.com ⓘ Closed
Nov. to mid-Mar. AX, DC, MC, VI

DUNGANNON, CO. TYRONE

🏨 Cohannon Inn $
Bedrooms are located behind the inn
complex in a separate block. The
main food and beverage areas have
been smartly upgraded and food is
available all day.
✉ 212 Ballynakilly Road (quarter
mile from exit 14 off M1, head north
towards Coalisland) ☎ 028 8772
4488; fax 028 8775 2217;
www.cohannon-inn.com ⓘ Closed
Dec. 25 AX, DC, MC, VI

OMAGH, CO. TYRONE

🏨 Mellon Country Inn $$
Set in the foothills of the Sperrin
Mountains, this hotel has stylish,
modern bedrooms, a restaurant with
an international menu, and the
Heaven on Earth spa.
✉ Castletown, Omagh. On A5 6
miles from Omagh, 1 mile from
Ulster American Folk Park
☎ 028 816 61224; fax 028 816
61891

ENNISKILLEN, CO. FERMANAGH

🏨 Killyhevlin $$–$$$
This hotel commands superb views
over Lough Erne from the
comfortable public rooms. Attractive

KEY TO SYMBOLS

- 🏨 hotel
- 🍽 restaurant
- ✉ address
- ☎ telephone number
- 🕐 days/times closed
- AX American Express
- DC Diners Club
- MC MasterCard
- VI VISA

Hotel

Price guide: double room with breakfast for two people:

$$$ over €180/UK£110
$$ €110–€180/UK£70–£110
$ up to €110/UK£70

Restaurant

Price guide: dinner per person, excluding drinks

$$$ over €50/UK£30
$$ €25–€50/UK£15–£30
$ up to €25/UK£15

Afternoon Tea

In properties owned by the National Trust conservation organization, the on-site tearooms are well known for the quality of their cakes and biscuits, and those in Northern Ireland have the added benefit of the Ulster tradition of home baking. Recipes include a sumptuous variety of breads, potato cakes, soda breads, barm brack (a fruity tea cake) and cookies. To finish off a visit to one of the magnificent stately homes with afternoon tea is a treat not to be missed.

---

rooms and up-to-the-minute health club and spa. An ideal base for exploring the sights of Fermanagh.
✉ Dublin Road. 2 miles south, off A4 ☎ 0286 632 3481; fax 0286 632 4726; www.killlyhevlin.com 🕐 Closed Dec. 24–25 AX, DC, MC, VI

LETTERKENNY, CO. DONEGAL;

🍽 The Lemon Tree Restaurant $$

This restaurant in the center of the town, bedecked with flowers outside and terracotta tiles and peach-toned walls inside, serves excellent food. The emphasis is on locally sourced produce all prepared in the open kitchen for all to see.
✉ 39 Lower Main Street ☎ 074 91 25788 🕐 Dinner daily, lunch Sun. only AX, MC, V

LIMAVADY, CO. LONDONDERRY

🏨 Radisson Roe Park Hotel and Golf Resort $$$

In a stunning spot, this country-house offers superb sporting and leisure facilities.
✉ On the A2 Londonderry–Limavady road, 1 mile from Limavady ☎ 028 7772 2222; fax 028 7772 2313; www.radissonroepark.com AX, DC, MC, VI

LONDONDERRY, CO. LONDONDERRY

🍽 The Grill Room at Da Vinci's Hotel $

This excellent restaurant specializes in wonderful seafoods such as grilled seabass with tikka crust and lime-cherry relish and other variations of classic dishes. Also serves food in the bar.
✉ 15 Culmore Road ☎ 028 7127 9111 AX, MC, VI

🏨 Tower Hotel Derry $$

This contemporary and stylish hotel is within the city walls. Modern bedrooms are fully equipped and those on the upper floors enjoy superb views. The Mediterranean-style restaurant offers a contemporary menu.
✉ Butcher Street, off the Diamond ☎ 028 7137 1000; fax 028 7137 1234; www.towerhotelderry.com 🕐 Closed late Dec. AX, DC, MC, VI

NEWCASTLE, CO. DOWN

🏨 Enniskeen House $$

The Porter family's hotel enjoys superb views to the Mountains of Mourne. Public areas and bedrooms are traditional in style. Wholesome fare is offered in two dining areas.
✉ 98 Bryansford Road (from Newcastle town center follow signs for Tollymore Forest Park; hotel is 1 mile on left) ☎ 02843 722 392; fax 02843 724 084 🕐 Closed mid-Nov. to mid-Mar. AX, MC, VI

PORTAFERRY, CO. DOWN

🏨 Portaferry $$

Portaferry is a charming hotel with a restaurant. Many bedrooms enjoy views over Strangford Lough.
✉ 10 The Strand (on Lough Shore opposite ferry terminal) ☎ 02842 728 231; fax 02842 728 999 ; www.portafe3rryhotel.com AX, DC, MC, VI

PORTBALLINTRAE, CO. ANTRIM

🏨 Bayview $$

Bayview is found in the heart of this picturesque village. Close to the Giant's Causeway, this small hotel of 25 rooms is an ideal destination for a leisurely break.
✉ 2 Bayhead Road ☎ 028 2073 4100; fax 028 2073 4330; www.bayviewhotelni.com 🕐 Closed Dec. 25 AX, DC, MC, VI

PORTRUSH, CO. ANTRIM

🏨 Ramada Portrush $$

Located in the center of Portrush, the hotel overlooks the Atlantic Ocean. Relax in the Counties Café Bar and Restaurant after a day in the outdoors. It is in an ideal location for outdoor pursuits and sightseeing.
✉ 73 Main Street ☎ 028 7082 6100; fax 028 7082 6160; www.ramadaportrush.com 🕐 Closed Dec. 25 AX, DC, MC, VI

ROSSNOWLAGH, CO. DONEGAL

🏨 Sandhouse $$–$$$

A hotel with good cuisine and service. Rooms have sea views, and a conservatory lounge offers a retreat.
✉ Donegal Bay. On coast road 5 miles north of Ballyshannon ☎ 071 985 1777; fax 071 985 2100; www.sandhouse-hotel.ie 🕐 Closed Dec.–Jan. AX, DC, MC, VI

Essential Information

Planning advice and practical travel tips

The information in this guide has been compiled for U.S. citizens traveling as tourists.

Travelers who are not U.S. citizens, or who are traveling on business, should check with their embassies and tourist offices for information on the countries they wish to visit.

Entry requirements are subject to change at short notice, and travelers are advised to check the current situation before they travel.

Ireland – Essential Information

Before you Go

Passports

The most important document you'll need before you travel is a passport. Passport application forms can be obtained from any federal or state court or post office authorized to accept passport applications. U.S. passport agencies have offices in all major cities; check the Yellow Pages. (U.S. Government, State Department) for the one nearest you. You also can request an application form by calling the National Passport Information Center at (887) 487 2778. (Note: There is a credit card charge.) Comprehensive passport information and application forms are available on the U.S. State Government internet site at www.travel.state.gov.

Apply for your passport early as processing can take several months from the time of application until arrival. Rush service is available for an extra charge. Before departure, make sure your passport is valid for at least another six months after you are due to travel: some European countries require this.

There are no border formalities between Northern Ireland and the Republic if you are crossing by car, although it is always advisable to take your passort with you.

Travel visas are not necessary for American citizens traveling to either the Irish Republic or Northern Ireland (which is part of the United Kingdom), but if you'll be traveling on to other nations, check their entry requirements before you leave home.

Travel Insurance

Before departing make sure you are covered by insurance that will reimburse travel expenses if you need to cancel or cut short your trip due to unforeseen circumstances. You'll need coverage for property loss or theft, emergency health and dental treatment. Before taking out additional insurance, check to see if your current homeowner's insurance or medical coverage already covers you for travel abroad. If you make a claim, your insurance company will need proof of the incident or expenditure. Keep copies of any police report or medical bills or statements, to submit with your insurance claim.

National flag of the Republic of Ireland

Essential for Travelers

● Required ● Recommended ● Not required

Passport	●
Visa	●
Travel, medical insurance	●
Round-trip or onward airline ticket	●
Local currency	●
Traveler's checks	●
Credit cards	●
First-aid kit and medicines	●
Health inoculations	●

Essential for Drivers

● Required ● Recommended ● Not required

Driver's license	●
International Driving Permit	●
Car insurance (for non-rental cars)	●
Car registration (for non-rental cars)	●

*see also Driving section, page 118

When to Go

Weather in Ireland is impossible to predict. You can experience all four seasons in one day, but you can be certain that no conditions will last for long, and showers pass quickly. The warmest months are July and August, and rainfall in May, June and September is often lower. May and June are good months to visit, as schools are still in session and there are fewer crowds at major attractions. Temperatures rarely fall below freezing in the winter and you can pick up bargain accommodations deals during the low season, but some sights may be closed.

Important Addresses

Tourism Ireland (Republic and Northern Ireland)
345 Park Avenue
New York, NY 10154
☎ (2120 418-0800
fax (212) 371-9052

Republic of Ireland Tourist Board (Fáilte Ireland)
Baggot Street Bridge
Dublin 2, Republic of Ireland
☎ 01 602 4000; fax 01 855 6821

American Consulate (NI)
Danesfort House, 223 Stranmills Road
Belfast BT9 5GR, Northern Ireland
☎ 028 9038 6100; fax 028 9068 1301

American Embassy (Republic of Ireland)
42 Elgin Road, Ballsbridge
Dublin 4, Republic of Ireland
☎ 01 668 8777; fax 01 668 9946
American Citizens Services: 8:30–12:30 and 1–4;
closed Sat.–Sun. and Wed.

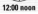

Ireland – Essential Information

Customs

 Duty-free limits on goods brought in from non-European Union countries: 200 cigarettes or 100 cigarillos or 50 cigars or 250 g. tobacco; 2 L. wine; 1 L. alcohol over 22% volume or 2 L. alcohol under 22% volume; 60 ml. perfume; 250 ml. toilet water; plus any other duty-free goods (including gifts) to the value of €175 ($121). There is no limit on the importation of tax-paid goods purchased within the European Union, if they are for your own personal use. There are no currency regulations. You can purchase $400 worth of personal goods before returning to the U.S. before a tax is levied; keep sales slips.

No unlicensed drugs, weapons, ammunition, obscene material, pets or other animals, counterfeit money or copied goods, meat or poultry.

Money

The Republic of Ireland's currency is the euro (€), which is divided into 100 cents (c)

Denominations of euro bills are 5, 10, 20, 50, 100, 200 and 500. There are coins of 1, 2, 5, 10, 20 and 50c and €1 and €2. In Northern Ireland the currency is the pound sterling (UK£) and it must be used in the following counties: Antrim, Armagh, Derry, Down, Fermanagh and Tyrone. The pound sterling is divided into 100 pence (p). The denominations of pound bills are 5, 10, 20 and 50. There are coins of 1, 2, 5, 10, 20 and 50p and £1 and £2. The pound sterling and the euro are not interchangeable.

Credit cards are accepted in hotels, large stores and upscale restaurants; check first in small or rural establishments. Exchange dollars or traveler's checks at a bank, exchange office, post office or large hotel.

Exchange rate at press time: $1 =63c; UK£0.50

Tips and Gratuities

Restaurants (where service is not included)	12–15%
Cafés/bars	10%
Taxis	10%
Porters	€1/50p per bag
Hairdressers	10%
Tour guides	€2/£1
Cloakroom attendants	€1/50p

Communications

Post Offices

 Buy stamps at post offices, some newsstands and tobacconists, large grocery stores and hotels. Hours for out-of-town

 post offices may vary. Mailboxes and vans are green in the Republic of Ireland and red in Northern Ireland.

Mail service in the Republic is notoriously slow and expensive. Postcards are cheaper to send than letters.

Telephones

 Older-style public call boxes are blue and cream and marked in Gaelic 'Telefón' and red in Northern Ireland, although they are being replaced by glass and metal booths. They take cash (10c/10p, 20c/20p,

 50c/50p or 21/£1 coins) or prepaid phone cards bought from newsstands, post offices and local stores.

Phoning within Ireland
All Irish phone numbers in this book include the area code; dial the number listed.

Phoning Ireland from abroad
The country code for Ireland is 353; for Northern Ireland 44. Note that Irish numbers in this book do not include the country code; you will need to prefix this if you are phoning from another country. To phone Ireland from the United States or Canada, omit the first zero from the Irish number and add the prefix 011 353; for Northern Ireland 011 44. (Note the number of digits in Irish area codes varies.)
RI example: 01 122 3344 becomes 011 353 1 122 3344.
NI example: 01 122 3344 becomes 011 44 1 122 3344.

Phoning from Ireland
To phone the United States or Canada from Ireland, prefix the area code and number with 001. Example: (111) 222-3333 becomes 001

Emergency Numbers

Police	999
Fire service	999
Ambulance	999

Emergency calls are free from phone booths.

Emergency phone numbers

☎ **Police 999 or 112**

Ireland – Essential Information

Hours of Operation

● Stores Mon.–Sat. ● Post offices Mon.–Sat.
●Offices Mon.–Fri. ● Museums/monuments
● Banks Mon.–Fri.   ●Pharmacies Mon.–Sat.

7 8 9 10 11 12 1 2 3 4 5 6 7

In addition to the times shown above, some stores stay open until 8 or 9 for late-night shopping on Thursday or Friday.

In smaller towns and rural areas some stores close in the afternoon on one day of the week.

Some banks in small towns close 12:30–1:30. Nearly all banks are closed on Saturday, and post offices close at 1 p.m. on Saturday.

Hours for museums and tourist sights vary and are subject to change; always check with the local tourist office. Many places close from October to March or have very limited opening times, although most major sights are open all year.

Pharmacies may close earlier on Saturday.

National Holidays

Banks, businesses and most stores close on these days. Museums also may have restricted hours.

Jan. 1	New Year's Day
Mar. 17	St. Patrick's Day
Mar./Apr.	Good Friday
Mar./Apr.	Easter Monday
1st Mon. of May	May Day Holiday
Last Mon. of May	Spring Holiday (NI)
1st Mon. of Jun.	June Holiday (RI)
Jul. 12	Orangeman's Day (NI)
1st Mon. of Aug.	August Holiday (RI)
Last Mon. of Aug. (NI)	Late Summer Holiday
Last Mon. of Oct.	October Holiday (RI)
Dec. 25	Christmas Day
Dec. 26	St. Stephen's Day

Restrooms

Identify restrooms in Gaelic-speaking areas by Fir (men) and Mná (women). A small charge is levied in restrooms at some railroad stations, but most other facilities are free. The standards of hygiene are moderate. You will be welcomed into any local pub if you need to use their facilities, but stop for a drink and a talk while you are there.

Health Advice

Medical Services

Private medical insurance is recommended. U.S. and Canadian visitors can receive treatment in emergency rooms, but are charged if admitted to a hospital bed. A general practitioner also will charge for services.

Dental Services

Dentists charge for treatment. Dental work is expensive, so check to see if it is covered by your medical insurance. Dentists are listed in the Yellow Pages, or ask at your embassy, hotel or at a tourist office. Alternatively, a list of dental practioners can be obtained from the Irish Dental Association; (☎ 01 295 0072).

Sun Advice

The sunniest months are May and June, with 5–6½ hours of sun a day (the extreme southwest is the sunniest). July and August are the warmest. During these months you should take sensible precautions against the sun.

Drugs

Pharmacies (also called chemists) sell a range of prescription and non-prescription medicines. If you need medicine outside regular hours, information about the nearest 24-hour facility should be posted on the door of all pharmacies.

Safe Water

Tap water is safe to drink throughout Ireland. If, however, you prefer mineral water you will find it widely available.

Personal Safety

Irish towns and cities are generally relaxed, safe places to be, and are regularly patrolled by police, especially in Northern Ireland. However, it is always best to use common-sense precautions when traveling.

● Keep valuables hidden when you're on the move; a money belt or neck purse is the best option.
● Never leave bags unattended.
● Avoid walking alone in dimly lit areas at night.
● If you have belongings stolen, report the incident immediately to the police and get a written report to provide to your insurance company as evidence for your claim.
● Security forces on both sides of the border are courteous to bona fide travelers.

Ireland – Essential Information

National Transportation

Air

Most European flights arrive in Dublin or Belfast; international flights land also in Shannon and Cork. Internal flights and those to the U.K. are very competitive. Fly with Aer Lingus (www.aerlingus.com) or Ryanair (www.ryanair.com). Aer Aran (www.aerann.ie) operate the Aran flyer with several daily flights between the Aran Islands and Galway.

Train

Ireland's rail company is Iarnród éireann (IÉ). Trains are the fastest way of covering long distances and are generally reliable and comfortable, but the network is limited and one-way tickets cost almost as much as round-trip tickets. Midweek is less expensive than weekends, and there are many special offers on fares. The Dublin to Belfast Express takes 2 hours, and there are eight to nine trains daily (less on Sundays). Round-trip tickets are available; for more information ☎ 01 836 6222. Rail runaround tickets (seven days of unlimited travel) are available from main Northern Ireland railroad stations (tel 028 9066 6630).

Bus

In the Republic, Bus Éireann operates a network of express bus routes serving most of the country and includes service to Belfast (some services run summer only); for information ☎ 01 836 6111. If you are traveling around Dublin, make sure you have plenty of change, as an exact fare policy is in operation. The number 41 bus from Eden Quay runs to Dublin Airport. Barratt Tours (☎ 061 384 700) in Limerick operates day tours in the summer season and on Wednesdays they run a tour combining a trip to Galway City with a cruise on Lough Corrib. In Northern Ireland, Ulsterbus Tours (☎ 028 9066 6630) has links between Belfast and about 23 towns, and also run ferry and coach tours to England, Scotland and Wales; unlimited travel tickets are available.

Ferry

There are several ferries a day from Belfast and Dublin to ports on the British mainland; taxis, trains and coaches operate a regular service from the ports to the cities. Combined train and ferry or bus and ferry tickets can be an inexpensive option from London to Dublin; try National Express (www.nationalexpress.com).
A car ferry runs between Ballyhack, Co. Wexford and Passage East, Co. Waterford (☎ 051 382 480). Another serves Killimer, Co. Clare and Tarbert, Co. Kerry, saving 60 miles over the road trip (☎ 065 90 53124). Traveling between Northern Ireland and London can be more expensive, for combination tickets try Scottish Citylink (☎ 08705 50 50 50). There are also ferries to several islands; ask for details at a local tourist office. Ringaskiddy's Ferryport, 10 miles southeast of Cork city, provides passenger and car ferry service to Brittany (Brittany Ferries ☎ 021 427 7801).

Electricity

Ireland has a 230-volt power supply. Electrical sockets either take plugs with two round pins or three square pins; American appliances will need a plug adapter and will require a transformer if they do not have a dual-voltage facility.

Photography

The light is frequently poor, so if you are using a 35mm camera you may need fast film. Bring a tripod for landscape work. Film and camera batteries are widely available. Digital equipment and developing facilities are also available in towns and cities.

If landscapes are your interest , there is a large variety to choose from. You'll find a plethora of castles as subject matter, but remember, if the weather is too poor for long shots, zoom in close and study detail. Film and camera batteries are readily available in Ireland, and you should be able to find good developing and printing facilities in most large towns and all digital camera requirements and printing facilities are readily available in larger towns. It is generally illegal to take film photos of the police and military barracks in Northern Ireland.

Media

The main newspapers in the Republic are the *Irish Times* and the *Irish Independent* ; they both provide great insights into Irish life and politics. The *Irish Examiner* is a serious and respected newspaper, commenting on world affairs. For arts reviews and listings, the *Sunday Tribune* is good; other Sunday papers include the *Sunday Independent* and *Sunday Business Post*. British papers are available the same day in major cities and in Northern Ireland. The local *Belfast Telegraph* is a popular evening paper. In the mornings, you can choose between the nationalist *Irish News* or the loyalist *News Letter*.

Republic of Ireland television broadcasting is operated by a state-sponsored body called RTE (Radio Telefís Éireann). It has three radio and four television channels. You can receive them all over Ireland and Northern Ireland. In much of the Republic, you can pick up BBC (radio and television) and Ulster television.

Driving Regulations

Drive on the Left

Drive on the left-hand side of the road on both sides of the border and, at traffic circles, yield to traffic approaching from your right.

Seat Belts

Must be worn in front seats at all times and in the rear seats where fitted.

Minimum Age

The minimum age for driving a car is 17. However, rental car firms will often stipulate a minimum age of 25.

Blood Alcohol

The legal blood alcohol limit is 0.08%. Random breath tests on drivers are carried out frequently, especially late at night, and the penalties for offenders are severe.

Tolls

The Westlink and Eastlink bridges around Dublin require tolls of about €1.55. Tolls are charged on the M1 (Drogheda by-pass) and M4 (Kinnegad–Enfield).

Additional Information

An International Driving Permit (IDP) is recommended; some rental firms require it, and it can speed up formalities if you are involved in an accident.

A Green Card (international motor insurance certificate) is recommended if you are driving a non-rental car.

Irish Republic roads vary tremendously and the road classification gives no reliable indication of the width or surface quality – some primary roads are little better than country lanes. In Northern Ireland the major roads are fast and well-maintained and seldom congested.

Speed Limits

Regulations
Traffic police can impose on-the-spot fines.

Limited-access highways
(motorways; blue)
120 k.p.h. (75 m.p.h.)

National roads (green) 100 k.p.h. (62 m.p.h.)
Regional (white) 80 k.p.h. (50 m.p.h)
Northern Ireland 96 k.p.h. (60 m.p.h)

Urban areas
50k.p.h (31 m.p.h.)

Car Rental

Car Rental

The leading rental companies have offices at airports, railroad stations and large ferry terminals. Hertz offers discounts to AAA members. If you are taking a rented car across the border from Northern Ireland into the Republic of Ireland, check with your rental company to see that you have the appropriate insurance.

Car rental is less expensive in Northern Ireland than in the Republic.

A local car rental firm is likely to offer cheaper rates than an international company, but it may not allow different pick-up and drop-off points.

Often, the cheapest way to book a car rental is to arrange a package deal in advance with a tour operator (fly and drive or rail and ferry-drive) rather than waiting until you arrive in Ireland. Early booking is advisable if you are traveling during the high season.

The minimum age for renting a car ranges from 18 to 25 depending on the model of the car. Some companies have a maximum age limit of 70.
For reservations:

	United States	Ireland
Alamo	(800) 426-5266	21 432 0755
Avis	(800) 331-1212	21 428 1111
Budget	(800) 527-0700	90 662 7744
Hertz	(800) 654-3080	01 676 7476

Fuel

Fuel

Gas is unleaded and sold in liters; diesel also is easily purchased. Gas stations in villages stay open until 8 or 9 p.m. and usually open after Mass on Sunday. Along main highways on both sides of the border, there are 24-hour gas stations: gas is considerably less expensive in Northern Ireland.

Parking

In some urban areas, parking is limited to certain times and periods. Where this is signed you must buy a disk from a newsstand or garage and display it on the dashboard of your car. Multi-story and pay and display parking can also be used in cities.

Park only in authorized areas in Northern Ireland; vehicles parked in unauthorized areas may cause a security alert and be removed by security forces.

AAA

AAA Affiliated Motoring Club
AA Ireland
56 Drury Street, Dublin 2
☎ 01 617 9999; fax 01 617 9990
If you break down while driving in the Republic of Ireland ☎ 1800 66 77 88
For breakdowns in Northern Ireland
☎ 0800 66 77 88
Not all automobile clubs offer full services to AAA members.

Breakdowns/Accidents

There are 24-hour emergency phones at regular intervals on highways: ☎ 999. Most car rental firms provide their own free rescue service; if your car is rented, follow the instructions given in the documentation. Use of a car repair service other than those authorized by your rental company may violate your agreement.

In the event of a breakdown, the vehicle should be moved off the highway whenever possible. Hazard warning lights should be used and, if available, a red warning triangle should be placed on the road at least 165 feet before the obstruction and on the same side of the road.

Road Signs

Driving in Ireland is still, generally speaking, a pleasure. Out of the big towns the roads are uncrowded and most drivers courteous. The farther west you go, the more patience you need: roads are narrower, steeper and more winding.

Road signs in the Republic of Ireland that give road distances are in the process of being changed: Older, black-and-white signs give distances in miles, while newer green-and-white signs give kilometers. In Northern Ireland, the distance signs are always in miles.

Keep left

Vehicles may pass on either side to reach same destination

Ahead only

One-way traffic

No entry for vehicular traffic

Give way to traffic on major road

Crossroads

National speed limit applies

Double curve, first to the left

No passing

Two-way traffic straight ahead

Ireland – Essential Information

Irish and American English

Although on the surface they are the same language, there are some quirky differences between American and Irish English. The Irish have become familiar with Americanisms through imported American television shows and movies, and on the whole will understand American visitors. However, note the possible misunderstanding if an Irish person directs you to the "first floor" of a building; the American equivalent is actually the second floor) Irish words and phrases are in the left column below; American words appear in the right column.

Hotels

bath	*bathtub*
book	*reserve*
caretaker/ porter	*janitor*
cot	*crib*
duvet	*quilt*
foyer	*lobby*
ground/ first floor	*first/second floor*
lavatory/ loo/toilet	*restroom*
lift	*elevator*

Eating Out

aubergine	*eggplant*
bacon butty	*bacon sandwich*
bacon rasher	*slice of bacon*
banger	*sausage*
bap	*hamburger bun*
bill	*check*
biscuit	*cookie*
chips	*french fries*
courgette	*zucchini*
crisps	*potato chips*
jacket potato	*potato in its skin*
kipper	*smoked herring*
lager	*light beer*
porridge	*oatmeal*
pudding	*dessert*
runner beans	*string beans*
sweets	*candy*
jam	*jelly*
jelly	*Jell-O*

Communications

call box	*telephone booth*
post box	*mail box*
post code	*zip code*
put through	*connect*
reverse charge	*call connect*
ring up	*call*

Money

bank note	*bill*
cashpoint	*ATM*
cheque	*check*
quid (colloquial)	*one pound (money)*
VAT	*value added tax*

Shopping

anorak	*parka*
bank holiday	*public holiday*
braces	*suspenders*
briefs	*jockey shorts*
carrier bag	*shopping bag*
chemist	*drugstore*
dinner jacket	*tuxedo*
ironmongers	*hardware store*
jumper	*sweater*
nappy	*diaper*
off licence	*liquor store*
pants	*briefs (underwear)*
public convenience	*restroom*
queue	*line of people*
tights	*pantyhose*
trousers	*pants/slacks*
shop assistant	*sales clerk*

Transportation

coach	*long distance bus*
left luggage office	*baggage room*
lost property	*lost and found*
return ticket	*round-trip ticket*
single ticket	*one-way ticket*
timetable	*schedule*
underground/	*subway*

Driving

boot	*trunk (of a car)*
bonnet	*hood (of a car)*
car park	*parking lot*
caravan	*house trailer*
dual carriageway	*divided highway*
estate car	*station wagon*
filling station	*gas station*
flyover	*overpass*
gear lever	*gear shift*
layby	*pull-off*
lorry	*truck*
manual	*stick shift*
motorway	*freeway*
pavement	*sidewalk*
petrol	*gas*
roundabout	*traffic circle*
zebra crossing	*pedestrian crossing*

Gaelic Place-name Spellings

Gaelic is the first language in an area of the west of Ireland, known as the Gaeltacht. Many English place-names have been changed to the Gaelic spelling, and this process is ongoing. Below is a list of place-names that have been changed so far.

English	Gaelic
Achill Sound	Gob an Choire
Aran Islands	Oileáin Árann
Árainn Mhór	Arranmore
Ballydavid	Head Ceann Baile Dháith
Ballyferriter	Baile an Fheirtéaraigh
Ballyskelligs	Bay Bá na Scealg
Barnatra	Barr na Trá
Belderg	Béal Deirg
Belmullet	Béalan Mhuirthead
Binghamstown	An Geata Mór
Blasket Islands	Na Blascaodai
Brandon Head	Pointe an Choma Dhóite
Bunbeg	An Bun Beag
Burtonport	Ailt an Chorráin
Caherdaniel	Cathair Dónall
Carrick	An Charraig
Carrowmore	An Cheathrú Mhór
Clear Island	Oileán Cléire
Cloghane	An Clochán
Clonbur	An Fhairche
Cloonboo	Cluáin Bú
Deenish Island	Dúinis
Dingle	An Daingean
Dingle Bay	Bá na Daingin
Dingle Harbour	Cuan an Daingin
Dingle Peninsula	Corca Dhuibhne
Dungloe	An Clochán Liath
Dunlewy	Dún Lúiche
Dunquin	Dún Chaoin
Doogort	Dumha Goirt
Glencolumbkille	Gleann Cholm Cille
Glendowan	Gleann Domhain
Gortahork	Gort an Choirce
Gorumna	Garumna
Great Blasket Island	An Blascaod Mór
Gweedore	Gaoth Dobhair
Inish Glkora	Inisglora Island
Inishmaan	Inis Mein
Inishmore	Inis Móir
Inisheer	Inis Óirr
Kilronan	Cill Rónáin
Kinvarra	Cinn Mhara
Lettermullan	Leitir Mealláin
Lettermore	Leitir Moir
Little Skellig	An Sceilg Bheag
Maam Cross	An Teach Dóite
Maum	An Mám

Place-names Continued

Moycullen	Maigh Cuilinn
St. Macdara's Island	Oileán Mhic Dara
Scariff Island	An Scairbh
Skellig Michael	An Sceilg Mhicil
Slea Head	Ceann Sléibhe
Ventry	Ceann Trá

Gaelic Words and Phrases

The following is a list of words that you may come across during your visit.

Bord Fáilte (Irish Tourist Board)	bord falty
Ceilidh (traditional dance night)	kaylee
Gaeilge (the Irish language)	gale-geh
Gaeltacht (Irish-speaking country)	gale-tackt
Garda (police)	gawrdah
Fleadh (traditional music evening)	flah
Taoiseach (prime minister)	teeschock

Meeting people

faílte (welcome)	fall-to
le do thoil (please)	le-do-hull
lá maith (good day)	law-ma
dia hduit (hello)	d-git
á (yes)	thaw
níl/ní hea (no)	ha/knee
oíche mhaith (good night)	eha-ma
cé mhéid? (how much?) k	-made
go raibh maith aguth (thank you)	go-reve-ma-agut
Conas taoi? (how are you?)	konus-thaw-too

Eating and Drinking

bialann (restaurant)	bee-lun
teach tábhairne (pub/bar)	tock-tairne
bricfeásta (breakfast)	brick-fasta
lón (lunch) loan	
dinnéar (dinner)	din-air
tábla (table)	taub-law
freastalaí (waiter)	fras-taul-ee
uisce (water)	ois-e
ascailte (open)	oscail-te
dúnta (closed)	doon-thaw

Here are a few terms that may be used in descriptions of many archeological sites, monuments and ruins in Ireland.

Dolmens Standing stones (usually three) surmounted by a massive capstone.

Passage graves Great stone tombs with a large burial chamber, entered through a long passage.

Court cairns These are the earliest megolithic chambered tombs.

Crannogs Artificial islands built in lakes or marshy places.

Clochans Known as "beehives," these remarkable stone buildings were erected without mortar as tiny oratories.

Index

A

Abbey Theatre 66
Abbeyleix 103
Achill Island 31, 55
addresses, important 214
Aillwee Cave 134, 135
air travel 217
  see also individual
  towns (essential
  information)
Albert Memorial 160, 167
American connections
  176
An Creagan Visitor
  Centre 195, 195
Andrew Jackson Centre
  177
Antrim Coast Road 175
Aran Islands 28-30, 38-39
Ardmore 125, 126
Ards Peninsula 172
Armagh 172-173
Armagh County Museum
  173
Armagh Friary 173
Armagh Observatory
  173
Ashford Castle 42, 43
Athlone 90
Athlone Castle 90
Athy 102
Atlantic Drive 55
Atlantic Highlands 190
Avoca Handweavers 91
Avondale House 91

B

Ballina 56
Ballintubber Abbey 57
Ballybunion 146
Ballycastle 174, 175
Ballyferriter 131-132
Ballymalloe Cookery
  School and Gardens
  117
Bank of Ireland 70, 86
banks 216
Bantry 126
Bantry House 126, 127
Battle of the Boyne site
  96
Beaghmore Stone Circles
  196, 197
Beara Peninsula 126-127
Belcoo 188
Belfast 155-168
  essential information
  159
  sights 160-168
  walk 167-168
Belfast Castle 161
Belfast City Hall 156-157,
  162, 168
Belfast Zoo 161
Bellanaleck 189
Belleek Pottery 180, 181
Belvoir Park Forest 161
Blackwater Bog Tour 90
Blarney Castle 117-118,
  123

Blarney Woollen Mills
  117-118
Blasket Islands 131
Blennerville Windmill and
  Steam Train 145, 146
Boa Island 186
Bonamargy Friary 174,
  175
Book of Kells 84, 96
Border Counties 152-153
Botanic Gardens 161-162
Boyle 40-1
Boyne Valley 92, 94-96
breakdowns 219
Bronte Homeland
  Interpretative Centre
  193
Browne's Hill Dolmen
  102
Brú Ború Heritage Centre
  129-130
Buncrana 198
Bundoran 51
Bunratty Castle and Folk
  Park 142, 143, 144
Burren 134
buses 217
Bushmills 179
Buttevant 123

C

Cahersiveen 138
Cahir 128-129
Cahir Castle 124, 128
Cairns Hill Forest Park 51-
  52
Caldragh 186, 187
car rental 218
Carlow 102
Carndonagh 198
Carrick-a-Rede Rope
  Bridge 174, 175
Carrick-on-Suir 129
Carrickfergus 177
Carrickfergus Castle 177
Carrowmore 49, 52
Cashel 103, 129-131
Cashel Folk Village 130
Castle Archdale Country
  Park 186, 189
Castlebar 41
Castle Caldwell 187
Castle Ward 171
Castlecove 139
Castledermot 102
Castlerea 42
Castwellan 192
Causeway Coast 178-179
Cave Hill Country Park
  162
Céide Fields 56, 57
céilí 144
Celbridge Abbey Gardens
  106, 107
Celtic Plantarum
  Dundrum 131
Charles Fort 141, 142
Chester Beatty Library
  and Gallery of Oriental
  Art 70
Christ Church Cathedral,
  Dublin 70-71
Christ Church Cathedral,
  Waterford 149
Claddagh rings 33

Clare, County 134-135
Clare Heritage and
  Genealogical Centre
  135
Clare Island 54
Clifden 45
Cliffs of Moher 135
climate and seasons 10,
  214
  see also individual
  towns (essential
  information)
Clonalis House 42
Clonmacnois 62, 63, 90
Cobh Heritage Centre –
  The Queenstown Story
  118
Cois No hAbhna 134, 135
Colin Glen Forest Park
  162-163
Cong 42-43, 57
Connacht 26-57
Connemara 28, 44-45
Connemara National Park
  45
Coole Park 46
Corca Dhuibhne Regional
  Museum 132, 133
Cork 114-122
  essential information
  sights 117-121
  walk 120-121
Cork Butter Museum 119
Cork City Gaol 118
Craggaunowen Project
  134, 135
Crawford Art Gallery 121
credit cards 215
Croagh Patrick 31, 54
Crom Estate 189
Crown Liquor Saloon
  159, 163
Curragh 102
currency 215
Cushendall 174
Custom House Visitor
  Centre 71
customs regulations 215

D

Dalkey 91-92
Dalkey Island 92
Delamont Country Park
  184
dental services 216
Derrynane House 139,
  140
Derrynane National
  Historic Park 139
Desmond Castle 141,
  142
Devenish Island 185,
  186, 188, 189
Dingle 132
Dingle Peninsula 131-133
discounts 24
Dixon Park 163
Donard Forest Park 192
Donegal 180-181
Donegal Castle 180, 181
Donegal County
  Museum 190
Donegal Railway
  Heritage Centre 180
Doolin 133

Dooney Rock Forest 51
Douglas Hyde Gallery 71
Down County Museum
  183, 184
Downpatrick 171, 183-
  184
Downpatrick Railway
  Museum 183, 184
Dowth 95
Drimnagh Castle 71-72
drinking water 216
driving 24-25, 214, 218-
  219
Drogheda 92-93
drugs and medicines 216
Drum Manor Forest Park
  195
Drumcliff 50
Dublin 63, 64-89
  essential information
  69
  excursions 68
  festivals and events 75
  literary figures 88-89
  pubs 78-79
  sights 70-87
  walk 86-87
Dublin Castle 71-72, 86
Dublin City Hall 72
Dublin Writers' Museum
  73
Dublin Zoo 73-74
Dún Aengus 38, 39
Dun Laoghaire 97
Dunbeg Fort 131
Dundrum Castle 193
Dungannon 184
Dunguaire Castle 46
Dunluce Castle 179
Dunmore Cave 99
Dunsoghly Castle 74
Dvblinia and the Viking
  World 74

E

Earhart Centre 191-192
electricity 217
emergency telephone
  numbers 215, 216, 217
Emo Court 102-103
English Market (Cork)
  118, 121
Ennis 134
Enniscrone 56
Enniskillen 185
Enniskillen Castle 185
Errigal Mountain 190
Exploris Aquarium 170,
  171

F

Fahan 198
farmhouse holidays 24
Fermanagh 186-189
ferry services 217
festivals and events 19,
  33, 75, 122, 147
Fethard 103
Fethard Folk, Farm and
  Transport Museum 103
First Presbyterian Church
  163
fishing 21
Flame – The Gasworks
  Museum of Ireland 177

Florence Court 189
Florence Court Forest
  Park 189
Fort Dunree 198
Fota Wildlife Park 118
Four Courts 74
Foxford Woollen Mills 56,
  57
Foynes Flying Boat
  Museum 143
French Armada Exhibition
  Centre 126, 127
Fry Model Railway
  Museum 104-105
Fuerty 53
Fungi the Dolphin 132

G
GAA Museum 76
Gaelic football 21
Gaelic words and
  phrases 221
Gallarus Oratory 132
Galway 32-37
  essential information
    34
  sights 35-36
  walk 37
Galway Arts Centre 35
Galway Atlantiaquaria 35
Galway City Museum
  35
Garinish Island 127
Genealogical research
  158
General Post Office 76
geography 9-10
Giant's Causeway 150,
  178, 179
Giant's Ring 163
Glebe Gallery 190
Glenbeigh 138
Glencar Lake 51
Glencolumbkille Folk
  Village 180-181
Glendalough 97
Glengarriff 127
Glens of Antrim 174-175
Glenveah National Park
  and Castle 190
golf 21
Gort 46
Gortin Glen Forest Park
  194, 195
Gougane Barra National
  Forest Park 127
GPA Bolton Library 130,
  131
Graiguenamanagh 101-
  102
Grand Opera House 164
Greencastle 193
Greyabbey 169
Grianan of Aileach 198
Guinness Storehouse
  76-77

H
Harbour Commissioner's
  Office 164
Hawks Well Theatre 48,
  49
health advice 216
high crosses 94, 96, 186
Hill of Allen 102

history of Ireland 13-16,
  22-23
Holy Cross Abbey 145
Horse Museum 102
horseracing 20
horseriding 21
hotels and restaurants
  200-212
Howth Castle Gardens
  98
Hugh Lane Gallery, The
  77
Hunt Museum 142, 143
hurling 20-21

I
Inch Abbey 183, 184
Inishbofin Island 45
Inishowen Peninsula 198
insurance 214
International Museum of
  Wine 141
Ionnad Cois Locha 190
Irish Famine Museum
  53
Irish Jewish Museum
  77
Irish Museum of Modern
  Art 77
Irish National Heritage
  Park 108-109
Irish personality 11
Isle of Innisfree 51

J
James Fort 141
James Joyce Centre 80
James Joyce Tower and
  Museum 97
Jameson Heritage
  Centre 118-119
Japanese Gardens 102,
  106
Jerpoint Abbey 100-101,
  103
John F. Kennedy Park and
  Arboretum 109
Joyce, James 36, 88, 97

K
Kanturk Castle 123
Kavanagh, Patrick 152-
  153, 193
Kearney 170
Kells 96
Kenmare 139
Kerry County Museum
  145
Kerry the Kingdom 145,
  146
Kildare 102
Kilkenny 98-99
Kilkenny Castle 99
Kilkenny Design Centre
  99
Killala 56
Killarney 136-137
Killiney Bay 92
Killorglin 138
Killybegs 180
Killyleagh 171
Kilmainham Gaol 80
Kilronan Abbey 41
King House 40, 41
King John's Castle,

Limerick 142, 143
Kinlough 51
Kinsale 141
Knappogue Castle 135,
  144
Knock 30, 56, 57
Knowth 92, 95
Kylemore Abbey and
  Garden 44, 45

L
Lagan Boat Company
  164
Lagan Valley Regional
  Park 164
language 220-221
Larne 174-175
Leinster 58-109
Leinster House 80
Leisureland 36
Letterfrack 45
Letterkenny 190
Limerick 142-143
Linen Hall Library 164
Lisdoonvarna 135
Lismore 124-125, 143
Lissadell House 50, 52
Listowel 143
literature 12
Locke's Distillery 90, 91
Londonderry (Derry) 191-
  192
Lough Erne 153, 185, 189
Lough Gill 51
Lough Gur Stone Age
  Centre 143
Lough Key Forest Park
  40-41
Lough Navar Forest 185
Luas tram system 69
Lynch's Castle 37

M
MacCool, Finn 199
Macgillycuddy Reeks 136
Malahide 104-105
Malahide Castle 104-105
Mallow 123
Manorhamilton 51
Marble Arch Cave 188-
  189
Marble Arch Forest 189
Marsh's Library 81
medical services 216
medieval castle
  banquets 144
Mellifont Abbey 94-95
Midleton Distillery
  118–119
Minnowburn Beeches
  164
Misgaun Maeve 52
Mitchelstown Caves
  124
Mizen Head 112, 126,
  127
Monasterboice 94
monastic learning 15
Monea 187
money 215
Moore, Thomas 88-89,
  91
Mount Juliet 101
Mount Stewart Gardens
  169-170, 171

Mount Usher Gardens
  106
Mountains of Mourne 9,
  192-193
Movilla Abbey 169
Muckross Abbey 140
Muckross House 136,
  137, 140
Muckross Traditional
  Farms 136-137, 140
Munster 110-149
Murlough Bay 174
Murlough Nature
  Reserve 193
Museum of Country Life
  41
museum/monument
  opening hours 216
music 17, 79
Mussendon Temple 178,
  179

N
National Botanic Gardens
  106
National Gallery 81
national holidays 216
National Library of
  Ireland 81-82
National Maritime
  Museum 97
National Museum of
  Ireland – Archaeology
  and History 82
National Museum of
  Ireland – Decorative
  Arts and History 82
National Stud 102, 103
Navan Fort 172, 173
Nendrum Monastic Site
  171
New Ross 101
Newbridge House 105
Newgrange 92, 93, 95
Newgrange Farm 92-93
Newport 55
newspapers 217
Newtownards 169
Nora Barnacle House 36
North Mayo Family
  Heritage Centre 56, 57
Number Twenty-Nine
  (Dublin) 82

O
Oceanand Country
  Museum 45
O'Connell, Daniel 16,
  139
Odyssey 164
Old Jameson Distillery
  82–83
O'Malley, Grace 54, 55
opening hours 216
Omagh 194-195
Ormond Castle 129
Oscar Wilde House 83

P
Palace Stables Heritage
  Centre 173
Parke's Castle 51, 52
parking 218

224

Parknasilla 139
Parnell, Charles Stewart 16, 91
passports and visas 214
Patrick Kavanagh Rural and Resource Centre 193
Peatlands Park 184
personal safety 216
pharmacies 216
Phoenix Park 73-74
photography 25, 217
police 215, 216
Portaferry 170
Portavogie 170
Portlaoise 102
Portrush 178-179
postal services 215, 216
Powerscourt Gardens 106-107
public transportation 217 see also individual towns (essential information)
pubs with music 79

Q
Queen's University 164
Quiet Man Heritage Cottage and Archaeological Historical Centre 42, 43

R
Radio Telefís Éireann Museum 118
radio and television 217
Rathlin Island 174
Reginald's Tower 148, 149
restrooms 216
Ring of Kerry 138-140
River Shannon 90, 153
Rock of Cashel 129, 130
Rockfleet Castle 55
Roscommon 53
Rose of Tralee 19, 147
Ross Castle 137
Roundstone 44-45
Roundstone Bog 45

Roundstone Musical Instruments 44-45
Royal Hospital Kilmainham 77
Royal Inniskilling Fusiliers Museum 185
Royal Irish Fusiliers Museum 173
Royal Tara China Visitor Centre 36
Russborough House 105
Ryan, Cornelius 89

S
St. Anne's Cathedral 165
St. Anne's Church 119
St. Anne's Park Rose Garden 107
St. Audoen's Church of Ireland and Roman Catholic Church 83
St. Canice's Cathedral 99
St. Columb's Cathdral 191, 192
St. Cowey's Wells 170
St. Declan's Oratory 126
St. Fiachra's Garden 106
St. Fin Barre's Cathedral 119, 120, 121
St. Malachy's Church 165
St. Michan's Church 83
St. Nicholas Collegiate Church 36
St. Patrick 14, 15, 95, 173, 182
St. Patrick Centre 183, 184
St. Patrick's Cathedral 83-84
St. Patrick's Trian and Land of Lilliput 172, 173
St. Stephen's Green 84, 87
Scrabo Tower 169
Shandon 119
Shaw, George Bernard 89, 91-92, 127, 139
Sheelin Lace Museum 185
shopping 216

Siamsa Tire 145, 146
Silent Valley Mountain Park 192, 193
Sinclair Seaman's Church 164-165
Skellig Islands 137
Sky Drive 45
Slane 95-96
Slieve Gullion Forest Park 192, 193
Sligo 48-49
Sligo County Museum and Art Gallery 49
Sneem 139
Sperrin Mountains 196-197
sport 20-21
Staigue Fort 139
Stormont 165
Strandhill 52
Strangford 171
Strangford Castle 184
Strangford Lough 169-171
Streedagh 51
Strokestown Park House 53
survival guide 24-25
swimming 25
Swiss Cottage 128, 129

T
Tara 96
telephones 215
Temple Bar 67, 86
Temple Cowey 170
Thomastown 100
Thoor Ballylee 46
Thurles 103, 145
time zones 215
Timoleague Abbey 141
tipping 215
Torc Waterfall 140
tourist information see individual towns (essential information)
Tower Museum 191, 192
train services 217
Tralee 145
Tramore 146
Transport Museum 98
traveler's checks 215

Trinity College 84-85
Tuam 56
Tullyboy Farm 41
Tullynally Castle Gardens 107
Tyrone Crystal 184

U
Ulster Folk and Transport Museum 165-166, 169
Ulster Museum 166
Ulster and Northern Ireland 9-10, 150-199
Ulster Way 153
Ulster–American Folk Park 176, 194, 195
University College Cork 119
U.S. Grant Ancestral Homestead 184

V
Valentia Island 137, 138

W
Waterford 148-149
Waterford Crystal Factory 148-149
Waterford Heritage Museum 148-149
Waterford Museum of Treasures 148-149
Waterville 138
Wellbrook Beetling Mill 194-195
Westport 53-54
Westport House 54
Wexford 108-109
Wexford Wildfowl Reserve 109
whiskey 80, 174, 179
White Island 186
Wilson Ancestral Home 197
The Wood 132, 133

Y
Yeats Country 50-52
Yeats, W.B. 46, 47, 49, 89
Youghal 125

The Automobile Association wishes to thank the following photographers, companies and picture libraries for their assistance in the preparation of this book.

Abbreviations for the picture credits are as follows – (t) top; (b) bottom; (l) left; (r) right; (c) centre.

Alamy 21 (Joe Fox), 147 (INSADCO Photography), 148 (Rough Guides), 166 (Pixel Pusher), 196/197 (David Lyons), 198 (Gareth McCormack); Belfast Visitor and Convention Bureau 166/167; © DACS, 2007 88; Digital Vision 122; Hugh Lane Gallery 77; Illustrated London News 12; Mary Evans Picture Library 182, 199; Rex Features 176; Shannon Heritage 144; World Pictures/Photoshot 33

The remaining pictures are held in the Associations own library (AA World Travel Library) with contributions from the following photographers:

AA 6, 146b, 179; Liam Blake 4/5 26, 28, 36, 40, 40/41, 42/43, 44, 52, 53; Jamie Blandford 110, 113, 117, 119, 121, 124/125, 126, 127, 131, 132/133, 136/137, 138, 140; Chris Coe 20, 25, 150, 153, 159, 165, 168, 192, 200; Ian Burgum 56; Ian Dawson 18; Steve Day 10/11, 13, 17, 29, 30/31, 72/73, 75, 82, 101, 108/109; Michael Diggin 145, 146t; Derek Forss 141, 142, 177; Christopher Hill 35, 43, 47, 49, 51, 54, 57t, 180/181, 185; Stephen Hill 3, 38, 39, 46, 124, 215b; Jill Johnson 143; Caroline Jones 114/115; T King 76; Simon McBride 19, 62/63, 64, 130/131, 134/135; George Munday 9, 91, 156/157, 160, 161, 162, 163, 169, 171, 172, 173, 175, 178, 183, 187, 188/189, 190, 193, 194/195; Ken Paterson 194; Michael Short 15, 61, 70, 78, 85, 87, 93, 96, 98, 99, 103, 105, 106/107; Slide File 97, 104/105; Jonathan Smith 200; Stephen Whitehorne 58, 67, 71, 74, 79, 80, 81, 83, 84, 88, 215t; Peter Zollier 94/95, 128/129

Index and Acknowledgments